The Evolution of the Dragon

The Evolution of the Dragon

By
G. Elliot Smith, M.A., M.D., F.R.S.

Athens ‡ Manchester

The Evolution of the Dragon

Published by: Old Book Publishing Ltd

Book Cover Design: Old Book Publishing Ltd

Copyright © 2015 Old Book Publishing Ltd
All rights reserved.

Title of original: The Evolution of the Dragon

Originally Published in 1919 by Longmans, Green & Company

ISBN-10: 1-78107-179-3
ISBN-13: 978-1-78107-179-3

EDITOR'S NOTE

Old Book Publishing Ltd takes care in preserving the wording and images of the original books. For this reason we have invested in technology that enables us to enhance the quality of such reproduction. This investment helps overcome problems encountered when reproducing old books, such as stains, coloured paper, discolouration of ink, yellowed pages, see-through and onion skin type paper.

This reproduction book, produced from digital images of the original, may contain occasional defects such as missing pages or blemishes due to the original source content or were introduced by the scanning process.

These are scanned pages and the quality of print represents accurately the print quality of the original book, though we may have been able to enhance it.

As this book has been scanned and/or reformatted from the original we cannot guarantee that it is error-free or contains the full content of the original.

However, we believe that this work is culturally important, and despite its imperfections, have elected to bring it back into print as part of our commitment to the preservation of printed works.

Old Book Publishing

THE EVOLUTION OF THE DRAGON

Published for the John Rylands Library at
THE UNIVERSITY PRESS (H. M. McKechnie, Secretary)
12 Lime Grove, Oxford Road, MANCHESTER

LONGMANS, GREEN & COMPANY
London: 39 Paternoster Row
New York: 443-449 Fourth Avenue, and Thirtieth Street
Chicago: Prairie Avenue and Twenty-fifth Street
Bombay: Hornby Road
Calcutta: 6 Old Court House Street
Madras: 167 Mount Road

THE EVOLUTION OF
THE DRAGON

BY

G. ELLIOT SMITH, M.A., M.D., F.R.S.
PROFESSOR OF ANATOMY IN THE UNIVERSITY OF MANCHESTER

ILLUSTRATED

MANCHESTER: AT THE UNIVERSITY PRESS
LONGMANS, GREEN & COMPANY
LONDON, NEW YORK, CHICAGO, BOMBAY, CALCUTTA, MADRAS
1919

PREFACE.

SOME explanation is due to the reader of the form and scope of these elaborations of the lectures which I have given at the John Rylands Library during the last three winters.

They deal with a wide range of topics, and the thread which binds them more or less intimately into one connected story is only imperfectly expressed in the title " The Evolution of the Dragon ".

The book has been written in rare moments of leisure snatched from a variety of arduous war-time occupations; and it reveals only too plainly the traces of this disjointed process of composition. On 23 February, 1915, I presented to the Manchester Literary and Philosophical Society an essay on the spread of certain customs and beliefs in ancient times under the title " On the Significance of the Geographical Distribution of the Practice of Mummification," and in my Rylands Lecture two weeks later I summed up the general conclusions.[1] In view of the lively controversies that followed the publication of the former of these addresses, I devoted my next Rylands Lecture (9 February, 1916) to the discussion of " The Relationship of the Egyptian Practice of Mummification to the Development of Civilization ". In preparing this address for publication in the *Bulletin* some months later so much stress was laid upon the problems of " Incense and Libations " that I adopted this more concise title for the elaboration of the lecture which forms the first chapter of this book. This will explain why so many matters are discussed in that chapter which have little or no connexion either with " Incense and Libations " or with " The Evolution of the Dragon ".

The study of the development of the belief in water's life-giving

---

[1] " The Influence of Ancient Egyptian Civilisation in the East and in America," *Bulletin of the John Rylands Library*, January-March, 1916.

attributes, and their personification in the gods Osiris, Ea, Soma [Haoma] and Varuna, prepared the way for the elucidation of the history of "Dragons and Rain Gods" in my next lecture (Chapter II). What played a large part in directing my thoughts dragon-wards was the discussion of certain representations of the Indian Elephant upon Precolumbian monuments in, and manuscripts from, Central America (*Nature*, 25 Nov., 1915; 16 Dec., 1915; and 27 Jan., 1916). For in the course of investigating the meaning of these remarkable designs I discovered that the Elephant-headed rain-god of America had attributes identical with those of the Indian Indra (and of Varuna and Soma) and the Chinese dragon. The investigation of these identities established the fact that the American rain-god was transmitted across the Pacific from India via Cambodia.

The intensive study of dragons impressed upon me the importance of the part played by the Great Mother, especially in her Babylonian *avatar* as Tiamat, in the evolution of the famous wonder-beast. Under the stimulus of Dr. Rendel Harris's Rylands Lecture on "The Cult of Aphrodite," I therefore devoted my next address (14 November, 1917) to the "Birth of Aphrodite" and a general discussion of the problems of Olympian obstetrics.

Each of these addresses was delivered as an informal demonstration of large series of lantern projections; and, as Mr. Guppy insisted upon the publication of the lectures in the *Bulletin*, it became necessary, as a rule, many months after the delivery of each address, to rearrange my material and put into the form of a written narrative the story which had previously been told mainly by pictures and verbal comments upon them.

In making these elaborations additional facts were added and new points of view emerged, so that the printed statements bear little resemblance to the lectures of which they pretend to be reports. Such transformations are inevitable when one attempts to make a written report of what was essentially an ocular demonstration, unless every one of the numerous pictures is reproduced.

Each of the first two lectures was printed before the succeeding lecture was set up in type. For these reasons there is a good deal of repetition, and in successive lectures a wider interpretation of evidence mentioned in the preceding addresses. Had it been possible to revise the whole book at one time, and if the pressure of other duties had permitted me to devote more time to the work, these blemishes might have been eliminated and a coherent story made out of what is little more than a collection of data and tags of comment. No one is more conscious than the writer of the inadequacy of this method of presenting an argument of such inherent complexity as the dragon story : but my obligation to the Rylands Library gave me no option in the matter : I had to attempt the difficult task in spite of all the unpropitious circumstances. This book must be regarded, then, not as a coherent argument, but merely as some of the raw material for the study of the dragon's history. In my lecture (13 November, 1918) on "The Meaning of Myths," which will be published in the *Bulletin of the John Rylands Library*, I have expounded the general conclusions that emerge from the studies embodied in these three lectures ; and in my forthcoming book, "The Story of the Flood," I have submitted the whole mass of evidence to examination in detail, and attempted to extract from it the real story of mankind's age-long search for the elixir of life.

In the earliest records from Egypt and Babylonia it is customary to portray a king's beneficence by representing him initiating irrigation works. In course of time he came to be regarded, not merely as the giver of the water which made the desert fertile, but as himself the personification and the giver of the vital powers of water. The fertility of the land and the welfare of the people thus came to be regarded as dependent upon the king's vitality. Hence it was not illogical to kill him when his virility showed signs of failing and so imperilled the country's prosperity. But when the view developed that the dead king acquired a new grant of vitality in the other world he became the god Osiris, who was able to confer even greater boons of life-giving to the land and people than was the case before. He was the Nile, and he fertilized the land. The original dragon was a beneficent creature, the personification of water, and was identified with kings and gods.

But the enemy of Osiris became an evil dragon, and was identified with Set.

The dragon-myth, however, did not really begin to develop until an ageing king refused to be slain, and called upon the Great Mother, as the giver of life, to rejuvenate him. Her only elixir was human blood; and to obtain it she was compelled to make a human sacrifice. Her murderous act led to her being compared with and ultimately identified with a man-slaying lioness or a cobra. The story of the slaying of the dragon is a much distorted rumour of this incident; and in the process of elaboration the incidents were subjected to every kind of interpretation and also confusion with the legendary account of the conflict between Horus and Set.

When a substitute was obtained to replace the blood the slaying of a human victim was no longer logically necessary: but an explanation had to be found for the persistence of this incident in the story. Mankind (no longer a mere individual human sacrifice) had become sinful and rebellious (the act of rebellion being complaints that the king or god was growing old) and had to be destroyed as a punishment for this treason. The Great Mother continued to act as the avenger of the king or god. But the enemies of the god were also punished by Horus in the legend of Horus and Set. The two stories hence became confused the one with the other. The king Horus took the place of the Great Mother as the avenger of the gods. As she was identified with the moon, he became the Sun-god, and assumed many of the Great Mother's attributes, and also became her son. In the further development of the myth, when the Sun-god had completely usurped his mother's place, the infamy of her deeds of destruction seems to have led to her being confused with the rebellious men who were now called the followers of Set, Horus's enemy. Thus an evil dragon emerged from this blend of the attributes of the Great Mother and Set. This is the Babylonian Tiamat. From the amazingly complex jumble of this tissue of confusion all the incidents of the dragon-myth were derived.

When attributes of the Water-god or his enemy became assimilated with those of the Great Mother and the Warrior Sun-god, the animals with which these deities were identified came to be regarded individually and collectively as concrete expressions of the Water-god's powers. Thus the cow and the gazelle, the falcon and the eagle, the lion and the serpent, the fish and the crocodile became symbols of the life-giving and the life-destroying powers of water, and composite monsters or dragons were invented by combining parts of these various creatures to express the different manifestations of the vital powers of water. The process of elaboration of the attributes of these monsters led to the development of an amazingly complex myth: but the story became still further involved when the dragon's life-controlling powers became confused with man's vital spirit and identified with the good or evil genius which was regarded as the guest, welcome or unwelcome, of every individual's body, and the arbiter of his destiny. In my remarks on the *ka* and the *fravashi* I have merely hinted at the vast complexity of these elements of confusion.

Had I been familiar with [Archbishop] Söderblom's important monograph,[1] when I was writing Chapters I and III, I might have attempted to indicate how vital a part the confusion of the individual *genius* with the mythical wonder-beast has played in the history of the myths relating to the latter. For the identification of the dragon with the vital spirit of the individual explains why the stories of the former appealed to the selfish interest of every human being. At the time the lecture on "Incense and Libations" was written, I had no idea that the problems of the *ka* and the *fravashi* had any connexion with those relating to the dragon. But in the third chapter a quotation from Professor Langdon's account of "A Ritual of Atonement for a Babylonian King" indicates that the Babylonian equivalent of the *ka* and the *fravashi*, "my god who walks at my side," presents many points of affinity to a dragon.

When in the lecture on "Incense and Libations" I ventured to make the daring suggestion that the ideas underlying the Egyptian conception of the *ka* were substantially identical with those entertained by

---

[1] Nathan Söderblom, "Les Fravashis Étude sur les Traces dans le Mazdéisme d'une Ancienne Conception sur la Survivance des Morts," Paris, 1899.

the Iranians in reference to the *fravashi*, I was not aware of the fact that such a comparison had already been made. In [Archbishop] Söderblom's monograph, which contains a wealth of information in corroboration of the views set forth in Chapter I, the following statement occurs: "L'analyse, faite par M. Brede-Kristensen (*Ægypternes forestillinger om livet efter döden*, 14 ss. Kristiania, 1896) du *ka* égyptien, jette une vive lumière sur notre question, par la frappante analogie qui semble exister entre le sens originaire de ces deux termes *ka* et *fravashi*" (p. 58, note 4). "La similitude entre le *ka* et la *fravashi* a été signalée déjà par Nestor Lhote, *Lettres écrites d'Égypte*, note, selon Maspero, *Études de mythologie et d'archéologie égyptiennes*, I, 47, note 3."

In support of the view, which I have submitted in Chapter I, that the original idea of the *fravashi*, like that of the *ka*, was suggested by the placenta and the fœtal membranes, I might refer to the specific statement (Farvardin-Yasht, XXIII, 1) that "les fravashis tiennent en ordre l'enfant dans le sein de sa mère et l'enveloppent de sorte qu'il ne meurt pas" (*op. cit.*, Söderblom, p. 41, note 1). The *fravashi* "nourishes and protects" (p. 57): it is "the nurse" (p. 58): it is always feminine (p. 58). It is in fact the placenta, and is also associated with the functions of the Great Mother. "Nous voyons dans fravashi une personification de la force vitale, conservée et exercée aussi après la mort. La fravashi est le principe de vie, la faculté qu'a l'homme de se soutenir par la nourriture, de manger, d'absorber et ainsi d'exister et de se développer. Cette étymologie et le rôle attribué à la fravashi dans le développement de l'embryon, des animaux, des plantes rappellent en quelque sorte, comme le remarque M. Foucher, l'idée directrice de Claude Bernard. Seulement la fravashi n'a jamais été une abstraction. La fravashi est une puissance vivante, un *homunculus in homine*, un être personnifié comme du reste toutes les sources de vie et de mouvement que l'homme non civilisé aperçoit dans son organisme.

Il ne faut pas non plus considérer la fravashi comme un double de l'homme, elle en est plutôt une partie, un hôte intime qui continue son existence après la mort aux mêmes conditions qu'avant, et qui oblige les vivants à lui fournir les aliments nécessaires" (*op. cit.*, p. 59).

Thus the *fravashi* has the same remarkable associations with nourishment and placental functions as the *ka*. As a further suggestion of its connexion with the Great Mother as the inaugurator of the year, and in virtue of her physiological (uterine) functions the moon-controlled measurer of the month, it is important to note that " Le 19e jour de chaque mois est également consecré aux fravashis en général. Le premier mois porte aussi le nom de Farvardîn. Quant aux formes des fêtes mensuelles, elles semblent conformes à celles que nous allons rappeler [les fêtes célébrées en l'honneur des mortes] " (*op. cit.*, p. 10).

But the *fravashi* was not only associated with the Great Mother, but also with the Water-god or Good Dragon, for it controlled the waters of irrigation and gave fertility to the soil (*op. cit.*, p. 36). The *fravashi* was also identified with the third member of the primitive Trinity, the Warrior Sun-god, not merely in the general sense as the adversary of the powers of evil, but also in the more definite form of the Winged Disk (*op. cit.*, pp. 67 and 68).

In all these respects the *fravashi* is brought into close association with the dragon, so that in addition to being "the divine and immortal element" (*op. cit.*, p. 51), it became the genius or spirit that possesses a man and shapes his conduct and regulates his behaviour. It was in fact the expression of a crude attempt on the part of the early psychologists of Iran to explain the working of the instinct of self-preservation.

In the text of Chapters I and III I have referred to the Greek, Babylonian, Chinese, and Melanesian variants of essentially the same conception. Söderblom refers to an interesting parallel among the Karens, whose *kelah* corresponds to the Iranian *fravashi* (p. 54, Note 2 : compare also A. E. Crawley, "The Idea of the Soul," 1909).

In the development of the dragon-myth astronomical factors played a very obtrusive part : but I have deliberately refrained from entering into a detailed discussion of them, because they were not primarily the real causal agents in the origin of the myth. When the conception of a sky-world or a heaven became drawn into the dragon story it came to play so prominent a part as to convince most writers that the myth was primarily and essentially astronomical. But it is clear that originally the myth was concerned solely with the regulation of irrigation systems and the search upon earth for an elixir of life.

When I put forward the suggestion that the annual inundation of the Nile provided the information for the first measurement of the year, I was not aware of the fact that Sir Norman Lockyer ("The Dawn of Astronomy," 1894, p. 209), had already made the same claim and substantiated it by much fuller evidence than I have brought together here.

In preparing these lectures I have received help from so large a number of correspondents that it is difficult to enumerate all of them. But I am under a special debt of gratitude to Dr. Alan Gardiner for calling my attention to the fact that the common rendering of the Egyptian word *didi* as "mandrake" was unjustifiable, and to Mr. F. Ll. Griffith for explaining its true meaning and for lending me the literature relating to this matter. Miss Winifred M. Crompton, the Assistant Keeper of the Egyptian Department in the Manchester Museum, gave me very material assistance by bringing to my attention some very important literature which otherwise would have been overlooked; and both she and Miss Dorothy Davison helped me with the drawings that illustrate this volume. Mr. Wilfrid Jackson gave me much of the information concerning shells and cephalopods which forms such an essential part of the argument, and he also collected a good deal of the literature which I have made use of. Dr. A. C. Haddon, F.R.S., of Cambridge, lent me a number of books and journals which I was unable to obtain in Manchester; and Mr. Donald A. Mackenzie, of Edinburgh, has poured in upon me a stream of information, especially upon the folklore of Scotland and India. Nor must I forget to acknowledge the invaluable help and forbearance of Mr. Henry Guppy, of the John Rylands Library, and Mr. Charles W. E. Leigh, of the University Library. To all of these and to the still larger number of correspondents who have helped me I offer my most grateful thanks.

During the three years in which these lectures were compiled I

PREFACE

have been associated with Dr. W. H. R. Rivers, F.R.S., and Mr. T. H. Pear in their psychological work in the military hospitals, and the influence of this interesting experience is manifest upon every page of this volume.

But perhaps the most potent factor of all in shaping my views and directing my train of thought has been the stimulating influence of Mr. W. J. Perry's researches, which are converting ethnology into a real science and shedding a brilliant light upon the early history of civilization.

G. ELLIOT SMITH.

9 *December*, 1918.

CONTENTS.

CHAPTER I.
INCENSE AND LIBATIONS . . . . PAGE 1

CHAPTER II.
DRAGONS AND RAIN GODS 76

CHAPTER III.
THE BIRTH OF APHRODITE 140

LIST OF ILLUSTRATIONS.

	FACING PAGE
Fig. 1.—The conventional Egyptian representation of the burning of incense and the pouring of libations	2
Fig. 2.—Water-colour sketch by Mrs. Cecil Firth, representing a restoration of the early mummy found at Medûm by Professor Flinders Petrie, now in the Museum of the Royal College of Surgeons in London	16
Fig. 3.—A mould taken from a life-mask found in the Pyramid of Teta by Mr. Quibell	17
Fig. 4.—Portrait statue of an Egyptian lady of the Pyramid Age	18
Fig. 5.—Statue of an Egyptian noble of the Pyramid Age to show the technical skill in the representation of life-like eyes	52
Fig. 6.—Representation of the ancient Mexican worship of the Sun	70
Fig. 7.—A mediæval picture of a Chinese Dragon upon its cloud (after the late Professor W. Anderson)	80
Fig. 8.—A Chinese Dragon (after de Groot)	80
Fig. 9.—Dragon from the Ishtar Gate of Babylon	81
Fig. 10.—Babylonian Weather God	81
Fig. 11.—Reproduction of a picture in the Maya Codex Troano representing the Rain-god *Chac* treading upon the Serpent's head, which is interposed between the earth and the rain the god is pouring out of a bowl. A Rain-goddess stands upon the Serpent's tail	84
Fig. 12.—Another representation of the elephant-headed Rain-god. He is holding thunderbolts, conventionalized in a hand-like form. The serpent is converted into a sac, holding up the rain-waters	84
Fig. 13.—A page (the 36th) of the Dresden Maya Codex	86
Fig. 14.—A. The so-called "sea-goat" of Babylonia, a creature compounded of the antelope and fish of Ea.—B. The "sea-goat" as the vehicle of Ea or Marduk.—C to K—a series of varieties of the *makara* from the Buddhist Rails at Buddha Gaya and Mathura, circa 70 B.C.—70 A.D., after Cunningham ("Archæological Survey of India," Vol. III, 1873, Plates IX and XXIX).—L. The *makara* as the vehicle of Varuna, after Sir George Birdwood. It is not difficult to understand how, in the course of the easterly diffusion of culture, such a picture should develop into the Chinese Dragon or the American elephant-headed god	88
Fig. 15.—Photograph of a Chinese embroidery in the Manchester School of Art representing the Dragon and the Pearl-Moon Symbol	98

LIST OF ILLUSTRATIONS

FACING PAGE

Fig. 16.—The God of Thunder (from a Chinese drawing (? 17th Century) in the John Rylands Library) 136

Fig. 17.—From Joannes de Turrecremata's "Meditationes seu Contemplationes". *Rome: Ulrich Han*, 1467 137

Fig. 18.—(*a*) The Archaic Egyptian slate palette of Narmer showing, perhaps, the earliest design of Hathor (at the upper corners of the palette) as a woman with cow's horns and ears (compare Flinders Petrie "The Royal Tombs of the First Dynasty," Part I, 1900, Plate XXVII, Fig. 71). The pharaoh is wearing a belt from which are suspended four cow-headed Hathor figures in place of the cowry-amulets of more primitive peoples. This affords corroboration of the view that Hathor assumed the functions originally attributed to the cowry-shell. (*b*) The king's *sporran*, where Hathor-heads (*H*) take the place of the cowries of the primitive girdle 150

Fig. 19.—The front of Stela B (famous for the realistic representations of the Indian elephant at its upper corners), one of the ancient Maya monuments at Copan, Central America (after Maudslay's photograph and diagram). The girdle of the chief figure is decorated both with shells (*Oliva* or *Conus*) and amulets representing human faces corresponding to the Hathor-heads on the Narmer palette (Fig. 18) 151

Fig. 20.—Diagrams illustrating the form of cowry-belts worn in (*a*) East Africa and (*b*) Oceania respectively. (*c*) Ancient Indian girdle (from the figure of Sirima Devata on the Bharat Tope), consisting of strings of pearls and precious stones, and what seem to be (fourth row from the top) models of cowries. (*d*) The Copan girdle (from Fig. 19) in which both shells and heads of deities are represented. The two objects suspended from the belt between the heads recall Hathor's sistra 153

Fig. 21.—(*a*) A slate triad found by Professor G. A. Reisner in the temple of the Third Pyramid at Giza. It shows the Pharaoh Mycerinus supported on his right side by the goddess Hathor, represented as a woman with the moon and the cow's horns upon her head, and on the left side by a nome goddess, bearing upon her head the jackal-symbol of her nome. (*b*) The Ecuador Aphrodite. Bas-relief from Cerro-Jaboncillo (after Saville, "Antiquities of Manabi, Ecuador," Preliminary Report, 1907, Plate XXXVIII). A grotesque composite monster intended to represent a woman (compare Saville's Plates XXXV, XXXVI, and XXXIX), whose head is a conventionalized Octopus, whose body is a *Loligo*, and whose limbs are human 164

Fig. 22.—(*a*) *Sepia officinalis*, after Tryon, "Cephalopoda". (*b*) *Loligo vulgaris*, after Tryon. (*c*) The position usually adopted by the resting Octopus, after Tryon 168

Fig. 23.—A series of Mycenæan conventionalizations of the Argonaut and the Octopus (after Tümpel), which provided the basis for Houssay's theory of the origin of the triskele (*a*, *c*, and *d*) and swastika (*b* and *e*), and Siret's theory to explain the design of Bes's face (*f* and *g*) 172

Fig. 24.—(*a*) and (*b*) Two Mycenæan pots (after Schliemann). (*a*) The so-called "owl-shaped" vase is really a representation of the Mother-Pot in the form of a conventionalized Octopus (Houssay). (*b*) The other vase represents the Octopus Mother-Pot, with a jar upon her head and another in her hands—a three-fold representation of the Great Mother as a pot. (*c*) A Cretan vase from Gournia in which the Octopus-motive is represented as a decoration

LIST OF ILLUSTRATIONS

FACING PAGE

upon the pot instead of in its form. (*d*), (*e*), (*f*), (*g*), and (*h*) A series of coins from Central Greece (after Head) showing a series of conventionalizations of the Octopus, with its pot-like body and palm-tree-like arms (*f*). (*i*) *Sepia officinalis* (after Tryon). (*h*) and (*l*) The so-called "spouting vases" in the hands of the Babylonian god Ea, from a cylinder seal of the time of Gudea, Patesi of Tello, after Ward ("Seal Cylinders, etc.," p. 215) 180

Fig. 25.—(*a*) Winged Disk from the Temple of Thothmes I. (*b*) Persian design of Winged Disk above the Tree of Life (Ward, "Seal Cylinders of Western Asia," Fig. 1109). (*c*) Assyrian or Syro-Hittite design of the Winged Disk and Tree of Life in an extremely conventionalized form (Ward, Fig. 1310). (*d*) Assyrian conventionalized Winged Disk and Tree of Life, from the design upon the dress of Assurnazipal (Ward, Fig. 670). (*e*) Part of the design from a tablet of the time of Dungi (Ward, Fig. 663). (*f*) Design on a Cretan sarcophagus from Hagia Triada (Blinckenberg, Fig. 9). (*g*) Double axe from a gold signet from Acropolis Treasure, Mycenæ (after Sir Arthur Evans, "Mycenæan Tree and Pillar Cult," p. 10). (*h*) Assyrian Winged Disk (Ward, Fig. 608). (*i*) "Primitive Chaldean Winged Gate" (Ward, Fig. 349). (*k*) Persian Winged Disk (Ward, Fig. 1144). (*l*) An Assyrian Tree of Life and Winged Disk crudely conventionalized (Ward, Fig. 691). (*m*) Assyrian Tree of Life and Winged Disk in which the god is riding in a crescent replacing the Disk (Ward, Fig. 695) 184

Fig. 26.—(*a*) An Egyptian picture of Hathor between the mountains of the horizon (on which trees are growing) (after Budge, "Gods of the Egyptians," Vol. II, p. 101). (*b*) The mountains of the horizon supporting a cow's head as a surrogate of Hathor, from a stele found at Teima in Northern Arabia, now in the Louvre (after Sir Arthur Evans, *op. cit.*, p. 39). (*c*) The Mesopotamian sun-god Shamash rising between the Eastern Mountains, the Gates of Dawn (Ward, *op. cit.*, p. 373). (*d*) The familiar Egyptian representation of the sun rising between the Eastern Mountains (the splitting of the mountain giving birth to "the ridiculous mouse"—Smintheus). (*e*) Part of the design from a Mycenæan vase from Old Salamis (after Evans, p. 9). (*f*) Part of the design from a lentoid gem from the Idæan Cave, now in the Candia Museum (after Evans, Fig. 25). (*g*) The Eastern Mountains supporting the pillar-form of the goddess (after Evans, Fig. 66). (*h*) Another Mycenæan design comparable with (*e*). (*i*) Design from a signet-ring from Mycenæ (after Evans, Fig. 34). (*k*) The famous sculpture above the Lion Gate at Mycenæ . . 188

ILLUSTRATIONS IN THE TEXT.

PAGE

Fig. 1.—Early representation of a "Dragon" compounded of the forepart of an eagle and the hindpart of a lion (from an Archaic Cylinder seal from Susa, after Jequier) 79

Fig. 2.—The earliest Babylonian conception of the Dragon Tiamat (from a Cylinder-seal in the British Museum, after L. W. King) 79

Fig. 3.—Wm. Dennis's drawing of the "Flying Dragon" depicted on the rocks at Piasa, Illinois 94

Fig. 4.—Two representations of Astarte (Qetesh) 155

Fig. 5.—*Pterocera bryonia*, the Red Sea spider-shell 170

LIST OF ILLUSTRATIONS

PAGE

Fig. 6.—(a) Picture of a bowl of water—the hieroglyphic sign equivalent to *hm* (the word *hmt* means "woman"—Griffith, "Beni Hasan," Part III, Plate VI, Fig. 88 and p. 29). (b) "A basket of sycamore figs"—Wilkinson's "Ancient Egyptians," Vol. I, p. 323. (c) and (d) are said by Wilkinson to be hieroglyphic signs meaning "wife" and are apparently taken from (b). But (c) is identical with (i), which, according to Griffith (p. 14), represents a bivalve shell (g, from Plate III, Fig. 3), more usually placed obliquely (h). The varying conventionalizations of (a) or (b) are shown in (d), (e), and (f) (Griffith, "Hieroglyphics," p. 34). (k) The sign for a lotus leaf, which is a phonetic equivalent of the sign (h), and, according to Griffith ("Hieroglyphics," p. 26), "is probably derived from the same root, on account of its shell-like outline". (l) The hieroglyphic sign for a pot of water in such words as *Nu* and *Nut*. (m) A "pomegranate" (replacing a bust of Tanit) upon a sacred column at Carthage (Arthur J. Evans, "Mycenæan Tree and Pillar Cult," p. 46). (n) The form of the body of an octopus as conventionalized on the coins of Central Greece (compare Fig. 24 (d)) 179

Fig. 7.—(a) An Egyptian design representing the sun-god Horus emerging from a lotus, representing his mother Hathor (Isis). (b) Papyrus sceptre often carried by goddesses and animistically identified with them either as an instrument of life-giving or destruction. (c) Conventionalized lily—the prototype of the trident and the thunder-weapon. (d) A water-plant associated with the Nile-gods 180

Fig. 8.—(a) "Ceremonial forked object," or "magic wand," used in the ceremony of "opening the mouth," possibly connected with (b) (a bicornuate uterus), according to Griffith ("Hieroglyphics," p. 60). (c) The Egyptian sign for a key. (d) The double axe of Crete and Egypt 191

Fig. 9.—The Egyptian emblem for gold, the sign *nub* 222

CHAPTER I.

INCENSE AND LIBATIONS.[1]

The dragon was primarily a personification of the life-giving and life-destroying powers of water. This chapter is concerned with the genesis of this biological theory of water and its relationship to the other germs of civilization.

IT is commonly assumed that many of the elementary practices of civilization, such as the erection of rough stone buildings, whether houses, tombs, or temples, the crafts of the carpenter and the stonemason, the carving of statues, the customs of pouring out libations or burning incense, are such simple and obvious procedures that any people might adopt them without prompting or contact of any kind with other populations who do the same sort of things. But if such apparently commonplace acts be investigated they will be found to have a long and complex history. None of these things that seem so obvious to us was attempted until a multitude of diverse circumstances became focussed in some particular community, and constrained some individual to make the discovery. Nor did the quality of obviousness become apparent even when the enlightened discoverer had gathered up the threads of his predecessor's ideas and woven them into the fabric of a new invention. For he had then to begin the strenuous fight against the opposition of his fellows before he could induce them to accept his discovery. He had, in fact, to contend against their preconceived ideas and their lack of appreciation of the significance of the progress he had made before he could persuade them of its "obviousness". That is the history of most inventions since the world began. But it is begging the question to pretend that because tradition has made such inventions seem simple and obvious to us it is unnecessary to inquire into their history or to assume that any people or any individual simply did these things without any instruction when the spirit moved it or him so to do.

[1] An elaboration of a Lecture on the relationship of the Egyptian practice of mummification to the development of civilization delivered in the John Rylands Library, on 9 February, 1916.

The customs of burning incense and making libations in religious ceremonies are so widespread and capable of being explained in such plausible, though infinitely diverse, ways that it has seemed unnecessary to inquire more deeply into their real origin and significance. For example, Professor Toy [1] disposes of these questions in relation to incense in a summary fashion. He claims that " when burnt before the deity " it is " to be regarded as food, though in course of time, when the recollection of this primitive character was lost, a conventional significance was attached to the act of burning. A more refined period demanded more refined food for the gods, such as ambrosia and nectar, but these also were finally given up."

This, of course, is a purely gratuitous assumption, or series of assumptions, for which there is no real evidence. Moreover, even if there were any really early literature to justify such statements, they explain nothing. Incense-burning is just as mysterious if Prof. Toy's claim be granted as it was before.

But a bewildering variety of other explanations, for all of which the merit of being " simple and obvious " is claimed, have been suggested. The reader who is curious about these things will find a luxurious crop of speculations by consulting a series of encyclopædias.[2] I shall content myself by quoting only one more. " Frankincense and other spices were indispensable in temples where bloody sacrifices formed part of the religion. The atmosphere of Solomon's temple must have been that of a sickening slaughter-house, and the fumes of incense could alone enable the priests and worshippers to support it. This would apply to thousands of other temples through Asia, and doubtless the palaces of kings and nobles suffered from uncleanliness and insanitary arrangements and required an antidote to evil smells to make them endurable." [3]

It is an altogether delightful anachronism to imagine that religious ritual in the ancient and aromatic East was inspired by such squeamishness as a British sanitary inspector of the twentieth century might experience !

---

[1] " Introduction to the History of Religions," p. 486.
[2] He might start upon this journey of adventure by reading the article on " Incense " in Hastings' *Encyclopædia of Religion and Ethics.*
[3] Samuel Laing, " Human Origins," Revised by Edward Clodd, 1903, p. 38.

Fig. 1.—The conventional Egyptian representation of the Burning of Incense and the Pouring of Libations
(Period of the New Empire)—after Lepsius

But if there are these many diverse and mutually destructive reasons in explanation of the origin of incense-burning, it follows that the meaning of the practice cannot be so "simple and obvious". For scholars in the past have been unable to agree as to the sense in which these adjectives should be applied.

But no useful purpose would be served by enumerating a collection of learned fallacies and exposing their contradictions when the true explanation has been provided in the earliest body of literature that has come down from antiquity. I refer to the Egyptian "Pyramid Texts".

Before this ancient testimony is examined certain general principles involved in the discussion of such problems should be considered. In this connexion it is appropriate to quote the apt remarks made, in reference to the practice of totemism, by Professor Sollas.[1] "If it is difficult to conceive how such ideas . . . originated at all, it is still more difficult to understand how they should have arisen repeatedly and have developed in much the same way among races evolving independently in different environments. It is at least simpler to suppose that all [of them] have a common source . . . and may have been carried . . . to remote parts of the world."

I do not think that anyone who conscientiously and without bias examines the evidence relating to incense-burning, the arbitrary details of the ritual and the peculiar circumstances under which it is practised in different countries, can refuse to admit that so artificial a custom must have been dispersed throughout the world from some one centre where it was devised.

The remarkable fact that emerges from an examination of these so-called "obvious explanations" of ethnological phenomena is the failure on the part of those who are responsible for them to show any adequate appreciation of the nature of the problems to be solved. They know that incense has been in use for a vast period of time, and that the practice of burning it is very widespread. They have been so familiarized with the custom and certain more or less vague excuses for its perpetuation that they show no realization of how strangely irrational and devoid of obvious meaning the procedure is. The reasons usually given in explanation of its use are for the most part merely paraphrases of the traditional meanings that in the course of

[1] "Ancient Hunters," 2nd Edition, pp. 234 and 235.

history have come to be attached to the ritual act or the words used to designate it. Neither the ethnologist nor the priestly apologist will, as a rule, admit that he does not know why such ritual acts as pouring out water or burning incense are performed, and that they are wholly inexplicable and meaningless to him. Nor will they confess that the real inspiration to perform such rites is the fact of their predecessors having handed them down as sacred acts of devotion, the meaning of which has been entirely forgotten during the process of transmission from antiquity. Instead of this they simply pretend that the significance of such acts is obvious. Stripped of the glamour which religious emotion and sophistry have woven around them, such pretended explanations become transparent subterfuges, none the less real because the apologists are quite innocent of any conscious intention to deceive either themselves or their disciples. It should be sufficient for them that such ritual acts have been handed down by tradition as right and proper things to do. But in response to the instinctive impulse of all human beings, the mind seeks for reasons in justification of actions of which the real inspiration is unknown.

It is a common fallacy to suppose that men's actions are inspired mainly by reason. The most elementary investigation of the psychology of everyday life is sufficient to reveal the truth that man is not, as a rule, the pre-eminently rational creature he is commonly supposed to be.[1] He is impelled to most of his acts by his instincts, the circumstances of his personal experience, and the conventions of the society in which he has grown up. But once he has acted or decided upon a course of procedure he is ready with excuses in explanation and attempted justification of his motives. In most cases these are not the real reasons, for few human beings attempt to analyse their motives or in fact are competent without help to understand their own feelings and the real significance of their actions. There is implanted in man the instinct to interpret for his own satisfaction his feelings and sensations, i.e. the meaning of his experience. But of necessity this is mostly of the nature of rationalizing, i.e. providing satisfying interpretations of thoughts and decisions the real meaning of which is hidden.

Now it must be patent that the nature of this process of rationalization will depend largely upon the mental make-up of the individual—

[1] On this subject see Elliot Smith and Pear, " Shell Shock and its Lessons," Manchester University Press, 1917, p. 59.

of the body of knowledge and traditions with which his mind has become stored in the course of his personal experience. The influences to which he has been exposed, daily and hourly, from the time of his birth onward, provide the specific determinants of most of his beliefs and views. Consciously and unconsciously he imbibes certain definite ideas, not merely of religion, morals, and politics, but of what is the correct and what is the incorrect attitude to assume in most of the circumstances of his daily life. These form the staple currency of his beliefs and his conversation. Reason plays a surprisingly small part in this process, for most human beings acquire from their fellows the traditions of their society which relieves them of the necessity of undue thought. The very words in which the accumulated traditions of his community are conveyed to each individual are themselves charged with the complex symbolism that has slowly developed during the ages, and tinges the whole of his thoughts with their subtle and, to most men, vaguely appreciated shades of meaning.[1] During this process of acquiring the fruits of his community's beliefs and experiences every individual accepts without question a vast number of apparently simple customs and ideas. He is apt to regard them as obvious, and to assume that reason led him to accept them or be guided by them, although when the specific question is put to him he is unable to give their real history.

Before leaving these general considerations[2] I want to emphasize certain elementary facts of psychology which are often ignored by those who investigate the early history of civilization.

First, the multitude and the complexity of the circumstances that are necessary to lead men to make even the simplest invention render the concatenation of all of these conditions wholly independently on a second occasion in the highest degree improbable. Until very definite and conclusive evidence is forthcoming in any individual case it can safely be assumed that no ethnologically significant innovation in customs or beliefs has ever been made twice.

Those critics who have recently attempted to dispose of this claim by referring to the work of the Patent Office thereby display a singular

[1] An interesting discussion of this matter by the late Professor William James will be found in his "Principles of Psychology," Vol. I, pp. 261 *et seq.*

[2] For a fuller discussion of certain phases of this matter see my address on "Primitive Man," in the *Proceedings of the British Academy*, 1917, especially pp. 23-50.

lack of appreciation of the real point at issue. For the ethnological problem is concerned with different populations who are assumed *not* to share any common heritage of acquired knowledge, nor to have had any contact, direct or indirect, the one with the other. But the inventors who resort to the Patent Office are all of them persons supplied with information from the storehouse of our common civilization ; and the inventions which they seek to protect from imitation by others are merely developments of the heritage of all civilized peoples. Even when similar inventions are made apparently independently under such circumstances, in most cases they can be explained by the fact that two investigators have followed up a line of advance which has been determined by the development of the common body of knowledge.

This general discussion suggests another factor in the working of the human mind.

When certain vital needs or the force of circumstances compel a man to embark upon a certain train of reasoning or invention the results to which his investigations lead depend upon a great many circumstances. Obviously the range of his knowledge and experience and the general ideas he has acquired from his fellows will play a large part in shaping his inferences. It is quite certain that even in the simplest problem of primitive physics or biology his attention will be directed only to some of, and not all, the factors involved, and that the limitations of his knowledge will permit him to form a wholly inadequate conception even of the few factors that have obtruded themselves upon his attention. But he may frame a working hypothesis in explanation of the factors he had appreciated, which may seem perfectly exhaustive and final, as well as logical and rational to him, but to those who come after him, with a wider knowledge of the properties of matter and the nature of living beings, and a wholly different attitude towards such problems, the primitive man's solution may seem merely a ludicrous travesty.

But once a tentative explanation of one group of phenomena has been made it is the method of science no less than the common tendency of the human mind to buttress this theory with analogies and fancied homologies. In other words the isolated facts are built up into a generalisation. It is important to remember that in most cases this mental process begins very early ; so that the analogies play a very obtrusive part in the building up of theories. As a rule a multitude of such influences play a part consciously or unconsciously in shaping any belief. Hence the historian is faced with the difficulty, often quite insuperable, of ascertaining (among scores of factors that definitely played some part in the building up of a great generalization) the real foundation upon which the vast edifice has been erected. I refer to these elementary matters here for two reasons. First, because they are so often overlooked by ethnologists; and secondly, because in these pages I shall have to discuss a series of historical events in which a bewildering number of factors played their part. In sifting out a certain number of them, I want to make it clear that I do not pretend to have discovered more than a small minority of the most conspicuous threads in the complex texture of the fabric of early human thought.

Another fact that emerges from these elementary psychological considerations is the vital necessity of guarding against the misunderstandings necessarily involved in the use of words. In the course of long ages the originally simple connotation of the words used to denote many of our ideas has become enormously enriched with a meaning which in some degree reflects the chequered history of the expression of human aspirations. Many writers who in discussing ancient peoples make use of such terms, for example, as "soul," "religion," and "gods," without stripping them of the accretions of complex symbolism that have collected around them within more recent times, become involved in difficulty and misunderstanding.

For example, the use of the terms "soul" or "soul-substance" in much of the literature relating to early or relatively primitive people is fruitful of misunderstanding. For it is quite clear from the context that in many cases such people meant to imply nothing more than "life" or "vital principle," the absence of which from the body for any prolonged period means death. But to translate such a word simply as "life" is inadequate because all of these people had some theoretical views as to its identity with the "breath" or to its being in the nature of a material substance or essence. It is naturally impossible to find any one word or phrase in our own language to express the exact idea, for among every people there are varying shades of meaning which cannot adequately express the symbolism distinctive of each place and society. To meet this insuperable difficulty perhaps the term "vital essence" is open to least objection.

In my last Rylands lecture [1] I sketched in rough outline a tentative explanation of the world-wide dispersal of the elements of the civilization that is now the heritage of the world at large, and referred to the part played by Ancient Egypt in the development of certain arts, customs, and beliefs. On the present occasion I propose to examine certain aspects of this process of development in greater detail, and to study the far-reaching influence exerted by the Egyptian practice of mummification, and the ideas that were suggested by it, in starting new trains of thought, in stimulating the invention of arts and crafts that were unknown before then, and in shaping the complex body of customs and beliefs that were the outcome of these potent intellectual ferments.

In speaking of the relationship of the practice of mummification to the development of civilization, however, I have in mind not merely the influence it exerted upon the moulding of culture, but also the part played by the trend of philosophy in the world at large in determining the Egyptian's conceptions of the wider significance of embalming, and the reaction of these effects upon the current doctrines of the meaning of natural phenomena.

No doubt it will be asked at the outset, what possible connexion can there be between the practice of so fantastic and gruesome an art as the embalming of the dead and the building up of civilization? Is it conceivable that the course of the development of the arts and crafts, the customs and beliefs, and the social and political organizations—in fact any of the essential elements of civilization—has been deflected a hair's breadth to the right or left as the outcome, directly or indirectly, of such a practice?

In previous essays and lectures [2] I have indicated how intimately this custom was related, not merely to the invention of the arts and crafts of the carpenter and stonemason and all that is implied in the building up of what Professor Lethaby has called the "matrix of civilization," but also to the shaping of religious beliefs and ritual practices,

[1] "The Influence of Ancient Egyptian Civilization in the East and in America," *The Bulletin of the John Rylands Library*, Jan.-March, 1916.
[2] "The Migrations of Early Culture," 1915, Manchester University Press: "The Evolution of the Rock-cut Tomb and the Dolmen," *Essays and Studies Presented to William Ridgeway*, Cambridge, 1913, p. 493: "Oriental Tombs and Temples," *Journal of the Manchester Egyptian and Oriental Society*, 1914-1915, p. 55.

INCENSE AND LIBATIONS

which developed in association with the evolution of the temple and the conception of a material resurrection. I have also suggested the far-reaching significance of an indirect influence of the practice of mummification in the history of civilization. It was mainly responsible for prompting the earliest great maritime expeditions of which the history has been preserved.[1] For many centuries the quest of resins and balsams for embalming and for use in temple ritual, and wood for coffin-making, continued to provide the chief motives which induced the Egyptians to undertake sea-trafficking in the Mediterranean and the Red Sea. The knowledge and experience thus acquired ultimately made it possible for the Egyptians and their pupils to push their adventures further afield. It is impossible adequately to estimate the vastness of the influence of such intercourse, not merely in spreading abroad throughout the world the germs of our common civilization, but also, by bringing into close contact peoples of varied histories and traditions, in stimulating progress. Even if the practice of mummification had exerted no other noteworthy effect in the history of the world, this fact alone would have given it a pre-eminent place.

Another aspect of the influence of mummification I have already discussed, and do not intend to consider further in this lecture. I refer to the manifold ways in which it affected the history of medicine and pharmacy. By accustoming the Egyptians, through thirty centuries, to the idea of cutting the human corpse, it made it possible for Greek physicians of the Ptolemaic and later ages to initiate in Alexandria the systematic dissection of the human body which popular prejudice forbade elsewhere, and especially in Greece itself. Upon this foundation the knowledge of anatomy and the science of medicine has been built up.[2] But in many other ways the practice of mummification exerted far-reaching effects, directly and indirectly, upon the development of medical and pharmaceutical knowledge and methods.[3]

---

[1] "Ships as Evidence of the Migrations of Early Culture," Manchester University Press, 1917, p. 37.

[2] "Egyptian Mummies," *Journal of Egyptian Archæology*, Vol. I, Part III, July, 1914, p. 189.

[3] Such, for example, as its influence in the acquisition of the means of preserving the tissues of the body, which has played so large a part in the development of the sciences of anatomy, pathology, and in fact biology in general. The practice of mummification was largely responsible for the attainment of a knowledge of the properties of many drugs and especially

There is then this *prima-facie* evidence that the Egyptian practice of mummification was closely related to the development of architecture, maritime trafficking, and medicine. But what I am chiefly concerned with in the present lecture is the discussion of the much vaster part it played in shaping the innermost beliefs of mankind and directing the course of the religious aspirations and the scientific opinions, not merely of the Egyptians themselves, but also of the world at large, for many centuries afterward.

It had a profound influence upon the history of human thought. The vague and ill-defined ideas of physiology and psychology, which had probably been developing since Aurignacian times [1] in Europe, were suddenly crystallized into a coherent structure and definite form by the musings of the Egyptian embalmer. But at the same time, if the new philosophy did not find expression in the invention of the first deities, it gave them a much more concrete form than they had previously presented, and played a large part in the establishment of the foundations upon which all religious ritual was subsequently built up, and in the initiation of a priesthood to administer the rites which were suggested by the practice of mummification.

The Beginning of Stone-Working.

During the last few years I have repeatedly had occasion to point out the fundamental fallacy underlying much of the modern speculation in ethnology, and I have no intention of repeating these strictures here.[2] But it is a significant fact that, when one leaves the writings of professed ethnologists and turns to the histories of their special subjects written by scholars in kindred fields of investigation, views such

of those which restrain putrefactive changes. But it was not merely in the acquisition of a knowledge of material facts that mummification exerted its influence. The humoral theory of pathology and medicine, which prevailed for so many centuries and the effects of which are embalmed for all time in our common speech, was closely related in its inception to the ideas which I shall discuss in these pages. The Egyptians themselves did not profit to any appreciable extent from the remarkable opportunities which their practice of embalming provided for studying human anatomy. The sanctity of these ritual acts was fatal to the employment of such opportunities to gain knowledge. Nor was the attitude of mind of the Egyptians such as to permit the acquisition of a real appreciation of the structure of the body.

[1] See my address, "Primitive Man," *Proc. Brit. Academy*, 1917.

[2] See, however, *op. cit. supra*; also "The Origin of the Pre-Columbian Civilization of America," *Science*, N.S., Vol. XLV, No. 1158, pp. 241-246, 9 March, 1917.

as I have been setting forth will often be found to be accepted without question or comment as the obvious truth.

There is an excellent little book entitled "Architecture," written by Professor W. R. Lethaby for the Home University Library, that affords an admirable illustration of this interesting fact. I refer to this particular work because it gives lucid expression to some of the ideas that I wish to submit for consideration. "Two arts have changed the surface of the world, Agriculture and Architecture" (p. 1). "To a large degree architecture" [which he defines as "the matrix of civilization"] "is an Egyptian art" (p. 66) : for in Egypt "we shall best find the origins of architecture as a whole" (p. 21).

Nevertheless Professor Lethaby bows the knee to current tradition when he makes the wholly unwarranted assumption that Egypt probably learnt its art from Babylonia. He puts forward this remarkable claim in spite of his frank confession that "little or nothing is known of a primitive age in Mesopotamia. At a remote time the art of Babylonia was that of a civilized people. As has been said, there is a great similarity between this art and that of dynastic times in Egypt. Yet it appears that Egypt borrowed of Asia, rather than the reverse." [He gives no reasons for this opinion, for which there is no evidence, except possibly the invention of bricks for building.] "If the origins of art in Babylonia were as fully known as those in Egypt, the story of architecture might have to begin in Asia instead of Egypt" (p. 67).

But later on he speaks in a more convincing manner of the known facts when he says (p. 82) :—

When Greece entered on her period of high-strung life the time of first invention in the arts was over—the heroes of Craft, like Tubal Cain and Daedalus, necessarily belong to the infancy of culture. The phenomenon of Egypt could not occur again ; the mission of Greece was rather to settle down to a task of gathering, interpreting, and bringing to perfection Egypt's gifts. The arts of civilization were never developed in water-tight compartments, as is shown by the uniformity of custom over the modern world. Further, if any new nation enters into the circle of culture it seems that, like Japan, it must 'borrow the capital'. The art of Greece could hardly have been more self-originated than is the science of Japan. Ideas of the temple and of the fortified town must have spread from the East, the square-roomed house, columnar orders, fine masonry, were all Egyptian.

Elsewhere[1] I have pointed out that it was the importance which

---

[1] *Op. cit. supra.*

the Egyptian came to attach to the preservation of the dead and to the making of adequate provision for the deceased's welfare that gradually led to the aggrandisement of the tomb. In course of time this impelled him to cut into the rock,[1] and, later still, suggested the substitution of stone for brick in erecting the chapel of offerings above ground. The Egyptian burial customs were thus intimately related to the conceptions that grew up with the invention of embalming. The evidence in confirmation of this is so precise that every one who conscientiously examines it must be forced to the conclusion that man did not instinctively select stone as a suitable material with which to erect temples and houses, and forthwith begin to quarry and shape it for such purposes.

There was an intimate connexion between the first use of stone for building and the practice of mummification. It was probably for this reason, and not from any abstract sense of "wonder at the magic of art," as Professor Lethaby claims, that "ideas of sacredness, of ritual rightness, of magic stability and correspondence with the universe, and of perfection of form and proportion" came to be associated with stone buildings.

At first stone was used only for such sacred purposes, and the pharaoh alone was entitled to use it for his palaces, in virtue of the fact that he was divine, the son and incarnation on earth of the sun-god. It was only when these Egyptian practices were transplanted to other countries, where these restrictions did not obtain, that the rigid wall of convention was broken down.

Even in Rome until well into the Christian era "the largest domestic and civil buildings were of plastered brick". "Wrought masonry seems to have been demanded only for the great monuments, triumphal arches, theatres, temples and above all for the Coliseum." (Lethaby, *op. cit.* p. 120).

Nevertheless Rome was mainly responsible for breaking down the hieratic tradition which forbade the use of stone for civil purposes. "In Roman architecture the engineering element became paramount. It was this which broke the moulds of tradition and recast construction into modern form, and made it free once more" (p. 130).

---

[1] For the earliest evidence of the cutting of stone for architectural purposes, see my statement in the *Report of the British Association for* 1914, p. 212.

But Egypt was not only responsible for inaugurating the use of stone for building. For another forty centuries she continued to be the inventor of new devices in architecture. From time to time methods of building which developed in Egypt were adopted by her neighbours and spread far and wide. The shaft-tombs and *mastabas* of the Egyptian Pyramid Age were adopted in various localities in the region of the Eastern Mediterranean,[1] with certain modifications in each place, and in turn became the models which were roughly copied in later ages by the wandering dolmen-builders. The round tombs of Crete and Mycenae were clearly only local modifications of their square prototypes, the Egyptian Pyramids of the Middle Kingdom. " While this Ægean art gathered from, and perhaps gave to, Egypt, it passed on its ideals to the north and west of Europe, where the productions of the Bronze Age clearly show its influence" (Lethaby, p. 78) in the chambered mounds of the Iberian peninsula and Brittany, of New Grange in Ireland and of Maes Howe in the Orkneys.[2] In the East the influence of these Ægean modifications may possibly be seen in the Indian *stupas* and the *dagabas* of Ceylon, just as the stone stepped pyramids there reveal the effects of contact with the civilizations of Babylonia and Egypt.

Professor Lethaby sees the influence of Egypt in the orientation of Christian churches (p. 133), as well as in many of their structural details (p. 142); in the domed roofs, the iconography, the symbolism, and the decoration of Byzantine architecture (p. 138); and in Mohammedan buildings wherever they are found.

For it was not only the architecture of Greece, Rome, and Christendom that received its inspiration from Egypt, but that of Islâm also. These buildings were not, like the religion itself, in the main Arabic in origin. " Primitive Arabian art itself is quite negligible. When the new strength of the followers of the Prophet was consoli-

---

[1] Especially in Crete, Palestine, Syria, Asia Minor, Southern Russia, and the North African Littoral.

[2] For an account of the evidence relating to these monuments, with full bibliographical references, see Déchelette, " Manuel d'Archéologie préhistorique Celtique et Gallo-Romaine," T. 1, 1912, pp. 390 *et seq.*; also Sophus Müller, " Urgeschichte Europas," 1905, pp. 74 and 75; and Louis Siret, " Les Cassitérides et l'Empire Colonial des Phéniciens," *L'Anthropologie*, T. 20, 1909, p. 313.

dated with great rapidity into a rich and powerful empire, it took over the arts and artists of the conquered lands, extending from North Africa to Persia" (p. 158); and it is known how this influence spread as far west as Spain and as far east as Indonesia. "The Pharos at Alexandria, the great lighthouse built about 280 B.C., almost appears to have been the parent of all high and isolated towers. . . . Even on the coast of Britain, at Dover, we had a Pharos which was in some degree an imitation of the Alexandrian one." The Pharos at Boulogne, the round towers of Ravenna, and the imitations of it elsewhere in Europe, even as far as Ireland, are other examples of its influence. But in addition the Alexandrian Pharos had "as great an effect as the prototype of Eastern minarets as it had for Western towers" (p. 115).

I have quoted so extensively from Professor Lethaby's brilliant little book to give this independent testimony of the vastness of the influence exerted by Egypt during a span of nearly forty centuries in creating and developing the "matrix of civilization". Most of this wider dispersal abroad was effected by alien peoples, who transformed their gifts from Egypt before they handed on the composite product to some more distant peoples. But the fact remains that the great centre of original inspiration in architecture was Egypt.

The original incentive to the invention of this essentially Egyptian art was the desire to protect and secure the welfare of the dead. The importance attached to this aim was intimately associated with the development of the practice of mummification.

With this tangible and persistent evidence of the general scheme of spread of the arts of building I can now turn to the consideration of some of the other, more vital, manifestations of human thought and aspirations, which also, like the "matrix of civilization" itself, grew up in intimate association with the practice of embalming the dead.

I have already mentioned Professor Lethaby's reference to architecture and agriculture as the two arts that have changed the surface of the world. It is interesting to note that the influence of these two ingredients of civilization was diffused abroad throughout the world in intimate association the one with the other. In most parts of the world the use of stone for building and Egyptian methods of architecture made their first appearance along with the peculiarly distinctive form of agriculture and irrigation so intimately associated with early Babylonia and Egypt.[1]

But agriculture also exerted a most profound influence in shaping the early Egyptian body of beliefs.

I shall now call attention to certain features of the earliest mummies, and then discuss how the ideas suggested by the practice of the art of embalming the dead were affected by the early theories of agriculture and the mutual influence they exerted one upon the other.

The Origin of Embalming.

I have already explained[2] how the increased importance that came to be attached to the corpse as the means of securing a continuance of existence led to the aggrandizement of the tomb. Special care was taken to protect the dead and this led to the invention of coffins, and to the making of a definite tomb, the size of which rapidly increased as more and more ample supplies of food and other offerings were made. But the very measures thus taken the more efficiently to protect and tend the dead defeated the primary object of all this care. For, when buried in such an elaborate tomb, the body no longer became desiccated and preserved by the forces of nature, as so often happened when it was placed in a simple grave directly in the hot dry sand.

It is of fundamental importance in the argument set forth here to remember that these factors came into operation before the time of the First Dynasty. They were responsible for impelling the Proto-Egyptians not only to invent the wooden coffin, the stone sarcophagus, the rock-cut tomb, and to begin building in stone, but also to devise measures for the artificial preservation of the body.

But in addition to stimulating the development of the first real architecture and the art of mummification other equally far-reaching results in the region of ideas and beliefs grew out of these practices.

From the outset the Egyptian embalmer was clearly inspired by two ideals: (*a*) to preserve the actual tissues of the body with a minimum disturbance of its superficial appearance; and (*b*) to preserve a likeness of the deceased as he was in life. At first it

---

[1] W. J. Perry, "The Geographical Distribution of Terraced Cultivation and Irrigation," *Memoirs and Proc. Manch. Lit. and Phil. Soc.*, Vol. 60, 1916.

[2] *Op. cit. supra.*

was naturally attempted to make this simulacrum of the body itself if it were possible, or alternatively, when this ideal was found to be unattainable, from its wrappings or by means of a portrait statue. It was soon recognized that it was beyond the powers of the early embalmer to succeed in mummifying the body itself so as to retain a recognizable likeness to the man when alive : although from time to time such attempts were repeatedly made,[1] until the period of the XXI Dynasty, when the operator clearly was convinced that he had at last achieved what his predecessors, for perhaps twenty-five centuries, had been trying in vain to do.

Early Mummies.

In the earliest known (Second Dynasty) examples of Egyptian attempts at mummification[2] the corpse was swathed in a large series of bandages, which were moulded into shape to represent the form of the body. In a later (probably Fifth Dynasty) mummy, found in 1892 by Professor Flinders Petrie at Medûm, the superficial bandages had been impregnated with a resinous paste, which while still plastic was moulded into the form of the body, special care being bestowed upon the modelling of the face[3] and the organs of reproduction, so as to leave no room for doubt as to the identity and the sex. Professor Junker has described[4] an interesting series of variations of these practices. In two graves the bodies were covered with a layer of stucco plaster. First the corpse was covered with a fine linen cloth : then the plaster was put on, and modelled into the form of the body (p. 252). But in two other cases it was not the whole body that was

---

[1] See my volume on " The Royal Mummies," General Catalogue of the Cairo Museum.

[2] G. Elliot Smith, " The Earliest Evidence of Attempts at Mummification in Egypt," *Report British Association*, 1912, p. 612: compare also J. Garstang, " Burial Customs of Ancient Egypt," London, 1907, pp. 29 and 30. Professor Garstang did not recognize that mummification had been attempted.

[3] G. Elliot Smith, " The History of Mummification in Egypt," *Proc. Royal Philosophical Society of Glasgow*, 1910 : also " Egyptian Mummies," *Journal of Egyptian Archæology*, Vol. I, Part III, July, 1914, Plate. XXXI.

[4] " Excavations of the Vienna Imperial Academy of Sciences at the Pyramids of Gizah, 1914," *Journal of Egyptian Archæology*, Vol. I, Oct. 1914, p. 250.

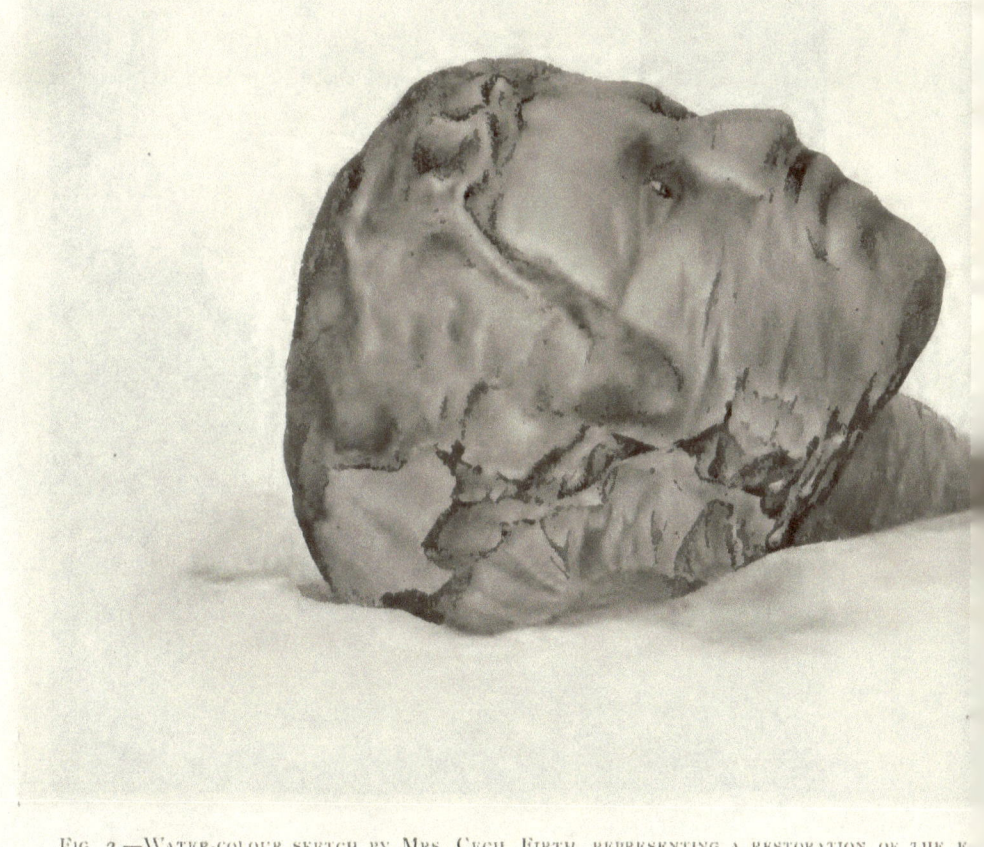

FIG. 2.—WATER-COLOUR SKETCH BY MRS. CECIL FIRTH, REPRESENTING A RESTORATION OF THE H
BY PROF. FLINDERS PETRIE, NOW IN THE MUSEUM OF THE ROYAL COLLEGE OF SUR

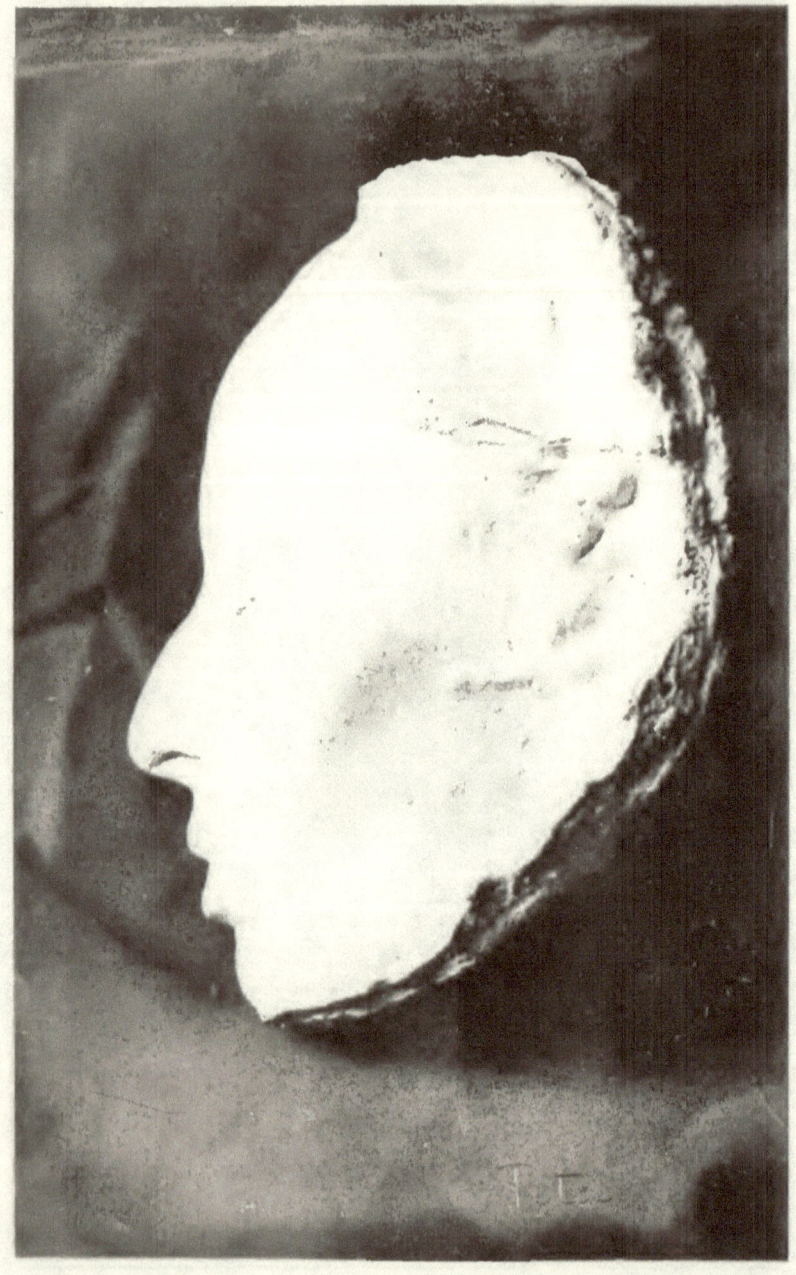

FIG. 3.—A MOULD TAKEN FROM A LIFE-MASK FOUND IN THE PYRAMID OF TETA BY MR. QUIBELL

INCENSE AND LIBATIONS

covered with this layer of stucco, but only the head. Professor Junker claims that this was done " apparently because the head was regarded as the most important part, as the organs of taste, sight, smell, and hearing were contained in it". But surely there was the additional and more obtrusive reason that the face affords the means of identifying the individual! For this modelling of the features was intended primarily as a restoration of the form of the body which had been altered, if not actually destroyed. In other cases, where no attempt was made to restore the features in such durable materials as resin or stucco, the linen-enveloped head was modelled, and a representation of the eyes painted upon it so as to enhance the life-like appearance of the face.

These facts prove quite conclusively that the earliest attempts to reproduce the features of the deceased and so preserve his likeness, were made upon the wrapped mummy itself. Thus the mummy was intended to be the portrait as well as the actual bodily remains of the dead. In view of certain differences of opinion as to the original significance of the funerary ritual, which I shall have occasion to discuss later on (see p. 20), it is important to keep these facts clearly in mind.

A discovery made by Mr. J. E. Quibell in the course of his excavations at Sakkara[1] suggests that, as an outcome of these practices a new procedure may have been devised in the Pyramid Age—the making of a death-mask. For he discovered what may be the mask taken directly from the face of the Pharaoh Teta (Fig. 3).

About this time also the practice originated of making a life-size portrait statue of the dead man's head and placing it along with the actual body in the burial chamber. These "reserve heads," as they have been called, were usually made of fine limestone, but Junker found one made of Nile mud.[2]

Junker believes that there was an intimate relationship between the plaster-covered heads and the reserve-heads. They were both expressions of the same idea, to preserve a simulacrum of the deceased when his actual body had lost all recognizable likeness to him as he

---

[1] " Excavations at Saqqara," 1907-8, p. 113.

[2] The great variety of experiments that were being made at the beginning of the Pyramid Age bears ample testimony to the fact that the original inventors of these devices were actually at work in Lower Egypt at that time.

was when alive. The one method aimed at combining in the same object the actual body and the likeness; the other at making a more life-like portrait apart from the corpse, which could take the place of the latter when it decayed.

Junker states further that "it is no chance that the substitute-heads . . . entirely, or at any rate chiefly, are found in the tombs that have no statue-chamber and probably possessed no statues. The statues [of the whole body] certainly were made, at any rate partly, with the intention that they should take the place of the decaying body, although later the idea was modified. The placing of the substitute-head in [the burial chamber of] the mastaba therefore became unnecessary at the moment when the complete figure of the dead [placed in a special hidden chamber, now commonly called the *serdab*] was introduced." The ancient Egyptians themselves called the *serdab* the *pr-twt* or "statue-house," and the group of chambers, forming the tomb-chapel in the mastaba, was known to them as the "*ka*-house".[1]

It is important to remember that, even when the custom of making a statue of the deceased became fully established, the original idea of restoring the form of the mummy itself or its wrappings was never abandoned. The attempts made in the XVIII, and XXI and XXII Dynasties to pack the body of the mummy itself and by artificial means give it a life-like appearance afford evidence of this. In the New Empire and in Roman times the wrapped mummy was sometimes modelled into the form of a statue. But throughout Egyptian history it was a not uncommon practice to provide a painted mask for the wrapped mummy, or in early Christian times simply a portrait of the deceased.

With this custom there also persisted a remembrance of its original significance. Professor Garstang records the fact that in the XII Dynasty,[2] when a painted mask was placed upon the wrapped mummy, no statue or statuette was found in the tomb. The under-

---

[1] Aylward M. Blackman, "The *Ka*-House and the Serdab," *Journal of Egyptian Archæology*, Vol. III, Part IV, Oct., 1916, p. 250. The word *serdab* is merely the Arabic word used by the native workmen, which has been adopted and converted into a technical term by European archæologists.

[2] *Op. cit.* p. 171.

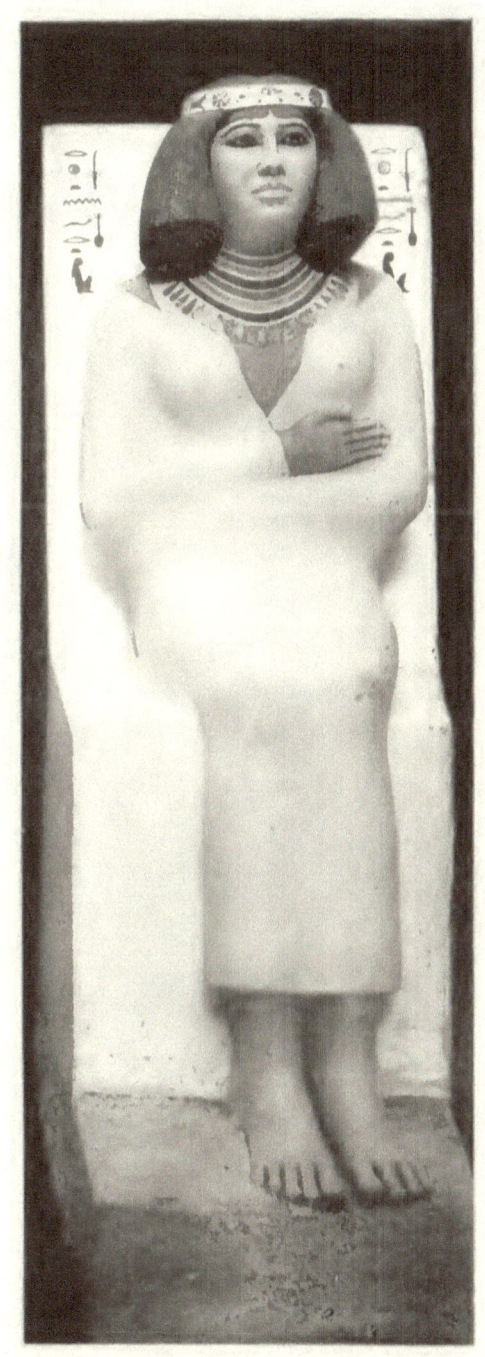

Fig. 4.—Portrait Statue of an Egyptian Lady of the Pyramid Age

takers apparently realized that the mummy¹ which was provided with the life-like mask was therefore fulfilling the purposes for which statues were devised. So also in the New Empire the packing and modelling of the actual mummy so as to restore its life-like appearance were regarded as obviating the need for a statue.

I must now return to the further consideration of the Old Kingdom statues. All these varied experiments were inspired by the same desire, to preserve the likeness of the deceased. But when the sculptors attained their object, and created those marvellous life-like portraits, which must ever remain marvels of technical skill and artistic feeling (Fig. 4), the old ideas that surged through the minds of the Pre-dynastic Egyptians, as they contemplated the desiccated remains of the dead, were strongly reinforced. The earlier people's thoughts were turned more specifically than heretofore to the contemplation of the nature of life and death by seeing the bodies of their dead preserved whole and incorruptible; and, if their actions can be regarded as an expression of their ideas, they began to wonder what was lacking in these physically complete bodies to prevent them from feeling and acting like living beings. Such must have been the results of their puzzled contemplation of the great problems of life and death. Otherwise the impulse to make more certain the preservation of the body by the invention of mummification and to retain a life-like representation of the deceased by means of a sculptured statue remains inexplicable. But when the corpse had been rendered incorruptible and the deceased's portrait had been fashioned with realistic perfection the old ideas would recur with renewed strength. The belief then took more definite shape that if the missing elements of vitality could be restored to the statue, it might become animated and the dead man would live again in his vitalized statue. This prompted a more intense and searching investigation of the problems concerning the nature of the elements of vitality of which the corpse was deprived at the time of death. Out of these inquiries in course of time a highly complex system of philosophy developed.²

[1] It is a remarkable fact that Professor Garstang, who brought to light perhaps the best, and certainly the best-preserved, collection of Middle Kingdom mummies ever discovered, failed to recognize the fact that they had really been embalmed (*op. cit.* p. 171).

[2] The reader who wishes for fuller information as to the reality of these beliefs and how seriously they were held will find them still in active

But in the earlier times with which I am now concerned it found practical expression in certain ritual procedures, invented to convey to the statue the breath of life, the vitalising fluids, and the odour and sweat of the living body. The seat of knowledge and of feeling was believed to be retained in the body when the heart was left *in situ:* so that the only thing needed to awaken consciousness, and make it possible for the dead man to take heed of his friends and to act voluntarily, was to present offerings of blood to stimulate the physiological functions of the heart. But the element of vitality which left the body at death had to be restored to the statue, which represented the deceased in the *ka*-house.[1]

In my earlier attempts[2] to interpret these problems, I adopted the view that the making of portrait statues was the direct outcome of the practice of mummification. But Dr. Alan Gardiner, whose intimate knowledge of the early literature enables him to look at such problems from the Egyptian's own point of view, has suggested a modification of this interpretation. Instead of regarding the custom of making statues as an outcome of the practice of mummification, he thinks that the two customs developed simultaneously, in response to the twofold desire to preserve both the actual body and a representation of the features of the dead. But I think this suggestion does not give adequate recognition to the fact that the earliest attempts at funerary portraiture were made upon the wrappings of the actual mummies.[3] This fact and the evidence which I have already

operation in China. An admirable account of Chinese philosophy will be found in De Groot's "Religious System of China," especially Vol. IV, Book II. It represents the fully developed (New Empire) system of Egyptian belief modified in various ways by Babylonian, Indian and Central Asiatic influences, as well as by accretions developed locally in China.

[1] A. M. Blackman, "The *Ka*-House and the Serdab," *The Journal of Egyptian Archæology*, Vol. III, Part IV, Oct., 1916, p. 250.

[2] "Migrations of Early Culture," p. 37.

[3] Dr. Alan Gardiner (Davies and Gardiner, "The Tomb of Amenemhēt," 1915, p. 83, footnote) has, I think, overlooked certain statements in my writings and underestimated the antiquity of the embalmer's art; for he attributes to me the opinion that "mummification was a custom of relatively late growth".

The presence in China of the characteristically Egyptian beliefs concerning the animation of statues (de Groot, *op. cit.* pp. 339-356), whereas the practice of mummification, though not wholly absent, is not obtrusive, might perhaps be interpreted by some scholars as evidence in favour of the

INCENSE AND LIBATIONS

quoted from Junker make it quite clear that from the beginning the embalmer's aim was to preserve the body and to convert the mummy itself into a simulacrum of the deceased. When he realized that his technical skill was not adequate to enable him to accomplish this double aim, he fell back upon the device of making a more perfect and realistic portrait statue apart from the mummy. But, as I have already pointed out, he never completely renounced his ambition of transforming the mummy itself; and in the time of the New Empire he actually attained the result which he had kept in view for nearly twenty centuries.

In these remarks I have been referring only to funerary portrait statues. Centuries before the attempt was made to fashion them modellers had been making of clay and stone representations of cattle and human beings, which have been found not only in Predynastic graves in Egypt but also in so-called "Upper Palæolithic" deposits in Europe.

But the fashioning of realistic and life-size human portrait-statues for funerary purposes was a new art, which gradually developed in the way I have tried to depict. No doubt the modellers made use of the skill they had acquired in the practice of the older art of rough impressionism.

Once the statue was made a stone-house (the *serdab*) was provided for it above ground.[1] As the dolmen is a crude copy of the *serdab*[2] it can be claimed as one of the ultimate results of the practice

development of the custom of making statues independently of mummification. But such an inference is untenable. Not only is it the fact that in most parts of the world the practices of making statues and mummifying the dead are found in association the one with the other, but also in China the essential beliefs concerning the dead are based upon the supposition that the body is fully preserved (*see* de Groot, chap. XV.). It is quite evident that the Chinese customs have been derived directly or indirectly from some people who mummified their dead as a regular practice. There can be no doubt that the ultimate source of their inspiration to do these things was Egypt.

I need mention only one of many identical peculiarities that makes this quite certain. De Groot says it is "strange to see Chinese fancy depict the souls of the viscera as distinct individuals with animal forms" (p. 71). The same custom prevailed in Egypt, where the "souls" or protective deities were first given animal forms in the Nineteenth Dynasty (Reisner).

[1] The Arabic word conveys the idea of being "hidden underground," because the house is exposed by excavation.

[2] *Op. cit. supra*, Ridgeway Essays; also *Man*, 1913, p. 193.

of mummification. It is clear that the conception of the possibility of a life beyond the grave assumed a more concrete form when it was realized that the body itself could be rendered incorruptible and its distinctive traits could be kept alive by means of a portrait statue. There are reasons for supposing that primitive man did not realize or contemplate the possibility of his own existence coming to an end.[1] Even when he witnessed the death of his fellows he does not appear to have appreciated the fact that it was really the end of life and not merely a kind of sleep from which the dead might awake. But if the corpse were destroyed or underwent a process of natural disintegration the fact was brought home to him that death had occurred. If these considerations, which early Egyptian literature seems to suggest, be borne in mind, the view that the preservation of the body from corruption implied a continuation of existence becomes intelligible. At first the subterranean chambers in which the actual body was housed were developed into a many-roomed house for the deceased, complete in every detail.[2] But when the statue took over the function of representing the deceased, a dwelling was provided for it above ground. This developed into the temple where the relatives and friends of the dead came and made the offerings of food which were regarded as essential for the maintenance of existence.

The evolution of the temple was thus the direct outcome of the ideas that grew up in connexion with the preservation of the dead. For at first it was nothing more than the dwelling place of the re-animated dead. But when, for reasons which I shall explain later (see p. 30), the dead king became deified, his temple of offerings became the building where food and drink were presented to the god, not merely to maintain his existence, but also to restore his consciousness, and so afford an opportunity for his successor, the actual king, to consult him and obtain his advice and help. The presentation of offerings and the ritual procedures for animating and restoring consciousness to the dead king were at first directed solely to these ends. But in course of time, as their original purpose became obscured, these services in the temple altered in character, and their meaning became

[1] See Alan H. Gardiner, "Life and Death (Egyptian)," Hastings' *Encyclopædia of Religion and Ethics*.

[2] See the quotation from Mr. Quibell's account in my statement in the *Report of the British Association for* 1914, p. 215.

rationalized into acts of homage and worship, and of prayer and supplication, and in much later times, acquired an ethical and moral significance that was wholly absent from the original conception of the temple services. The earliest idea of the temple as a place of offering has not been lost sight of. Even in our times the offertory still finds a place in temple services.

THE SIGNIFICANCE OF LIBATIONS.

The central idea of this lecture was suggested by Mr. Aylward M. Blackman's important discovery of the actual meaning of incense and libations to the Egyptians themselves.[1] The earliest body of literature preserved from any of the peoples of antiquity is comprised in the texts inscribed in the subterranean chambers of the Sakkara Pyramids of the Fifth and Sixth Dynasties. These documents, written forty-five centuries ago, were first brought to light in modern times in 1880-81; and since the late Sir Gaston Maspero published the first translation of them, many scholars have helped in the task of elucidating their meaning. But it remained for Blackman to discover the explanation they give of the origin and significance of the act of pouring out libations. "The general meaning of these passages is quite clear. The corpse of the deceased is dry and shrivelled. To revivify it the vital fluids that have exuded from it [in the process of mummification] must be restored, for not till then will life return and the heart beat again. This, so the texts show us, was believed to be accomplished by offering libations to the accompaniment of incantations" (*op. cit.* p. 70).

In the first three passages quoted by Blackman from the Pyramid Texts "the libations are said to be the actual fluids that have issued from the corpse". In the next four quotations "a different notion is introduced. It is not the deceased's own exudations that are to revive his shrunken frame but those of a divine body, the [god's fluid][2] that

[1] "The Significance of Incense and Libations in Funerary and Temple Ritual," *Zeitschrift für Ägyptische Sprache und Altertumskunde*, Bd. 50, 1912, p. 69.

[2] Mr. Blackman here quotes the actual word in hieroglyphics and adds the translation "god's fluid" and the following explanation in a footnote: "The Nile was supposed to be the fluid which issued from Osiris. The expression in the Pyramid texts may refer to this belief—the dead" [in the Pyramid Age it would have been more accurate if he had said the dead

came from the corpse of Osiris himself, the juices that dissolved from his decaying flesh, which are communicated to the dead sacrament-wise under the form of these libations."

This dragging-in of Osiris is especially significant. For the analogy of the life-giving power of water that is specially associated with Osiris played a dominant part in suggesting the ritual of libations. Just as water, when applied to the apparently dead seed, makes it germinate and come to life, so libations can reanimate the corpse. These general biological theories of the potency of water were current at the time, and, as I shall explain later (see p. 28), had possibly received specific application to man long before the idea of libations developed. For, in the development of the cult of Osiris [1] the general fertilizing power

king, in whose Pyramid the inscriptions were found] "being usually identified with Osiris—since the water used in the libations was Nile water."

[1] The voluminous literature relating to Osiris will be found summarized in the latest edition of "The Golden Bough" by Sir James Frazer. But in referring the reader to this remarkable compilation of evidence it is necessary to call particular attention to the fact that Sir James Frazer's interpretation is permeated with speculations based upon the modern ethnological dogma of independent evolution of similar customs and beliefs without cultural contact between the different localities where such similarities make their appearance.

The complexities of the motives that inspire and direct human activities are entirely fatal to such speculations, as I have attempted to indicate (see above, p. 195). But apart from this general warning, there are other objections to Sir James Frazer's theories. In his illuminating article upon Osiris and Horus, Dr. Alan Gardiner (in a criticism of Sir James Frazer's "The Golden Bough: Adonis, Attis, Osiris; Studies in the History of Oriental Religion," *Journal of Egyptian Archæology*, Vol. II, 1915, p. 122) insists upon the crucial fact that Osiris was primarily a king, and that "it is always as a *dead* king," "the rôle of the living king being invariably played by Horus, his son and heir".

He states further: "What Egyptologists wish to know about Osiris beyond anything else is how and by what means he became associated with the processes of vegetable life". An examination of the literature relating to Osiris and the large series of homologous deities in other countries (which exhibit *prima facie* evidence of a common origin) suggests the idea that the king who first introduced the practice of systematic irrigation thereby laid the foundation of his reputation as a beneficent reformer. When, for reasons which I shall discuss later on (see p. 220), the dead king became deified, his fame as the controller of water and the fertilization of the earth became apotheosized also. I venture to put forward this suggestion only because none of the alternative hypotheses that have been propounded

INCENSE AND LIBATIONS

of water when applied to the soil found specific exemplification in the potency of the seminal fluid to fertilize human beings. Malinowski has pointed out that certain Papuan people, who are ignorant of the fact that women are fertilized by sexual connexion, believe that they can be rendered pregnant by rain falling upon them (*op. cit. infra*). The study of folk-lore and early beliefs makes it abundantly clear that in the distant past which I am now discussing no clear distinction was made between fertilization and vitalization, between bringing new life into being and reanimating the body which had once been alive. The process of fertilization of the female and animating a corpse or a statue were regarded as belonging to the same category of biological processes. The sculptor who carved the portrait-statues for the Egyptian's tomb was called *sa'nkh*, "he who causes to live," and "the word 'to fashion' (*ms*) a statue is to all appearances identical with *ms*, 'to give birth'".[1]

Thus the Egyptians themselves expressed in words the ideas which an independent study of the ethnological evidence showed many other peoples to entertain, both in ancient and modern times.[2]

The interpretation of ancient texts and the study of the beliefs of less cultured modern peoples indicate that our expressions: "to give birth," "to give life," "to maintain life," "to ward off death," "to insure good luck," "to prolong life," "to give life to the dead," "to animate a corpse or a representation of the dead," "to give fertility," "to impregnate," "to create," represent a series of specializations of meaning which were not clearly differentiated the one from the other in early times or among relatively primitive modern people.

seem to be in acccordance with, or to offer an adequate explanation of, the body of known facts concerning Osiris.

It is a remarkable fact that in his lectures on "The Development of Religion and Thought in Ancient Egypt," which are based upon his own studies of the Pyramid Texts, and are an invaluable storehouse of information, Professor J. H. Breasted should have accepted Sir James Frazer's views. These seem to me to be altogether at variance with the renderings of the actual Egyptian texts and to confuse the exposition.

[1] Dr. Alan Gardiner, quoted in my "Migrations of Early Culture," p. 42: see also the same scholar's remarks in Davies and Gardiner, "The Tomb of Amenemhēt," 1915, p. 57, and "A new Masterpiece of Egyptian Sculpture," *The Journal of Egyptian Archæology*, Vol. IV, Part I, Jan., 1917.

[2] See J. Wilfrid Jackson, "Shells as Evidence of the Migrations of Early Culture," 1917, Manchester University Press.

The evidence brought together in Jackson's work clearly suggests that at a very early period in human history, long before the ideas that found expression in the Osiris story had materialized, men entertained in all its literal crudity the belief that the external organ of reproduction from which the child emerged at birth was the actual creator of the child, not merely the giver of birth but also the source of life.

The widespread tendency of the human mind to identify similar objects and attribute to them the powers of the things they mimic led primitive men to assign to the cowry-shell all these life-giving and birth-giving virtues. It became an amulet to give fertility, to assist at birth, to maintain life, to ward off danger, to ensure the life hereafter, to bring luck of any sort. Now, as the giver of birth, the cowry-shell also came to be identified with, or regarded as, the mother and creator of the human family ; and in course of time, as this belief became rationalized, the shell's maternity received visible expression and it became personified as an actual woman, the Great Mother, at first nameless and with ill-defined features. But at a later period, when the dead king Osiris gradually acquired his attributes of divinity, and a god emerged with the form of a man, the vagueness of the Great Mother who had been merely the personified cowry-shell soon disappeared and the amulet assumed, as Hathor, the form of a real woman, or, for reasons to be explained later, a cow.

The influence of these developments reacted upon the nascent conception of the water-controlling god, Osiris ; and his powers of fertility were enlarged to include many of the life-giving attributes of Hathor

Early Biological Theories.

Before the full significance of these procedures can be appreciated it is essential to try to get at the back of the Proto-Egyptian's mind and to understand his general trend of thought. I specially want to make it clear that the ritual use of water for animating the corpse or the statue was merely a specific application of the general principles of biology which were then current. It was no mere childish make-believe or priestly subterfuge to regard the pouring out of water as a means of animating a block of stone. It was a conviction for which the Proto-Egyptians considered there was a substantial scientific basis ; and their faith in the efficacy of water to animate the dead is to be regarded in the same light as any scientific inference which is made at the present time to give a specific application of some general theory considered to be well founded. The Proto-Egyptians clearly believed in the validity of the general biological theory of the life-giving properties of water. Many facts, no doubt quite convincing to them, testified to the soundness of their theory. They accepted the principle with the same confidence that modern people have adopted Newton's Law of Gravitation, and Darwin's theory of the Origin of Species, and applied it to explain many phenomena or to justify certain procedures, which in the light of fuller knowledge seem to modern people puerile and ludicrous. But the early people obviously took these procedures seriously and regarded their actions as rational. The fact that their early biological theory was inadequate ought not to mislead modern scholars and encourage them to fall into the error of supposing that the ritual of libations was not based upon a serious inference. Modern scientists do not accept the whole of Darwin's teaching, or possibly even Newton's " Law," but this does not mean that in the past innumerable inferences have been honestly and confidently made in specific application of these general principles.

It is important, then, that I should examine more closely the Proto-Egyptian body of doctrine to elucidate the mutual influence of it and the ideas suggested by the practice of mummification. It is not known where agriculture was first practised or the circumstances which led men to appreciate the fact that plants could be cultivated. In many parts of the world agriculture can be carried on without artificial irrigation, and even without any adequate appreciation on the part of the farmer of the importance of water. But when it came to be practised under such conditions as prevail in Egypt and Mesopotamia, the cultivator would soon be forced to realize that water was essential for the growth of plants, and that it was imperative to devise artificial means by which the soil might be irrigated. It is not known where or by whom this cardinal fact first came to be appreciated, whether by the Sumerians or the Egyptians or by some other people. But it is known that in the earliest records both of Egypt and Sumer the most significant manifestations of a ruler's wisdom were the making of irrigation canals and the controlling of water. Important as these facts are from their bearing upon the material prospects of the people, they had an infinitely more profound and far-reaching effect upon the beliefs of mankind. Groping after some explanation of the natural phenomenon that the earth became fertile when water was applied to it, and that seed burst into life under the same influence, the early biologist formulated the natural and not wholly illogical idea that water was the repository of life-giving powers. Water was equally necessary for the production of life and for the maintenance of life.

At an early stage in the development of this biological theory man and other animals were brought within the scope of the generalization. For the drinking of water was a condition of existence in animals. The idea that water played a part in reproduction was co-related with this fact.

Even at the present time many aboriginal peoples in Australia, New Guinea, and elsewhere, are not aware of the fact that in the process of animal reproduction the male exercises the physiological rôle of fertilization.[1]

There are widespread indications throughout the world that the appreciation of this elementary physiological knowledge was acquired at a relatively recent period in the history of mankind. It is difficult to believe that the fundamental facts of the physiology of fertilization in animals could long have remained unknown when men became breeders of cattle. The Egyptian hieroglyphs leave no doubt that the knowledge was fully appreciated at the period when the earliest picture-symbols were devised, for the verb "to beget" is represented by the male organs of generation. But, as the domestication of animals may have been earlier than the invention of agriculture, it is possible that the appreciation of the fertilizing powers of the male animal may have been definitely more ancient than the earliest biological theory of the fertilizing power of water.

I have discussed this question to suggest that the knowledge that animals could be fertilized by the seminal fluid was certainly brought within the scope of the wider generalization that water itself was endowed with fertilizing properties. Just as water fertilized the earth, so the semen fertilized the female. Water was

[1] Baldwin Spencer and Gillen, "The Northern Tribes of Central Australia"; "Across Australia"; and Spencer's "Native Tribes of the Northern Territory of Australia". For a very important study of the whole problem with special reference to New Guinea, see B. Malinowski, "Baloma: the Spirits of the Dead," etc., *Journal of the Royal Anthropological Institute*, 1916, p. 415.

INCENSE AND LIBATIONS

necessary for the maintenance of life in plants and was also essential in the form of drink for animals. As both the earth and women could be fertilized by water they were homologized one with the other. The earth came to be regarded as a woman, the Great Mother.[1] When the fertilizing water came to be personified in the person of Osiris his consort Isis was identified with the earth which was fertilized by water.[2]

One of the earliest pictures of an Egyptian king represents him using the hoe to inaugurate the making of an irrigation-canal.[3] This was the typical act of benevolence on the part of a wise ruler. It is not unlikely that the earliest organization of a community under a definite leader may have been due to the need for some systematized control of irrigation. In any case the earliest rulers of Egypt and Sumer were essentially the controllers and regulators of the water supply and as such the givers of fertility and prosperity.

Once men first consciously formulated the belief that death was not the end of all things,[4] that the body could be re-animated and

[1] The idea of the earth's maternal function spread throughout the greater part of the world.

[2] With reference to the assimilation of the conceptions of human fertilization and watering the soil and the widespread idea among the ancients of regarding the male as "he who irrigates," Canon van Hoonacker gave M. Louis Siret the following note:—

"In Assyrian the cuneiform sign for water is also used, *inter alia*, to express the idea of begetting (*banû*). Compare with this the references from Hebrew and Arabic writings. In Isaiah xlviii. 1, we read 'Hear ye this, O house of Jacob, which are called by the name of Israel, and are come forth out of the waters of Judah'; and in Numbers xxiv. 7, 'Water shall flow from his buckets and his seed shall be in many waters'.

"The Hebrew verb (*shangal*) which denotes sexual intercourse has, in Arabic (*sadjala*), the meaning 'to spill water'. In the Koran, Sur. 36, v. 6, the word *mâ'un* (water) is used to designate semen" (L. Siret, "Questions de Chronologie et d'Ethnographie Ibériques," Tome I, 1913, p. 250).

[3] Quibell, "Hieraconpolis, Vol, I, 260, 4.

[4] In using this phrase I want to make a clear distinction between the phase of culture in which it had never occurred to man that, in his individual case, life would come to an end, and the more enlightened stage, in which he fully realized that death would inevitably be his fate, but that in spite of it his real existence would continue.

It is clear that at quite an early stage in his history man appreciated the fact that he could kill an animal or his fellow-man. But for a long time he failed to realize that he himself, if he could avoid the process of me-consciousness and the will restored, it was natural that a wise ruler who, when alive, had rendered conspicuous services should after death continue to be consulted. The fame of such a man would grow with age; his good deeds and his powers would become apotheosized; he would become an oracle whose advice might be sought and whose help be obtained in grave crises. In other words the dead king would be "deified," or at any rate credited with the ability to confer even greater boons than he was able to do when alive.

It is no mere coincidence that the first "god" should have been a dead king, Osiris, nor that he controlled the waters of irrigation and was specially interested in agriculture. Nor, for the reasons that I have already suggested, is it surprising that he should have had phallic attributes, and in himself have personified the virile powers of fertilization.[1]

In attempting to explain the origin of the ritual procedures of burning incense and offering libations it is essential to realize that the creation of the first deities was not primarily an expression of religious belief, but rather an application of science to national affairs. It was the logical interpretation of the dominant scientific theory of the time for the practical benefit of the living; or in other words, the means devised for securing the advice and the active help of wise rulers after their death. It was essentially a matter of practical politics and applied science. It became "religion" only when the advancement of knowledge superseded these primitive scientific theories and left them as soothing traditions for the thoughts and aspirations of mankind to cherish. For by the time the adequacy of these theories of knowledge began to be questioned they had made an insistent appeal, and had come to be regarded as an essential prop to lend support to man's conviction of the reality of a life beyond the grave. A web of moral precept and the allurement of hope had been so woven around them that no force was able to strip away this body of consolatory

chanical destruction by which he could kill an animal or a fellow-man, would not continue to exist. The dead are supposed by many people to be still in existence so long as the body is preserved. Once the body begins to disintegrate even the most unimaginative of men can entirely repress the idea of death. But to primitive people the preservation of the body is equally a token that existence has not come to an end. The corpse is merely sleeping.

[1] Breasted, *op. cit.*, p. 28.

beliefs; and they have persisted for all time, although the reasoning by which they were originally built up has been demolished and forgotten several millennia ago.

It is not known where Osiris was born. In other countries there are homologous deities, such as Ea, Tammuz, Adonis, and Attis, which are certainly manifestations of the same idea and sprung from the same source. Certain recent writers assume that the germ of the Osiris-conception was introduced into Egypt from abroad. But if so, nothing is known for certain of its place of origin. In any case there can be no doubt that the distinctive features of Osiris, his real personality and character, were developed in Egypt.

For reasons which I have suggested already it is probable that the significance of water in cultivation was not realized until cereals were cultivated in some such place as Babylonia or Egypt. But there are very definite legends of the Babylonian Ea coming from abroad by way of the Persian Gulf.[1] The early history of Tammuz is veiled in obscurity.

Somewhere in South Western Asia or North Eastern Africa, probably within a few years of the development of the art of agriculture, some scientific theorist, interpreting the body of empirical knowledge acquired by cultivating cereals, propounded the view that water was the great life-giving element. This view eventually found expression in the Osiris-group of legends.

This theory found specific application in the invention of libations and incense. These practices in turn reacted upon the general body of doctrine and gave it a more sharply defined form. The dead king also became more real when he was represented by an actual embalmed body and a life-like statue, sitting in state upon his throne and holding in his hands the emblems of his high office.

Thus while, in the present state of knowledge, it would be unjustifiable to claim that the Osiris-group of deities was invented in Egypt, and certainly erroneous to attribute the general theory of the fertilizing properties of water to the practice of embalming, it is true that the latter was responsible for giving Osiris a much more concrete

[1] The possibility, or even the probability, must be borne in mind that the legend of Ea arising from the waters may be merely another way of expressing his primary attribute as the personification of the fertilizing powers of water.

and clearly-defined shape, of "making a god in the image of man," and for giving to the water-theory a much richer and fuller significance than it had before.

The symbolism so created has had a most profound influence upon the thoughts and aspirations of the human race. For Osiris was the prototype of all the gods; his ritual was the basis of all religious ceremonial; his priests who conducted the animating ceremonies were the pioneers of a long series of ministers who for more than fifty centuries, in spite of the endless variety of details of their ritual and the character of their temples, have continued to perform ceremonies that have undergone remarkably little essential change. Though the chief functions of the priest as the animator of the god and the restorer of his consciousness have now fallen into the background in most religions, the ritual acts (the incense and libations, the offerings of food and blood and the rest) still persist in many countries: the priest still appeals by prayer and supplication for those benefits, which the Proto-Egyptian aimed at securing when he created Osiris as a god to give advice and help. The prayer for rain is one of the earliest forms of religious appeal, but the request for a plentiful inundation was earlier still.

I have already said that in using the terms "god" and "religion" with reference to the earliest form of Osiris and the beliefs that grew up with reference to him a potent element of confusion is introduced.

During the last fifty centuries the meanings of those two words have become so complexly enriched with the glamour of a mystic symbolism that the Proto-Egyptian's conception of Osiris and the Osirian beliefs must have been vastly different from those implied in the words "god" and "religion" at the present time. Osiris was regarded as an actual king who had died and been reanimated. In other words he was a *man* who could bestow upon his former subjects the benefits of his advice and help, but could also display such human weaknesses as malice, envy, and all uncharitableness. Much modern discussion completely misses the mark by the failure to recognize that these so-called "gods" were really men, equally capable of acts of beneficence and of outbursts of hatred, and as one or the other aspect became accentuated the same deity could become a Vedic *deva* or an Avestan *dæva*, a *deus* or a devil, a god of kindness or a demon of wickedness.

The acts which the earliest "gods" were supposed to perform

were not at first regarded as supernatural. They were merely the boons which the mortal ruler was supposed to be able to confer, by controlling the waters of irrigation and rendering the land fertile. It was only when his powers became apotheosized with a halo of accumulated glory (and the growth of knowledge revealed the insecurity of the scientific basis upon which his fame was built up) that a priesthood, reluctant to abandon any of the attributes which had captured the popular imagination, made it an obligation of belief to accept these supernatural powers of the gods for which the student of natural phenomena refused any longer to be a sponsor. This was the parting of the ways between science and religion ; and thenceforth the attributes of the " gods" became definitely and admittedly superhuman.

As I have already stated (p. 23) the original object of the offering of libations was thus clearly for the purpose of animating the statue of the deceased and so enabling him to continue the existence which had merely been interrupted by the incident of death. In course of time, however, as definite gods gradually materialized and came to be represented by statues, they also had to be vitalized by offerings of water from time to time. Thus the pouring out of libations came to be an act of worship of the deity ; and in this form it has persisted until our own times in many civilized countries.

But not only was water regarded as a means of animating the dead, or statues representing the dead, and an appropriate act of worship, in that it vitalized an idol and the god dwelling in it was thus able to hear and answer supplications. Water also became an essential part of any act of ritual rebirth.[1] As a baptism it also symbolized the giving of life. The initiate was re-born into a new communion of faith. In scores of other ways the same conception of the life-giving properties of water was responsible for as many applications of the use of libations in inaugurating new enterprises, such as "baptising" ships and blessing buildings. It is important to remember that, according to early Egyptian beliefs, the continued existence of the dead was wholly dependent upon the attentions of the living. Unless this animating ceremony was performed not merely at the time of the funeral, but also at stated periods afterwards, and unless the friends of the deceased

---

[1] This occurred at a later epoch when the attributes of the water-controlling deity of fertility became confused with those of the birth-giving mother goddess (*vide infra*, p. 40).

periodically supplied food and drink, such a continuation of existence was impossible.

The development of these beliefs had far-reaching effects in other directions. The idea that a stone statue could be animated ultimately became extended to mean that the dead man could enter into and dwell in a block of stone, which he could leave or return to at will. From this arose the beliefs, which spread far and wide, that the dead, ancestors, kings, or deified kings, dwelt in stones; and that they could be consulted as oracles, who gave advice and counsel. The acceptance of this idea that the dead could be reanimated in a stone statue no doubt prepared the minds of the people to credit the further belief, which other circumstances were responsible for creating, that men could be turned into stone. In the next chapter I shall explain how these petrifaction stories developed.[1]

All the rich crop of myths concerning men and animals dwelling in stones which are to be found encircling the globe from Ireland to America, can be referred back to these early Egyptian attempts to solve the mysteries of death, and to acquire the means of circumventing fate.

These beliefs at first may have concerned human beings only. But in course of time, as the duty of revictualling an increasingly large number of tombs and temples tended to tax the resources of the people, the practice developed of substituting for the real things models, or even pictures, of food-animals, vegetables, and other requisites of the dead. And these objects and pictures were restored to life or reality by means of a ritual which was essentially identical with that used for animating the statue or the mummy of the deceased himself.[2]

It is well worth considering whether this may not be one of the basal factors in explanation of the phenomena which the late Sir Edward Tylor labelled "animism".

So far from being a phase of culture through which many, if not all, peoples have passed in the course of their evolution, may it not have been merely an artificial conception of certain things, which was

---

[1] For a large series of these stories see E. Sidney Hartland's "Legend of Perseus". But even more instructive, as revealing the intimate connexion of such ideas with the beliefs regarding the preservation of the body, see J. J. M. de Groot, "The Religious System of China," Vol. IV, Book II, 1901.

[2] In this connexion see de Groot, *op. cit.* pp. 356 and 415.

given so definite a form in Egypt, for the specific reasons at which I have just hinted, and from there spread far and wide ?

Against this view may be urged the fact that our own children talk in an animistic fashion. But is not this due in some measure to the unconscious influence of their elders ? Or at most is it not a vague and ill-defined attitude of anthropomorphism necessarily involved in all spoken languages, which is vastly different from what the ethnologist understands by " animism " [1] ?

But whether this be so or not, there can be no doubt that the " animism " of the early Egyptians assumed its precise and clear-cut distinctive features as the result of the growth of ideas suggested by the attempts to make mummies and statues of the dead and symbolic offerings of food and other funerary requisites.

Thus incidentally there grew up the belief in a power of magic by means of which these make-believe offerings could be transformed into realities. But it is important to emphasize the fact that originally the conviction of the genuineness of this transubstantiation was a logical and not unnatural inference based upon the attempt to interpret natural phenomena, and then to influence them by imitating what were regarded as the determining factors.[2]

In China these ideas still retain much of their primitive influence and directness of expression. Referring to the Chinese " belief in the identity of pictures or images with the beings they represent " de Groot states that the *kwan shuh* or " magic art " is a " main branch of Chinese witchcraft ". It consists essentially of " the infusion of a soul, life, and activity into likenesses of beings, to thus render them fit to work in some direction desired . . . this infusion is effected by blowing or breathing, or spurting water over the likeness: indeed breath or *khi*, or water from the mouth imbued with breath, is identical with *yang* substance or life." [3]

---

[1] The child certainly resembles primitive man in the readiness with which it attributes to even the crudest models of animals or human beings the feelings of living creatures.

[2] It became " magical " in our sense of the term only when the growth of knowledge revealed the fact that the measures taken were inadequate to attain the desired end; while the " magician " continued to make the pretence that he could attain that end by ultra-physical means.

[3] De Groot, *op. cit.* p. 356.

Incense.

So far I have referred in detail only to the offering of libations. But this was only one of several procedures for animating statues, mummies, and food-offerings. I have still to consider the ritual procedures of incense-burning and "opening the mouth".

From Mr. Blackman's translations of the Egyptian texts it is clear that the burning of incense was intended to restore to the statue (or the mummy) the odour of the living body, and that this was part of the procedure considered necessary to animate the statue. He says "the belief about incense [which is explained by a later document, the *Ritual of Amon*] apparently does not occur in the Old Kingdom religious texts that are preserved to us, yet it may quite well be as ancient as that period. That is certainly Erman's view" (*op. cit.* p. 75).

He gives the following translation of the relevant passage in the *Ritual of Amon* (XII, 11): "The god comes with body adorned which he has fumigated with the eye of his body, the incense of the god which has issued from his flesh, the sweat of the god which has fallen to the ground, which he has given to all the gods. . . . It is the Horus eye. If it lives, the people live, thy flesh lives, thy members are vigorous" (*op. cit.* p. 72). In his comments upon this passage Mr. Blackman states: "In the light of the Pyramid libation-formulæ the expressions in this text are quite comprehensible. Like the libations the grains of incense are the exudations of a divinity,[1] 'the fluid which issued from his flesh,' the god's sweat descending to the ground. . . . Here incense is not merely the 'odour of the god,' but the grains of resin are said to be the god's sweat" (*op. cit.* p. 72). "Both rites, the pouring of libations and the burning of incense, are performed for the same purpose—to revivify the body [or the statue] of god and man by restoring to it its lost moisture" (p. 75).

In attempting to reconstitute the circumstances which led to the

---

[1] As I shall explain later (see page 38), the idea of the divinity of the incense-tree was a result of, and not the reason for, the practice of incense-burning. As one of the means by which the resurrection was attained incense became a giver of divinity; and by a simple process of rationalization the tree which produced this divine substance became a god.

The reference to the "eye of the body" (see p. 55) means the life-giving god or goddess who is the "eye" of the sky, *i.e.* the god with whom the dead king is identified.

INCENSE AND LIBATIONS

invention of incense-burning as a ritual act, the nature of the problem to be solved must be recalled. Among the most obtrusive evidences of death were the coldness of the skin, the lack of perspiration and of the odour of the living. It is important to realize what the phrase "odour of the living" would convey to the Proto-Egyptian. From the earliest Predynastic times in Egypt it had been the custom to make extensive use of resinous material as an essential ingredient (what a pharmacist would call the adhesive "vehicle") of cosmetics. One of the results of this practice in a hot climate must have been the association of a strong aroma of resin or balsam with a living person.[1] Whether or not it was the practice to burn incense to give pleasure to the living is not known. The fact that such a procedure was customary among their successors may mean that it was really archaic; or on the other hand the possibility must not be overlooked that it may be merely the later vulgarization of a practice which originally was devised for purely ritual purposes. The burning of incense before a corpse or statue was intended to convey to it the warmth, the sweat, and the odour of life.

When the belief became well established that the burning of incense was potent as an animating force, and especially a giver of life to the dead, it naturally came to be regarded as a divine substance in the sense that it had the power of resurrection. As the grains of incense consisted of the exudation of trees, or, as the ancient texts express it, "their sweat," the divine power of animation in course of time became transferred to the trees. They were no longer merely the source of the life-giving incense, but were themselves animated by the deity whose drops of sweat were the means of conveying life to the mummy.

The reason why the deity which dwelt in these trees was usually identified with the Mother-Goddess will become clear in the course of the subsequent discussion (p. 38). It is probable that this was due mainly to the geographical circumstance that the chief source of incense was Southern Arabia, which was also the home of the primitive goddesses of fertility. For they were originally nothing more than personifications of the life-giving cowry amulets from the Red Sea.

Thus Robertson Smith's statement that "the value of the gum of the acacia as an amulet is connected with the idea that it is a clot of

[1] It would lead me too far afield to enter into a discussion of the use of scents and unguents, which is closely related to this question.

menstruous blood, i.e., that the tree is a woman "[1] is probably an inversion of cause and effect. It was the value attached to the gum that conferred animation upon the tree. The rest of the legend is merely a rationalization based upon the idea that the tree was identified with the mother-goddess. The same criticism applies to his further contention (p. 427) with reference to " the religious value of incense," which he claims to be due to the fact that " like the gum of the *samora* (acacia) tree, . . . it was an animate or divine plant ".

Many factors played a part in the development of tree-worship, but it is probable the origin of the sacredness of trees must be assigned to the fact that it was acquired from the incense and the aromatic woods which were credited with the power of animating the dead. But at a very early epoch many other considerations helped to confirm and extend the conception of deification. When Osiris was buried, a sacred sycamore grew up as " the visible symbol of the imperishable life of Osiris ".[2] But the sap of trees was brought into relationship with life-giving water and thus constituted another link with Osiris. The sap was also regarded as the blood of trees and the incense that exuded as the sweat. Just as the water of libation was regarded as the fluid of the body of Osiris, so also, by this process of rationalization, the incense came to possess a similar significance.

For reasons precisely analogous to those already explained in the case of libations, the custom of burning incense, from being originally a ritual act for animating the funerary statue, ultimately developed into an act of homage to the deity.

But it also acquired a special significance when the cult of sky-gods developed,[3] for the smoke of the burning incense then came to be regarded as the vehicle which wafted the deceased's soul to the sky or conveyed there the requests of the dwellers upon earth.[4]

" The soul of a human being is generally conceived [by the

[1] " The Religion of the Semites," p. 133. [2] Breasted, p. 28.
[3] For reasons explained on a subsequent page (56).
[4] It is also worth considering whether the extension of this idea may not have been responsible for originating the practice of cremation—as a device for transferring, not merely the animating incense and the supplications of the living, but also the body of the deceased to the sky-world. This, of course, did not happen in Egypt, but in some other country which adopted the Egyptian practice of incense-burning, but was not hampered by the religious conservatism that guarded the sacredness of the corpse.

Chinese] as possessing the shape and characteristics of a human being, and occasionally those of an animal ; . . . the spirit of an animal is the shape of this animal or of some being with human attributes and speech. But plant spirits are never conceived as plant-shaped, nor to have plant-characters . . . whenever forms are given them, they are mostly represented as a man, a woman, or a child, and often also as an animal, dwelling in or near the plant, and emerging from it at times to do harm, or to dispense blessings. . . . Whether conceptions on the animation of plants have never developed in Chinese thought and worship before ideas about human ghosts . . . had become predominant in mind and custom, we cannot say : but the matter seems probable " (De Groot, *op. cit.* pp. 272, 273). Tales of trees that shed blood and that cry out when hurt are common in Chinese literature (p. 274) [as also in Southern Arabia] ; also of trees that lodge or can change into maidens of transcendant beauty (p. 276).

It is further significant that amongst the stories of souls of men taking up their residence in and animating trees and plants, the human being is usually a woman, accompanied by " a fox, a dog, an old raven or the like " (p. 276).

Thus in China are found all the elements out of which Dr. Rendel Harris believes the Aphrodite cult was compounded in Cyprus,[1] the animation of the anthropoid plant, its human cry, its association with a beautiful maiden and a dog.[2]

The immemorial custom of planting trees on graves in China is supposed by De Groot (p. 277) to be due to " the desire to strengthen the soul of the buried person, thus to save his body from corruption, for which reason trees such as pines and cypresses, deemed to be bearers of great vitality for being possessed of more *shen* than other trees, were used preferably for such purposes". But may not such beliefs also be an expression of the idea that a tree growing upon a grave is developed from and becomes the personification of the deceased ? The significance of the selection of pines and cypresses may be compared to that associated with the so-called " cedars " in Babylonia, Egypt, and Phœnicia, and the myrrh- and frankincense- producing trees in Arabia and East Africa. They have come to be

[1] " The Ascent of Olympus," 1917.
[2] For a collection of stories relating to human beings, generally women, dwelling in trees, see Hartland's " Legend of Perseus ".

accredited with "soul-substance," since their use in mummification, and as incense and for making coffins, has made them the means for attaining a future existence. Hence in course of time they came to be regarded as charged with the spirit of vitality, the *shen* or "soul-substance".

In China also it was because the woods of the pine or fir and the cyprus were used for making coffins and grave-vaults and that pine-resin was regarded as a means of attaining immortality (De Groot, *op. cit.* pp. 296 and 297) that such veneration was bestowed upon these trees. "At an early date, Taoist seekers after immortality transplanted that animation [of the hardy long-lived fir and cypress [1]] into themselves by consuming the resin of those trees, which, apparently, they looked upon as coagulated soul-substance, the counterpart of the blood in men and animals" (p. 296).

In India the *amrita*, the god's food of immortality, was sometimes regarded as the sap exuded from the sacred trees of paradise.

Elsewhere in these pages it is explained how the vaguely defined Mother "Goddess" and the more distinctly anthropoid Water "God," which originally developed quite independently the one of the other, ultimately came to exert a profound and mutual influence, so that many of the attributes which originally belonged to one of them came to be shared with the other. Many factors played a part in this process of blending and confusion of sex. As I shall explain later, when the moon came to be regarded as the dwelling or the impersonation of Hathor, the supposed influence of the moon over water led to a further assimilation of her attributes with those of Osiris as the controller of water, which received definite expression in a lunar form of Osiris.

But the link that is most intimately related to the subject of this address is provided by the personification of the Mother-Goddess in incense-trees. For incense thus became the sweat or the tears of the Great Mother just as the water of libation was regarded as the fluid of Osiris.

---

[1] The fact that the fir and cypress are "hardy and long-lived" is not the reason for their being accredited with these life-prolonging qualities. But once the latter virtues had become attributed to them the fact that the trees were "hardy and long-lived" may have been used to bolster up the belief by a process of rationalization.

The Breath of Life.

Although the pouring of libations and the burning of incense played so prominent a part in the ritual of animating the statue or the mummy, the most important incident in the ceremony was the "opening of the mouth," which was regarded as giving it the breath of life.

Elsewhere[1] I have suggested that the conception of the heart and blood as the vehicles of life, feeling, volition, and knowledge may have been extremely ancient. It is not known when or under what circumstances the idea of the breath being the "life" was first entertained. The fact that in certain primitive systems of philosophy the breath was supposed to have something to do with the heart suggests that these beliefs may be a constituent element of the ancient heart-theory. In some of the rock-pictures in America, Australia, and elsewhere the air-passages are represented leading to the heart. But there can be little doubt that the practice of mummification gave greater definiteness to the ideas regarding the "heart" and "breath," which eventually led to a differentiation between their supposed functions.[2] As the heart and the blood were obviously present in the dead body they could no longer be regarded as the "life". The breath was clearly the "element" the lack of which rendered the body inanimate. It was therefore regarded as necessary to set the heart working. The heart then came to be looked upon as the seat of knowledge, the organ that feels and wills during waking life. All the pulsating motions of the body seem to have been regarded, like the act of respiration, as expressions of the vital principle or "life," which Dutch ethnological writers refer to as "soul substance". The neighbourhood of certain joints where the pulse can be felt most readily, and the top of the head, where pulsation can be felt in the infant's fontanelle, were therefore regarded by some Asiatic peoples as the places where the substance of life could leave or enter the body.

It is possible that in ancient times this belief was more widespread

---

[1] "Primitive Man," *Proceedings of the British Academy*, 1917, p. 41.
It is important to remember that the real meaning of respiration was quite unknown until modern science revealed the part played by oxygen.

[2] The enormous complexity and intricacy of the interrelation between the functions of the "heart," and the "breath" is revealed in Chinese philosophy (see de Groot, *op. cit.* Chapter VII. *inter alia*).

than it is now. It affords an explanation of the motive for trephining the skull among ancient peoples, to afford a more ready passage for the "vital essence" to and from the skull.

In his lecture on "The Socratic Doctrine of the Soul,"[1] Professor John Burnet has expounded the meaning of early Greek conceptions of the soul with rare insight and lucidity. Originally, the word ψυχή meant "breath," but, by historical times, it had already been specialized in two distinct ways. It had come to mean *courage* in the first place, and secondly the *breath of life*, the presence or absence of which is the most obvious distinction between the animate and the inanimate, the "ghost" which a man "gives up" at death. But it may also quit the body temporarily, which explains the phenomenon of swooning (λιποψυχία). It seemed natural to suppose it was also the thing that can roam at large when the body is asleep, and even appear to another sleeping person in his dream. Moreover, since we can dream of the dead, what then appears to us must be just what leaves the body at the moment of death. These considerations explain the world-wide belief in the "soul" as a sort of double of the real bodily man, the Egyptian *ka*,[2] the Italian *genius*, and the Greek ψυχή.

Now this double is not identical with whatever it is in us that feels and wills during our waking life. That is generally supposed to be blood and not breath.

What we feel and perceive have their seat in the heart: they belong to the body and perish with it.

It is only when the shades have been allowed to drink blood that consciousness returns to them for a while.

At one time the ψυχή was supposed to dwell with the body in the grave, where it had to be supported by the offerings of the survivors, especially by libations (χοαί).

An Egyptian psychologist has carried the story back long before the times of which Professor Burnet writes. He has explained "his conception of the functions of the 'heart (mind) and tongue'. 'When

---

[1] Second Annual Philosophical Lecture, Henriette Hertz Trust, *Proceedings of the British Academy*, Vol. VII, 26 Jan., 1916.

[2] The Egyptian *ka*, however, was a more complex entity than this comparison suggests.

the eyes see, the ears hear, and the nose breathes, they transmit to the heart. It is he (the heart) who brings forth every issue and it is the tongue which repeats the thought of the heart.'"[1]

"There came the saying that Atum, who created the gods, stated concerning Ptah-Tatenen : ' He is the fashioner of the gods. ... He made likenesses of their bodies to the satisfaction of their hearts. Then the gods entered into their bodies of every wood and every stone and every metal.'"[2]

That these ideas are really ancient is shown by the fact that in the Pyramid Texts Isis is represented conveying the breath of life to Osiris by "causing a wind with her wings".[3] The ceremony of "opening the mouth" which aimed at achieving this restoration of the breath of life was the principal part of the ritual procedure before the statue or mummy. As I have already mentioned (p. 25), the sculptor who modelled the portrait statue was called "he who causes to live," and the word "to fashion" a statue is identical with that which means "to give birth". The god Ptah created man by modelling his form in clay. Similarly the life-giving sculptor made the portrait which was to be the means of securing a perpetuation of existence, when it was animated by the " opening of the mouth," by libations and incense.

As the outcome of this process of rationalization in Egypt a vast crop of creation-legends came into existence, which have persisted with remarkable completeness until the present day in India, Indonesia, China, America, and elsewhere. A statue of stone, wood, or clay is fashioned, and the ceremony of animation is performed to convey to it the breath of life, which in many places is supposed to be brought down from the sky.[4]

In the Egyptian beliefs, as well as in most of the world-wide legends that were derived from them, the idea assumed a definite form that the vital principle (often referred to as the "soul," "soul-substance," or "double") could exist apart from the body. Whatever

---

[1] Breasted, *op. cit.* pp. 44 and 45.
[2] *Op. cit.* pp. 45 and 46. [3] *Ibid.* p. 28.
[4] W. J. Perry has collected the evidence preserved in a remarkable series of Indonesian legends in his recent book, "The Megalithic Culture of Indonesia". But the fullest exposition of the whole subject is provided in the Chinese literature summarized by de Groot (*op. cit.*).

the explanation, it is clear that the possibility of the existence of the vital principle apart from the body was entertained. It was supposed that it could return to the body and temporarily reanimate it. It could enter into and dwell within the stone representation of the deceased. Sometimes this so-called "soul" was identified[1] with the breath of life, which could enter into the statue as the result of the ceremony of "opening the mouth".

It has been commonly assumed by Sir Edward Tylor and those who accept his theory of animism that the idea of the "soul" was based upon the attempts to interpret the phenomena of dreams and shadows, to which Burnet has referred in the passage quoted above. The fact that when a person is sleeping he may dream of seeing absent people and of having a variety of adventures is explained by many peoples by the hypothesis that these are real experiences which befell the "soul" when it wandered abroad during its owner's sleep. A man's shadow or his reflection in water or a mirror has been interpreted as his double. But what these speculations leave out of account is the fact that these dream- and shadow-phenomena were probably merely the predisposing circumstances which helped in the development of (or the corroborative details which were added to and, by rationalization, incorporated in) the "soul-theory," which other circumstances were responsible for creating.[2]

I have already called attention (p. 5) to the fact that in many of the psychological speculations in ethnology too little account is taken of the enormous complexity of the factors which determine even the simplest and apparently most obvious and rational actions of men. I must again remind the reader that a vast multitude of influences, many of them of a subconscious and emotional nature, affect men's decisions and opinions. But once some definite state of feeling inclines a man to a certain conclusion, he will call up a host of other circumstances to buttress his decision, and weave them into a complex net of rationalization. Some such process undoubtedly took place in the development of "animism"; and though it is not possible yet to

---

[1] See, however, the reservations in the subsequent pages.
[2] The thorough analysis of the beliefs of any people makes this abundantly clear. De Groot's monograph is an admirable illustration of this (*op. cit.* Chapter VII.). Both in Egypt and China the conceptions of the significance of the shadow are later and altogether subsidiary.

reconstruct the whole history of the growth of the idea, there can be no question that these early strivings after an understanding of the nature of life and death, and the attempts to put the theories into practice to reanimate the dead, provided the foundations upon which has been built up during the last fifty centuries a vast and complex theory of the soul. In the creation of this edifice the thoughts and the aspirations of countless millions of peoples have played a part: but the foundation was laid down when the Egyptian king or priest claimed that he could restore to the dead the "breath of life" and, by means of the wand which he called "the great magician,"[1] could enable the dead to be born again. The wand is supposed by some scholars[2] to be a conventionalized representation of the uterus, so that its power of giving birth is expressed with literal directness. Such beliefs and stories of the "magic wand" are found to-day in scattered localities from the Scottish Highlands to Indonesia and America.

In this sketch I have referred merely to one or two aspects of a conception of vast complexity. But it must be remembered that, once the mind of man began to play with the idea of a vital essence capable of existing apart from the body and to identify it with the breath of life, an illimitable field was opened up for speculation. The vital principle could manifest itself in all the varied expressions of human personality, as well as in all the physiological indications of life. Experience of dreams led men to believe that the "soul" could also leave the body temporarily and enjoy varied experiences. But the concrete-minded Egyptian demanded some physical evidence to buttress these intangible ideas of the wandering abroad of his vital essence. He made a statue for it to dwell in after his death, because he was not able to make an adequately life-like reproduction of the dead man's features upon the mummy itself or its wrappings. Then he gradually persuaded himself that the life-substance could exist apart from the body as a "double" or "twin" which animated the statue.

Searching for material evidence to support his faith primitive man not unnaturally turned to the contemplation of the circumstances of his birth. All his beliefs concerning the nature of life can ultimately be referred back to the story of his own origin, his birth or creation.

When an infant is born it is accompanied by the after-birth or

[1] Alan H. Gardiner, Davies and Gardiner, *op. cit.* p. 59.
[2] F. Ll. Griffith, "A Collection of Hieroglyphs," 1898, p. 60.

placenta to which it is linked by the umbilical cord. The full comprehension of the significance of these structures is an achievement of modern science. To primitive man they were an incomprehensible marvel. But once he began to play with the idea that he had a double, a vital essence in his own shape which could leave the sleeping body and lead a separate existence, the placenta obviously provided tangible evidence of its reality. The considerations set forth by Blackman,[1] supplementing those of Moret, Murray and Seligman, and others, have been claimed as linking the placenta with the *ka*.

Much controversy has waged around the interpretation of the Egyptian word *ka*, especially during recent years. An excellent summary of the arguments brought forward by the various disputants up to 1912 will be found in Moret's "Mystères Égyptiens". Since then more or less contradictory views have been put forward by Alan Gardiner, Breasted, and Blackman. It is not my intention to intervene in a dispute as to the meaning of certain phrases in ancient literature; but there are certain aspects of the problems at issue which are so intimately related to my main theme as to make some reference to them unavoidable.

The development of the custom of making statues of the dead necessarily raised for solution the problem of explaining the deceased's two bodies, his actual mummy and his portrait statue. During life on earth his vital principle dwelt in the former, except on those occasions when the man was asleep. His actual body also gave expression to all the varied attributes of his personality. But after death the statue became the dwelling place of these manifestations of the spirit of vitality.

Whether or not the conception arose out of the necessities unavoidably created by the making of statues, it seems clear that this custom must have given more concrete shape to the belief that all of those elements of the dead man's individuality which left his body at the time of death could shift as a shadowy double into his statue.

At the birth of a king he is accompanied by a comrade or twin exactly reproducing all his features. This double or *ka* is intimately associated throughout life and in the life to come with the king's wel-

---

[1] Aylward M. Blackman, "Some Remarks on an Emblem upon the Head of an Ancient Egyptian Birth-Goddess," *Journal of Egyptian Archæology*, Vol. III, Part III, July, 1916, p. 199; and "The Pharaoh's Placenta and the Moon-God Khons," *ibid*. Part IV, Oct., 1916, p. 235.

fare. In fact Breasted claims that the *ka* " was a kind of superior genius intended to guide the fortunes of the individual *in the hereafter*" . . . there " he had his abode and awaited the coming of his earthly companion ".[1] At death the deceased " goes to his *ka*, to the sky ". The *ka* controls and protects the deceased : he brings him food which they eat together.

It is important clearly to keep in mind the different factors involved in the conception of the *ka* :—

(*a*) The statue of the deceased is animated by restoring to it the breath of life and all the other vital attributes of which the early Egyptian physiologist took cognisance.

(*b*) At the time of birth there came into being along with the child a " twin " whose destinies were closely linked with the child's.

(*c*) As the result of animating the statue the deceased also has restored to him his character, " the sum of his attributes," his individuality, later raised to the position of a protecting genius or god, a Providence who watches over his well-being.[2]

The *ka* is not simply identical with the breath of life or *animus*, as Burnet supposes (*op. cit. supra*), but has a wider significance. The adoption of the conception of the *ka* as a sort of guardian angel which finds its appropriate habitation in a statue that has been animated does not necessarily conflict with the view so concretely and unmistakably represented in the tomb-pictures that the *ka* is also a double who is born along with the individual.

This material conception of the *ka* as a double who is born with and closely linked to the individual is, as Blackman has emphasized,[3] very suggestive of Baganda beliefs and rites connected with the placenta. At death the circumstances of the act of birth are reconstituted, and for this rebirth the placenta which played an essential part in the original process is restored to the deceased. May not the original meaning of the expression " he goes to his *ka* " be a literal description of this re-union with his placenta ? The identification of the *ka* with the moon, the guardian of the dead man's welfare, may have enriched the symbolism.

---

[1] " Religion and Thought in Ancient Egypt," p. 52. Breasted denies that the *ka* was an element of the personality.

[2] For an abstruse discussion of this problem see Alan H. Gardiner, " Personification (Egyptian)," Hastings' *Encyclopædia of Religion and Ethics*, pp. 790 and 792.

[3] *Op. cit. supra*.

Blackman makes the suggestion that "on the analogy of the beliefs entertained by the Hamitic ruling caste in Uganda," according to Roscoe, "the placenta,[1] or rather its ghost, would have been supposed by the Ancient Egyptians to be closely connected with the individual's personality, as" he maintains was also the case with the god or protecting genius of the Babylonians.[2] "Unless united with his twin's [i.e. his placenta's] ghost the dead king was an imperfect deity, i.e. his directing intelligence was impaired or lacking," presumably because the placenta was composed of blood, which was regarded as the material of consciousness and intelligence.

In China, as the quotations from de Groot (see footnote) show, the placenta when placed under felicitous circumstances is able to ensure the child a long life and to control his mental and physical welfare.

In view of the claims put forward by Blackman to associate the placenta with the *ka*, it is of interest to note Moret's suggestion concerning the fourteen forms of the *ka*, to which von Bissing assigns

---

[1] Mr. Blackman is puzzled to explain what "possible connexion there could be between the Pharaoh's placenta and the moon beyond the fact that it is the custom in Uganda to expose the king's placenta each new moon and anoint it with butter.

To those readers who follow my argument in the later pages of this discussion the reasoning at the back of this association should be plain enough. The moon was regarded as the controller of menstruation. The placenta (and also the child) was considered to be formed of menstrual blood. The welfare of the placenta was therefore considered to be under the control of the moon.

The anointing with butter is an interesting illustration of the close connexion of these lunar and maternal phenomena with the cow.

The placenta was associated with the moon also in China, as the following quotation shows.

According to de Groot (*op. cit.* p. 396), "in the *Siao 'rh fang* or Medicament for Babies, by the hand of Ts'ui Hing-kung [died 674 A.D.], it is said : 'The placenta should be stored away in a felicitous spot under the salutary influences of the sky or the moon . . . in order that the child may be ensured a long life'". He then goes on to explain how any interference with the placenta will entail mental or physical trouble to the child.

The placenta also is used as the ingredient of pills to increase fertility, facilitate parturition, to bring back life to people on the brink of death and it is the main ingredient "in medicines for lunacy, convulsions, epilepsy, etc." (p. 397). "It gives rest to the heart, nourishes the blood, increases the breath, and strengthens the *tsing*" (p. 396).

These attributes of the placenta indicate that the beliefs of the Baganda are not merely local eccentricities, but widespread and sharply defined interpretations of the natural phenomena of birth.

[2] *Op. cit.* p. 241.

the general significance " nourishment or offerings ". He puts the question whether they do not " personify the elements of material and intellectual prosperity, all that is necessary for the health of body and spirit " (*op. cit.* p. 209).

The placenta is credited with all the varieties of life-giving potency that are attributed to the Mother-Goddess. It therefore controls the welfare of the individual and, like all maternal amulets (*vide supra*), ensures his good fortune. But, probably by virtue of its supposed derivation from and intimate association with blood, it also ministered to his mental welfare.

In my last Rylands Lecture I referred to the probability that the essential elements of Chinese civilization were derived from the West. I had hoped that, before the present statement went to the printer, I would have found time to set forth in detail the evidence in substantiation of the reality of that diffusion of culture.

Briefly the chain of proof is composed of the following links : (*a*) the intimate cultural contact between Egypt, Southern Arabia, Sumer, and Elam from a period at least as early as the First Egyptian Dynasty ; (*b*) the diffusion of Sumerian and Elamite culture in very early times at least as far north as Russian Turkestan and as far east as Baluchistan ; (*c*) at some later period the quest of gold, copper, turquoise, and jade led the Babylonians (and their neighbours) as far north as the Altai and as far east as Khotan and the Tarim Valley, where their pathways were blazed with the distinctive methods of cultivation and irrigation ; (*d*) at some subsequent period there was an easterly diffusion of culture from Turkestan into the Shensi Province of China proper ; and (*e*) at least as early as the seventh century B.C. there was also a spread of Western culture to China by sea.[1]

I have already referred to some of the distinctively Egyptian traits in Chinese beliefs concerning the dead. Mingled with them are other equally definitely Babylonian ideas concerning the liver.

It must be apparent that in the course of the spread of a complex system of religious beliefs to so great a distance, only certain of their features would survive the journey. Handed on from people to people, each of whom would unavoidably transform them to some

---

[1] See " The Origin of Early Siberian Civilization," now being published in the *Memoirs and Proceedings of the Manchester Literary and Philosophical Society*.

extent, the tenets of the Western beliefs would become shorn of many of their details and have many excrescences added to them before the Chinese received them. In the crucible of the local philosophy they would be assimilated with Chinese ideas until the resulting compound assumed a Chinese appearance. When these inevitable circumstances are recalled the value of any positive evidence of Western influence is of special significance.

According to the ancient Chinese, man has two souls, the *kwei* and the *shen*. The former, which according to de Groot is definitely the more ancient of the two (p. 8), is the material, substantial soul, which emanates from the terrestrial part of the universe, and is formed of *yin* substance. In living man it operates under the name of *p'oh*, and on his death it returns to the earth and abides with the deceased in his grave.

The *shen* or immaterial soul emanates from the ethereal celestial part of the cosmos and consists of *yang* substance. When operating actively in the living human body, it is called *khi* or "breath," and *hwun;* when separated from it after death it lives forth as a refulgent spirit, styled *ming*.[1]

But the *shen* also, in spite of its sky-affinities, hovers about the grave and may dwell in the inscribed grave-stone (p. 6). There may be a multitude of *shen* in one body and many "soul-tablets" may be provided for them (p. 74).

Just as in Egypt the *ka* is said to "symbolize the force of life which resides in nourishment" (Moret, p. 212), so the Chinese refer to the ethereal part of the food as its *khi*, i.e. the "breath" of its *shen*.

The careful study of the mass of detailed evidence so lucidly set forth by de Groot in his great monograph reveals the fact that, in spite of many superficial differences and apparent contradictions, the early Chinese conceptions of the soul and its functions are essentially identical with the Egyptian, and must have been derived from the same source.

From the quotations which I have already given in the foregoing pages, it appears that the Chinese entertain views regarding the functions of the placenta which are identical with those of the Baganda, and a conception of the souls of man which presents unmistakable analogies with Egyptian beliefs. Yet these Chinese references do

[1] De Groot, .p 5.

not shed any clearer light than Egyptian literature does upon the problem of the possible relationship between the *ka* and the *placenta*.

In the Iranian domain, however, right on the overland route from the Persian Gulf to China, there seems to be a ray of light. According to the late Professor Moulton, " The later Parsi books tell us that the Fravashi is a part of a good man's identity, living in heaven and reuniting with the soul at death. It is not exactly a guardian angel, for it shares in the development or deterioration of the rest of the man." [1]

In fact the Fravashi is not unlike the Egyptian *ka* on the one side and the Chinese *shen* on the other. " They are the *Manes*, ' the good folk '" (p. 144) : they are connected with the stars in their capacity as spirits of the dead (p. 143), and they " showed their paths to the sun, the moon, the sun, and the endless lights," just as the *kas* guide the dead in the hereafter.

The Fravashis play a part in the annual All Soul's feast (p. 144), for which Breasted has provided an almost exact parallel in Egypt during the Middle Kingdom.[2] All the circumstances of the two ceremonies are essentially identical.

Now Professor Moulton suggests that the word Fravashi may be derived from the Avestan root *var*, " to impregnate," and *fravaši* mean " birth-promotion " (p. 142). As he associates this with childbirth the possibility suggests itself whether the " birth-promoter " may not be simply the placenta.

Loret (quoted by Moret, p. 202), however, derives the word *ka* from a root signifying " to beget," so that the Fravashi may be nothing more than the Iranian homologue of the Egyptian *ka*.

The connecting link between the Iranian and Egyptian conceptions may be the Sumerian instances given to Blackman [3] by Dr. Langdon.

The whole idea seems to have originated out of the belief that the sum of the individual attributes or vital expressions of a man's personality could exist apart from the physical body. The contemplation of the phenomena of sleep and death provided the evidence in corroboration of this.

At birth the newcomer came into the world physically connected with the placenta, which was accredited with the attributes of the life-giving and birth-promoting Great Mother and intimately related

[1] *Early Religious Poetry of Persia*, p. 145.
[2] *Op. cit.* p. 264.   [3] *Ibid.* p. 240.

to the moon and the earliest totem. It was obviously, also, closely concerned in the nutrition of the embryo, for was it not the stalk upon which the latter was growing like some fruit on its stem ? It was a not unnatural inference to suppose that, as the elements of the personality were not indissolubly connected with the body, they were brought into existence at the time of birth and that the placenta was their vehicle.

The Egyptians' own terms of reference to the sculptor of a statue show that the ideas of birth were uppermost in their minds when the custom of statue-making was first devised. Moret has brought together (*op. cit. supra*) a good deal of evidence to suggest the far-reaching significance of the conception of ritual rebirth in early Egyptian religious ceremonial. With these ideas in his mind the Egyptian would naturally attach great importance to the placenta in any attempt to reconstruct the act of rebirth, which would be regarded in a literal sense. The placenta which played an essential part in the original act would have an equally important rôle in the ritual of rebirth. [For a further comment upon the problem discussed in the preceding ten pages, see Appendix A, p. 73.]

The Power of the Eye.

In attempting to understand the peculiar functions attributed to the eye it is essential that the inquirer should endeavour to look at the problem from the early Egyptian's point of view. After moulding into shape the wrappings of the mummy so as to restore as far as possible the form of the deceased the embalmer then painted eyes upon the face. So also when the sculptor had learned to make finished models in stone or wood, and by the addition of paint had enhanced the life-like appearance, the statue was still merely a dead thing. What were needed above all to enliven it, literally and actually, in other words, to animate it, were the eyes ; and the Egyptian artist set to work and with truly marvellous skill reproduced the appearance of living eyes (Fig. 5), How ample was the justification for this belief will be appreciated by anyone who glances at the remarkable photographs recently published by Dr. Alan H. Gardiner.[1] The wonderful eyes will be seen to make the statue sparkle and live. To the concrete mind of the Egyptian this triumph of art was regarded

[1] "A New Masterpiece of Egyptian Sculpture," *The Journal of Egyptian Archæology*, Vol. IV, Part I, Jan., 1917.

FIG. 5.—STATUE OF AN EGYPTIAN NOBLE OF THE PYRAMID AGE TO SHOW THE TECHNICAL SKILL IN THE REPRESENTATION OF LIFE-LIKE EYES.

INCENSE AND LIBATIONS

not as a mere technical success or æsthetic achievement. The artist was considered to have made the statue really live; in fact, literally and actually converted it into a "living image". The eyes themselves were regarded as one of the chief sources of the vitality which had been conferred upon the statue.

This is the explanation of all the elaborate care and skill bestowed upon the making of artificial eyes. No doubt also it was largely responsible for giving definition to the remarkable belief in the animating power of the eye. But so many other factors of most diverse kinds played a part in building up the complex theory of the eye's fertilizing potency that all the stages in the process of rationalization cannot yet be arranged in orderly sequence.

I refer to the question here and suggest certain aspects of it that seem worthy of investigation merely for the purpose of stimulating some student of early Egyptian literature to look into the matter further.[1]

As death was regarded as a kind of sleep and the closing of the eyes was the distinctive sign of the latter condition the open eyes were not unnaturally regarded as clear evidence of wakefulness and life. In fact, to a matter-of-fact people the restoration of the eyes to the mummy or statue was equivalent to an awakening to life.

At a time when a reflection in a mirror or in a sheet of water was supposed to afford quite positive evidence of the reality of each individual's "double," and when the "soul," or more concretely, "life," was imagined to be a minute image or homunculus, it is quite likely that the reflection in the eye may have been interpreted as the "soul" dwelling within it. The eye was certainly regarded as peculiarly rich in "soul substance". It was not until Osiris received from Horus the eye which had been wrenched out in the latter's combat with Set that he "became a soul".[2]

It is a remarkable fact that this belief in the animating power of the eye spread as far east as Polynesia and America, and as far west as the British Islands.

[1] In all probability the main factor that was responsible for conferring such definite life-giving powers upon the eye was the identification of the moon with the Great Mother. The moon was the Eye of Re, the sky-god.

[2] Breasted, "Religion and Thought in Ancient Egypt," p. 59. The meaning of the phrase rendered "a soul" here would be more accurately given by the word "reanimated".

Of course the obvious physiological functions of the eyes as means of communication between their possessor and the world around him; the powerful influence of the eyes for expressing feeling and emotion without speech; the analogy between the closing and opening of the eyes and the changes of day and night, are all hinted at in Egyptian literature.

But there were certain specific factors that seem to have helped to give definiteness to these general ideas of the physiology of the eyes. The tears, like all the body moisture, came to share the life-giving attributes of water in general. And when it is recalled that at funeral ceremonies emotion found natural expression in the shedding of tears, it is not unlikely that this came to be assimilated with all the other water-symbolism of the funerary ritual. The early literature of Egypt, in fact, refers to the part played by Isis and Nephthys in the reanimation of Osiris, when the tears they shed as mourners brought life back to the god. But the fertilizing tears of Isis were life-giving in the wider sense. They were said to cause the inundation which fertilized the soil of Egypt, meaning presumably that the "Eye of Re" sent the rain.

There is the further possibility that the beliefs associated with the cowry may have played some part, if not in originating, at any rate in emphasizing the conception of the fertilizing powers of the eye. I have already mentioned the outstanding features of the symbolism of the cowry. In many places in Africa and elsewhere the similarity of this shell to the half-closed eyelids led to its use as an artificial "eye" in mummies. The use of the same objects to symbolize the female reproductive organs and the eyes may have played some part in transferring to the latter the fertility of the former. The gods were born of the eyes of Ptah. Might not the confusion of the eye with the genitalia have given a meaning to this statement? There is evidence of this double symbolism of these shells. Cowry shells have also been employed, both in the Persian Gulf and the Pacific, to decorate the bows of boats, probably for the dual purpose of representing eyes and conferring vitality upon the vessel. These facts suggest that the belief in the fertilizing power of the eyes may to some extent be due to this cowry-association. Even if it be admitted that all the known cases of the use of cowries as eyes of mummies are relatively late, and that it is not known to have been employed for such a purpose in Egypt, the mere fact that the likeness to the eyelids so readily suggests itself may have linked together the attributes of the cowry and the eye even in Predynastic times, when cowries were placed with the dead in the grave.

Hathor's identification with the "Eye of Re" may possibly have been an expression of the same idea. But the rôle of the "Eye of Re" was due primarily to her association with the moon (*vide infra*, p. 56).

The apparently hopeless tangle of contradictions involved in these conceptions of Hathor will have to be unravelled. For " no eye is to be feared more than thine (Re's) when it attacketh in the form of Hathor" (Maspero, *op. cit.* p. 165). If it was the beneficent life-giving aspect of the eye which led to its identification with Hathor, in course of time, when the reason for this connexion was lost sight of, it became associated with the malevolent, death-dealing *avatar* of the goddess, and became the expression of the god's anger and hatred toward his enemies. It is not unlikely that such a confusion may have been responsible for giving concrete expression to the general psychological fact that the eyes are obviously among the chief means for expressing hatred for and intimidating and "brow-beating" one's fellows. [In my lecture on "The Birth of Aphrodite" I shall explain the explicit circumstances that gave rise to these contradictions.]

It is significant that, in addition to the widespread belief in the "evil eye"—which in itself embodies the same confusion, the expression of admiration that works evil—in a multitude of legends it is the eye that produces petrifaction. The "stony stare" causes death and the dead become transformed into statues, which, however, usually lack their original attribute of animation. These stories have been collected by Mr. E. S. Hartland in his "Legend of Perseus".

There is another possible link in the chain of associations between the eye and the idea of fertility. I have already referred to the development of the belief that incense, which plays so prominent a part in the ritual for conferring vitality upon the dead, is itself replete with animating properties. "Glaser has already shown the *anti* incense of the Egyptian Punt Reliefs to be an Arabian word, *a-a-neic*, 'tree-eyes' (*Punt und die Südarabischen Reiche*, p. 7), and to refer to the large lumps . . . as distinguished from the small round drops, which are supposed to be tree-tears or the tree-blood."[1]

[1] Wilfred H. Schoff, "The Periplus of the Erythræan Sea," 1912, p. 164.

THE MOON AND THE SKY-WORLD.

There are reasons for believing that the chief episodes in Aphrodite's past point to the Red Sea for their inspiration, though many other factors, due partly to local circumstances and partly to contact with other civilizations, contributed to the determination of the traits of the Mediterranean goddess of love. In Babylonia and India there are very definite signs of borrowing from the same source. It is important, therefore, to look for further evidence to Arabia as the obvious bond of union both with Phœnicia and Babylonia.

The claim made in Roscher's *Lexicon der Mythologie* that the Assyrian Ishtar, the Phœnician Ashtoreth (Astarte), the Syrian Atargatis (Derketo), the Babylonian Belit (Mylitta) and the Arabian Ilat (Al-ilat) were all moon-goddesses has given rise to much rather aimless discussion, for there can be no question of their essential homology with Hathor and Aphrodite. Moreover, from the beginning, all goddesses—and especially this most primitive stratum of fertility deities—were for obvious reasons intimately associated with the moon.[1] But the cyclical periodicity of the moon which suggested the analogy with the similar physiological periodicity of women merely explains the association of the moon with women. The influence of the moon upon dew and the tides, perhaps, suggested its controlling power over water and emphasized the life-giving function which its association with women had already suggested. For reasons which have been explained already, water was associated more especially with fertilization by the male. Hence the symbolism of the moon came to include the control of both the male and the female processes of reproduction.[2]

The literature relating to the development of these ideas with refer-

---

[1] I am not concerned here with the explanation of the means by which their home became transferred to the planet Venus.

[2] In his discussion of the functions of the Fravashis in the Iranian Yasht, the late Professor Moulton suggested the derivation of the word from the Avestan root *var*, " to impregnate," so that *fravaśi* might mean " birth-promotion". But he was puzzled by a reference to water. " Less easy to understand is their intimate connexion with the Waters " (" Early Religious Poetry of Persia," pp. 142 and 143). But the Waters were regarded as fertilizing agents. This is seen in the Avestan Anahita, who was " the presiding genie of Fertility and more especially of the Waters " (W. J. Phythian-Adams, " Mithraism," 1915, p. 13).

ence to the moon has been summarized by Professor Hutton Webster.[1] He shows that " there is good reason for believing that among many primitive peoples the moon, rather than the sun, the planets or any of the constellations, first excited the imagination and aroused feelings of superstitious awe or of religious veneration ".

Special attention was first devoted to the moon when agricultural pursuits compelled men to measure time and determine the seasons. The influence of the moon on water, both the tides and dew, brought it within the scope of the then current biological theory of fertilization. This conception was powerfully corroborated by the parallelism of the moon's cycles and those of womankind, which was interpreted by regarding the moon as the controlling power of the female reproductive functions. Thus all of the earliest goddesses who were personifications of the powers of fertility came to be associated, and in some cases identified, with the moon.

In this way the animation and deification of the moon was brought about : and the first sky deity assumed not only all the attributes of the cowry, i.e. the female reproductive functions, but also, as the controller of water, many of those which afterwards were associated with Osiris. The confusion of the male fertilizing powers of Osiris with the female reproductive functions of Hathor and Isis may explain how in some places the moon became a masculine deity, who, however, still retained his control over womankind, and caused the phenomena of menstruation by the exercise of his virile powers.[2] But the moon-god was also a measurer of time and in this aspect was specially personified in Thoth.

The assimilation of the moon with these earth-deities was probably responsible for the creation of the first sky-deity. For once the conception developed of identifying a deity with the moon, and the Osirian beliefs associated with the deification of a dead king grew up, the moon became the impersonation of the spirit of womankind, some mortal woman who by death had acquired divinity.

After the idea had developed of regarding the moon as the spirit

[1] " Rest Days," New York, 1916, pp. 124 *et seq*.
[2] Wherever these deities of fertility are found, whether in Egypt, Babylonia, the Mediterranean Area, Eastern Asia, and America, illustrations of this confusion of sex are found. The explanation which Dr. Rendel Harris offers of this confusion in the case of Aphrodite seems to me not to give due recognition to its great antiquity and almost world-wide distribution.

of a dead person, it was only natural that, in course of time, the sun and stars should be brought within the scope of the same train of thought, and be regarded as the deified dead. When this happened, the sun not unnaturally soon leapt into a position of pre-eminence. As the moon represented the deified female principle the sun became the dominant male deity Re. The stars also became the spirits of the dead.

Once this new conception of a sky-world was adumbrated a luxuriant crop of beliefs grew up to assimilate the new beliefs with the old, and to buttress the confused mixture of incompatible ideas with a complex scaffolding of rationalization.

The sun-god Horus was already the son of Osiris. Osiris controlled not only the river and the irrigation canals, but also the rain-clouds. The fumes of incense conveyed to the sky-gods the supplications of the worshippers on earth. Incense was not only "the perfume that deifies," but also the means by which the deities and the dead could pass to their doubles in the newly invented sky-heaven. The sun-god Re was represented in his temple not by an anthropoid statue, but by an obelisk,[1] the gilded apex of which pointed to heaven and "drew down" the dazzling rays of the sun, reflected from its polished surface, so that all the worshippers could see the manifestations of the god in his temple.

These events are important, not only for creating the sky-gods and the sky-heaven, but possibly also for suggesting the idea that even a mere pillar of stone, whether carved or uncarved, upon which no attempt had been made to model the human form, could represent the deity, or rather could become the "body" to be animated by the god.[2] For once it was admitted, even in the home of these ancient ideas concerning the animation of statues, that it was not essential for the idol to be shaped into human form, the way was opened for less cultured peoples, who had not acquired the technical skill to carve statues, simply to erect stone pillars or unshaped masses of stone or

[1] L. Borchardt, "Das Re-heiligtum des Königs Ne-woser-re".
For a good exposition of this matter see A. Moret, "Sanctuaires de l'ancien Empire Égyptien," *Annales du Musée Guimet*, 1912, p. 265.

[2] It is possible that the ceremony of erecting the *dad* columns may have played some part in the development of these beliefs. (On this see A. Moret, "Mystères Égyptiens," 1913, pp. 13-17.)

wood for their gods to enter, when the appropriate ritual of animation was performed.[1]

This conception of the possibility of gods, men, or animals dwelling in stones spread in course of time throughout the world, but in every place where it is found certain arbitrary details of the methods of animating the stone reveal the fact that all these legends must have been derived from the same source.

The complementary belief in the possibility of the petrifaction of men and animals has a similarly extensive geographical distribution. The history of this remarkable incident I shall explain in the lecture on "Dragons and Rain Gods" (Chapter II.).[2]

The Worship of the Cow.

Intimately linked with the subjects I have been discussing is the worship of the cow. It would lead me too far afield to enter into the details of the process by which the earliest Mother-Goddesses became so closely associated or even identified with the cow, and why the cow's horns became associated with the moon among the emblems

---

[1] Many other factors played a part in the development of the stories of the birth of ancestors from stones. I have already referred to the origin of the idea of the cowry (or some other shell) as the parent of mankind. The place of the shell was often taken by roughly carved stones, which of course were accredited with the same power of being able to produce men, or of being a sort of egg from which human beings could be hatched. It is unlikely that the finding of fossilized animals played any leading rôle in the development of these beliefs, beyond affording corroborative evidence in support of them after other circumstances had been responsible for originating the stories. The more circumstantial Oriental stories of the splitting of stones giving birth to heroes and gods may have been suggested by the finding in pebbles of fossilized shells—themselves regarded already as the parents of mankind. But such interpretations were only possible because all the predisposing circumstances had already prepared the way for the acceptance of these specific illustrations of a general theory.

These beliefs may have developed before and quite independently of the ideas concerning the animation of statues; but if so the latter event would have strengthened and in some places become merged with the other story.

[2] For an extensive collection of these remarkable petrifaction legends in almost every part of the world, see E. Sidney Hartland's "The Legend of Perseus," especially Volumes I and III. These distinctive stories will be found to be complexly interwoven with all the matters discussed in this address.

of Hathor. But it is essential that reference should be made to certain aspects of the subject.

I do not think there is any evidence to justify the common theory that the likeness of the crescent moon to a cow's horns was the reason for the association. On the other hand, it is clear that both the moon and the cow became identified with the Mother-Goddess quite independently the one of the other, and at a very remote period.

It is probable that the fundamental factor in the development of this association of the cow and the Mother-Goddess was the fact of the use of milk as food for human beings. For if the cow could assume this maternal function she was in fact a sort of foster-mother of mankind; and in course of time she came to be regarded as the actual mother of the human race and to be identified with the Great Mother.

Many other considerations helped in this process of assimilation. The use of cattle not merely as meat for the sustenance of the living but as the usual and most characteristic life-giving food for the dead naturally played a part in conferring divinity upon the cow, just as an analogous relationship made incense a holy substance and was responsible for the personification of the incense-tree as a goddess. This influence was still further emphasized in the case of cattle because they also supplied the blood which was used for the ritual purpose of bestowing consciousness upon the dead, and in course of time upon the gods also, so that they might hear and attend to the prayers of supplicants.

Other circumstances emphasize the significance attached to the cow: but it is difficult to decide whether they contributed in any way to the development of these beliefs or were merely some of the practices which were the result of the divination of the cow. The custom of placing butter in the mouths of the dead, in Egypt, Uganda, and India, the various ritual uses of milk, the employment of a cow's hide as a wrapping for the dead in the grave, and also in certain mysterious ceremonies,[1] all indicate the intimate connexion between the cow and the means of attaining a rebirth in the life to come.

I think there are definite reasons for believing that once the cow became identified with the Mother-Goddess as the parent of mankind

---

[1] See A. Moret, *op. cit.* p. 81, *inter alia*.

the first step was taken in the development of the curious system of ideas now known as "totemism".

This, however, is a complex problem which I cannot stay to discuss here.

When the cow became identified with the Great Mother and the moon was regarded as the dwelling or the personification of the same goddess, the Divine Cow by a process of confused syncretism came to be regarded as the sky or the heavens, to which the dead were raised up on the cow's back. When Re became the dominant deity, he was identified with the sky, and the sun and moon were then regarded as his eyes. Thus the moon, as the Great Mother as well as the Eye of Re, was the bond of identification of the Great Mother with an eye. This was probably how the eye acquired the animating powers of the Giver of Life.

A whole volume might be written upon the almost world-wide diffusion of these beliefs regarding the cow, as far as Scotland and Ireland in the west, and in their easterly migration probably as far as America, to the confusion alike of its ancient artists and its modern ethnologists.[1]

As an illustration of the identification of the cow's attributes with those of the life-giving Great Mother, I might refer to the late Professor Moulton's commentary[2] on the ancient Iranian Gâthâs, where cow's flesh is given to mortals by Yima to make them immortal. "May we connect it with another legend whereby at the Regeneration Mithra is to make men immortal by giving them to eat the fat of the . . . primeval Cow from whose slain body, according to the Aryan legends adopted by Mithraism, mankind was first created?"[3]

---

[1] See the Copan sculptured monuments described by Maudslay in Godman and Salvin's "Biologia Centrali-Americana," Archæology, Plate 46, representing "Stela D," with two serpents in the places occupied by the Indian elephants in Stela B—concerning which see *Nature*, November 25, 1915. To one of these intertwined serpents is attached a cow-headed human dæmon. Compare also the Chiriqui figure depicted by by MacCurdy, "A Study of Chiriquian Antiquities," Yale University Press, 1911, fig. 361, p. 209.

[2] "Early Religious Poetry of Persia," pp. 42 and 43.

[3] *Op. cit.* p. 43. But I think these legends accredited to the Aryans owe their parentage to the same source as the Egyptian beliefs concerning the cow, and especially the remarkable mysteries upon which Moret has been endeavouring to throw some light—"Mystères Égyptiens," p. 43.

The Diffusion of Culture.

In these pages I have made no attempt to deal with the far-reaching and intricate problems of the diffusion abroad of the practices and beliefs which I have been discussing. But the thoughts and the aspirations of every cultured people are permeated through and through with their influence.

It is important to remember that in almost every stage of the development of these complex customs and ideas not merely the "finished product" but also the ingredients out of which it was built up were being scattered abroad.

I shall briefly refer to certain evidence from Asia and America in illustration of this fact and in substantiation of the reality of the diffusion to the East of some of the beliefs I have been discussing.

The unity of Egyptian and Babylonian ideas is nowhere more strikingly demonstrated than in the essential identity of the attributes of Osiris and Ea. It affords the most positive proof of the derivation of the beliefs from some common source, and reveals the fact that Egyptian and Sumerian civilizations must have been in intimate cultural contact at the beginning of their developmental history. "In Babylonia, as in Egypt, there were differences of opinion regarding the origin of life and the particular natural element which represented the vital principle." "One section of the people, who were represented by the worshippers of Ea, appear to have believed that the essence of life was contained in water. The god of Eridu was the source of the 'water of life'."[1]

"Offerings of water and food were made to the dead," not primarily so that they might be "prevented from troubling the living,"[2] but to supply them with the means of sustenance and to

---

[1] Donald A. Mackenzie, "Myths of Babylonia and Assyria," p. 44 et seq.

[2] Dr. Alan Gardiner has protested against the assertions of "some Egyptologists, influenced more by anthropological theorists than by the unambiguous evidence of the Egyptian texts," to the effect that "the funerary rites and practices of the Egyptians were in the main precautionary measures serving to protect the living against the dead" (Article "Life and Death (Egyptian)," Hastings' *Encyclopædia of Religion and Ethics*). I should like to emphasize the fact that the "anthropological theorists," who so frequently put forward these claims have little more justification for them than "some

reanimate them to help the suppliants. It is a common belief that these and other procedures were inspired by fear of the dead. But such a statement does not accurately represent the attitude of mind of the people who devised these funerary ceremonies. For it is not the enemies of the dead or those against whom he had a grudge that run a risk at funerals, but rather his friends ; and the more deeply he was attached to a particular person the greater the danger for the latter. For among many people the belief obtains that when a man dies he will endeavour to steal the " soul-substance " of those who are dearest to him so that they may accompany him to the other world. But as stealing the " soul-substance "[1] means death, it is easy to misunderstand such a display of affection. Hence most people who long for life and hate death do their utmost to evade such embarrassing tokens of love ; and most ethnologists, misjudging such actions, write about " appeasing the dead ". It was those whom the gods *loved* who died young.

Ea was not only the god of the deep, but also " lord of life," king of the river and god of creation. Like Osiris "he fertilized parched and sunburnt wastes through rivers and irrigating canals, and conferred upon man the sustaining ' food of life '. . . . The goddess of the dead commanded her servant to ' sprinkle the Lady Ishtar with the water of life ' " (*op. cit.* p. 44).

In Chapter III. of Mr. Mackenzie's book, from which I have just

Egyptologists". Careful study of the best evidence from Babylonia, India, Indonesia, and Japan, reveals the fact that anthropologists who make such claims have in many cases misinterpreted the facts. In an article on "Ancestor Worship" by Professor Nobushige Hozumi in A. Stead's " Japan by the Japanese " (1904) the true point of view is put very clearly : " The origin of ancestor-worship is ascribed by many eminent writers to the *dread of ghosts* and the sacrifices made to the souls of ancestors for the purpose of *propitiating* them. It appears to me more correct to attribute the origin of ancestor-worship to a contrary cause. It was the *love* of ancestors, not the *dread* of them" [Here he quotes the Chinese philosophers Shiu-ki and Confucius in corroboration] that impelled men to worship. "We celebrate the anniversary of our ancestors, pay visits to their graves, offer flowers, food and drink, burn incense and bow before their tombs, entirely from a feeling of love and respect for their memory, and no question of 'dread' enters our minds in doing so" (pp. 281 and 282). [See, however, Appendix B, p. 74.]

[1] For, as I have already explained, the idea so commonly and mistakenly conveyed by the term " soul-substance " by writers on Indonesian and Chinese beliefs would be much more accurately rendered simply by the word " life," so that the stealing of it necessarily means death.

quoted, there is an interesting collection of quotations clearly showing that the conception of the vitalizing properties of the body moisture of gods is not restricted to Egypt, but is found also in Babylonia and India, in Western Asia and Greece, and also in Western Europe.

It has been suggested that the name Ishtar has been derived from Semitic roots implying " she who waters," " she who makes fruitful ".[1]

Barton claims that : " The beginnings of Semitic religion as they were conceived by the Semites themselves go back to sexual relations . . . the Semitic conception of deity . . . embodies the truth—grossly indeed, but nevertheless embodies it—that 'God is love'" (*op. cit.* p. 107). [This statement, however, is very misleading—see Appendix C, p. 75.]

Throughout the countries where Semitic[2] influence spread the primitive Mother-Goddesses or some of their specialized variants are found. But in every case the goddess is associated with many distinctive traits which reveal her identity with her homologues in Cyprus, Babylonia, and Egypt.

Among the Sumerians " life comes on earth through the introduction of water and irrigation ".[3] " Man also results from a union between the water-gods."

The Akkadians held views which were almost the direct antithesis of these. To them "the watery deep is disorder, and the cosmos, the order of the world, is due to the victory of a god of light and spring over the monster of winter and water ; man is directly made by the gods ".[4]

" The Sumerian account of Beginnings centres around the production by the gods of water, Enki and his consort Nin-ella (or Dangal), of a great number of canals bringing rain to the desolate fields of a dry continent. Life both of vegetables and animals follows the profusion of the vivifying waters. . . . In the process of life's production besides Enki, the personality of his consort is very conspicuous. She is called

[1] Barton, *op. cit.* p. 105.
[2] The evidence set forth in these pages makes it clear that such ideas are not restricted to the Semites: nor is there any reason to suppose that they originated amongst them.
[3] Albert J. Carnoy, " Iranian Views of Origins in Connexion with Similar Babylonian Beliefs," *Journal of the American Oriental Society*, Vol. XXXVI, 1916, pp. 300-20.
[4] This is Professor Carnoy's summary of Professor Jastrow's views as expressed in his article " Sumerian and Akkadian Views of Beginnings ".

Nin-Ella, 'the pure Lady,' *Damgal-Nunna*, the 'great Lady of the Waters,' *Nin-Tu*, 'the Lady of Birth'" (p. 301). The child of Enki and Nin-ella was the ancestor of mankind.[1]

"In later traditions, the personality of that Great Lady seems to have been overshadowed by that of Ishtar, who absorbed several of her functions" (p. 301).

Professor Carnoy fully demonstrates the derivation of certain early so-called "Aryan" beliefs from Chaldea. In the Iranian account of the creation "the great spring Ardvī Sūra Anāhita is the life-increasing, the herd-increasing, the fold-increasing who makes prosperity for all countries (Yt. 5, 1) . . . that precious spring is worshipped as a goddess . . . and is personified as a handsome and stately woman. She is a fair maid, most strong, tall of form, high-girded. Her arms are white and thick as a horse's shoulder or still thicker. She is full of gracefulness" (Yt. 5, 7, 64, 78). "Professor Cumont thinks that Anāhita is Ishtar . . . she is a goddess of fecundation and birth. Moreover in Achæmenian inscriptions Anāhita is associated with Ahura Mazdāh and Mithra, a triad corresponding to the Chaldean triad: Sin-Shamash-Ishtar. Ἀνᾶιτις in Strabo and other Greek writers is treated as Ἀφροδίτη" (p. 302).

But in Mesopotamia also the same views were entertained as in Egypt of the functions of statues.

"The statues hidden in the recesses of the temples or erected on the summits of the 'Ziggurats' became imbued, by virtue of their consecration, with the actual body of the god whom they represented." Thus Marduk is said to "inhabit his image" (Maspero, *op. cit.* p. 64).

This is precisely the idea which the Egyptians had. Even at the present day it survives among the Dravidian peoples of India.[2] They make images of their village deities, which may be permanent or only temporary, but in any case they are regarded not as actual deities but as the "bodies" so to speak into which these deities can enter. They are sacred only when they are so animated by the goddess. The

---

[1] Jastrow's interpretation of a recently-discovered tablet published by Langdon under the title *The Sumerian Epic of Paradise, the Flood and the Fall of Man*.

[2] I have already (p. 43) mentioned the fact that it is still preserved in China also.

ritual of animation is essentially identical with that found in Ancient Egypt. Libations are poured out; incense is burnt; the bleeding right fore-leg of a buffalo constitutes the blood-offering.[1] When the deity is reanimated by these procedures and its consciousness restored by the blood-offering it can hear appeals and speak.

The same attitude towards their idols was adopted by the Polynesians. "The priest usually addressed the image, into which it was imagined the god entered when anyone came to inquire his will."[2]

But there are certain other aspects of these Indian customs that are of peculiar interest. In my Ridgeway essay (*op. cit. supra*) I referred to the means by which in Nubia the degradation of the oblong Egyptian *mastaba* gave rise to the simple stone circle. This type spread to the west along the North African littoral, and also to the Eastern desert and Palestine. At some subsequent time mariners from the Red Sea introduced this practice into India.

[It is important to bear in mind that two other classes of stone circles were invented. One of them was derived, not from the *mastaba* itself, but from the enclosing wall surrounding it (see my Ridgeway essay, Fig. 13, p. 531, and compare with Figs. 3 and 4, p. 510, for illustrations of the transformed *mastaba*-type). This type of circle (enclosing a dolmen) is found both in the Caucasus-Caspian area as well as in India. A highly developed form of this encircling type of structure is seen in the famous rails surrounding the Buddhist *stupas* and *dagabas*. A third and later form of circle, of which Stonehenge is an example, was developed out of the much later New Empire Egyptian conception of a temple.]

But at the same time, as in Nubia, and possibly in Libya, the *mastaba* was being degraded into the first of the three main varieties of stone circle, other, though less drastic, forms of simplification of the

---

[1] Henry Whitehead (Bishop of Madras), "The Village Deities of Southern India," Madras Government Museum, Bull., Vol. V, No. 3, 1907; Wilber Theodore Elmore, "Dravidian Gods in Modern Hinduism: A Study of the Local and Village Deities of Southern India," University Studies: University of Nebraska, Vol. XV, No. 1, Jan., 1915. Compare the sacrifice of the fore-leg of a living calf in Egypt—A. E. P. B. Weigall, "An Ancient Egyptian Funeral Ceremony," *Journal of Egyptian Archæology*, Vol. II, 1915, p. 10. Early literary references from Babylonia suggest that a similar method of offering blood was practised there.

[2] William Ellis, "Polynesian Researches," 2nd edition, 1832, Vol. I, p. 373.

mastaba were taking place, possibly in Egypt itself, but certainly upon the neighbouring Mediterranean coasts. In some respects the least altered copies of the *mastaba* are found in the so-called "giant's graves" of Sardinia and the "horned cairns" of the British Isles. But the real features of the Egyptian *serdab*, which was the essential part, the nucleus so to speak, of the *mastaba*, are best preserved in the so-called "holed dolmens" of the Levant, the Caucasus, and India. [They also occur sporadically in the West, as in France and Britain.]

Such dolmens and more simplified forms are scattered in Palestine,[1] but are seen to best advantage upon the Eastern Littoral of the Black Sea, the Caucasus, and the neighbourhood of the Caspian. They are found only in scattered localities between the Black and Caspian Seas. As de Morgan has pointed out,[2] their distribution is explained by their association with ancient gold and copper mines. They were the tombs of immigrant mining colonies who had settled in these definite localities to exploit these minerals.

Now the same types of dolmens, also associated with ancient mines,[3] are found in India. There is some evidence to suggest that these degraded types of Egyptian *mastabas* were introduced into India at some time after the adoption of the other, the Nubian modification of the *mastaba* which is represented by the first variety of stone circle.[4]

I have referred to these Indian dolmens for the specific purpose of illustrating the complexities of the processes of diffusion of culture. For not only have several variously specialized degradation-products of the same original type of Egyptian *mastaba* reached India, possibly by different routes and at different times, but also many of the ideas

[1] See H. Vincent, "Canaan d'après l'exploration récente," Paris, 1907, p. 395.

[2] "Les Premières Civilizations," Paris, 1909, p. 404: Mémoires de la Délégation en Perse, Tome VIII, archéol.; and Mission Scientifique au Caucase, Tome I.

[3] W. J. Perry, "The Relationship between the Geographical Distribution of Megalithic Monuments and Ancient Mines," *Memoirs and Proceedings of the Manchester Literary and Philosophical Society*, Vol. 60, Part I, 24th Nov., 1915.

[4] The evidence for this is being prepared for publication by Captain Leonard Munn, R.E., who has personally collected the data in Hyderabad.

that developed out of the funerary ritual in Egypt—of which the *mastaba* was merely one of the manifestations—made their way to India at various times and became secondarily blended with other expressions of the same or associated ideas there. I have already referred to the essential elements of the Egyptian funerary ritual—the statues, incense, libations, and the rest—as still persisting among the Dravidian peoples.

But in the Madras Presidency dolmens are found converted into Siva temples.[1] Now in the inner chamber of the shrine—which represents the homologue of the *serdab*—in place of the statue or bas-relief of the deceased or of the deity, which is found in some of them (see Plate I), there is the stone *linga-yoni* emblem in the position corresponding to that in which, in the later temple in the same locality (Kambaduru), there is an image of Parvati, the consort of Siva.

The earliest deities in Egypt, both Osiris and Hathor, were really expressions of the creative principle. In the case of Hathor, the goddess was, in fact, the personification of the female organs of reproduction.[2] In these early Siva temples in India these principles of creation were given their literal interpretation, and represented frankly as the organs of reproduction of the two sexes. The gods of creation were symbolized by models in stone of the creating organs. Further illustrations of the same principle are witnessed in the Indonesian megalithic monuments which Perry calls " dissoliths ".[3]

The later Indian temples, both Buddhist and Hindu, were developed from these early dolmens, as Mr. Longhurst's reports so clearly demonstrate. But from time to time there was an influx of new ideas from the West which found expression in a series of modifications of the architecture. Thus India provides an admirable illustration of this principle of culture contact. A series of waves of megalithic culture introduced purely Western ideas. These were developed by the local people in their own way, constantly intermingling a variety of cultural influences to weave them into a dis-

[1] Annual Report of the Archæological Department, Southern Circle, Madras, for the year 1915-1916. See for example Mr. A. H. Longhurst's photographs and plans (Plates I-IV) and especially that of the old Siva temple at Kambaduru, Plate IV (*b*).
[2] As I shall show in " The Birth of Aphrodite " (Chapter III).
[3] W. J. Perry, " The Megalithic Culture of Indonesia ".

INCENSE AND LIBATIONS

tinctive fabric, which was compounded partly of imported, partly of local threads, woven locally into a truly Indian pattern. In this process of development one can detect the effects of Mycenean accretions (see for example Longhurst's Plate XIII), probably modified during its indirect transmission by Phœnician and later influences; and also the more intimate part played by Babylonian, Egyptian, and, later, Greek and Persian art and architecture in directing the course of development of Indian culture.

Incidentally, in the course of the discussions in the foregoing pages, I have referred to the profound influence of Egyptian, Babylonian and Indian ideas in Eastern Asia. Perry's important book (*op. cit. supra*) reveals their efforts in Indonesia. Thence they spread across the Pacific to America.

In the "Migrations of Early Culture" (p. 114) I called attention to the fact that among the Aztecs water was poured upon the head of the mummy. This ritual procedure was inspired by the Egyptian idea of libations, for, according to Brasseur de Bourbourg, the pouring out of the water was accompanied by the remark "C'est cette eau que tu as reçue en venant au monde".

But incense-burning and blood-offering were also practised in America. In an interesting memoir [1] on the practice of blood-letting by piercing the ears and tongue, Mrs. Zelia Nuttall reproduces a remarkable picture from a "partly unpublished MS. of Sahagun's work preserved in Florence". "The image of the sun is held up by a man whose body is partly hidden, and two men, seated opposite to each other in the foreground, are in the act of piercing the helices or external borders of their ears." But in addition to these blood-offerings to the sun, two priests are burning incense in remarkably Egyptian-like censers, and another pair are blowing conch-shell trumpets.

But it was not merely the use of incense and libations and the identities in the wholly arbitrary attributes of the American pantheon that reveal the sources of their derivation in the Old World. When the Spaniards first visited Yucatan they found traces of a Maya baptismal rite which the natives called *zihil*, signifying "to be born again". At the ceremony also incense was burnt.[2]

[1] "A Penitential Rite of the Ancient Mexicans," Archæological and Ethnological Papers of the Peabody Museum, Harvard University, Vol. I, No. 7, 1904.
[2] Bancroft, *op. cit.* Vol. II, pp. 682 and 683.

The forehead, the face, the fingers and toes were moistened. "After they had been thus sprinkled with water, the priest arose and removed the cloths from the heads of the children, and then cut off with a stone knife a certain bead that was attached to the head from childhood." [1]

[The custom of wearing such a bead during childhood is found in Egypt at the present day.]

In the case of the girls, their mothers " divested them of a cord which was worn during their childhood, fastened round the loins, having a small shell that hung in front ('una conchuela asida que les venia a dar encima de la parte honesta'—Landa). The removal of this signified that they could marry." [2]

This use of shells is found in the Soudan and East Africa at the present day.[3] The girdle upon which the shells were hung is the prototype of the cestus of Hathor, Ishtar, Aphrodite, Kali and all the goddesses of fertility in the Old World. It is an admirable illustration of the fact that not only were the finished products, the goddesses and their fantastic repertory of attributes, transmitted to the New World, but also the earliest and most primitive ingredients out of which the complexities of their traits were compounded.

In Chapter III ("The Birth of Aphrodite") I shall explain what an important part the invention of this girdle played in the development of the material side of civilization and the even vaster influence it exerted upon beliefs and ethics. It represents the first stage in the evolution of clothing; and it was responsible for originating the belief in love-philtres and in the possibility of foretelling the future.

It would lead me too far from my main purpose in this book to discuss the widespread geographical distribution and historical associations of the customs of baptism and pouring libations among different peoples. I may, however, refer the reader to an article by Mr. Elsdon Best, entitled "Ceremonial Performances Pertaining to Birth, as Performed by the Maori of New Zealand in Past Times" (*Journal of the Royal Anthropological Institute*, Vol. XLIV, 1914, p. 127), which sheds a clear light upon the general problem.

The whole subject of baptismal ceremonies is well worth detailed study as a remarkable demonstration of the spread of culture in early times.

[1] *Op. cit.* p. 684. [2] *Ibid.* [3] See J. Wilfrid Jackson, *op. cit. supra.*

FIG. 6.—REPRESENTATION OF THE ANCIENT MEXICAN WORSHIP OF THE SUN

The image of the sun is held up by a man in front of his face; two men blow conch-shell trumpets; another pair burn incense; and a third pair make blood-offerings by piercing their ears—after Zelia Nuttall.

SUMMARY.

In these pages I have ranged over a very wide field of speculation, groping in the dim shadows of the early history of civilization. I have been attempting to pick up a few of the threads which ultimately became woven into the texture of human beliefs and aspirations, and to suggest that the practice of mummification was the woof around which the web of civilization was intimately intertwined.

I have already explained how closely that practice was related to the origin and development of architecture, which Professor Lethaby has called the "matrix of civilization," and how nearly the ideas that grew up in explanation and in justification of the ritual of embalming were affected by the practice of agriculture, the second great pillar of support for the edifice of civilization. It has also been shown how far-reaching was the influence exerted by the needs of the embalmer, which impelled men, probably for the first time in history, to plan and carry out great expeditions by sea and land to obtain the necessary resins and the balsams, the wood and the spices. Incidentally also in course of time the practice of mummification came to exert a profound effect upon the means for the acquisition of a knowledge of medicine and all the sciences ancillary to it.

But I have devoted chief attention to the bearing of the ideas which developed out of the practice and ritual of embalming upon the spirit of man. It gave shape and substance to the belief in a future life; it was perhaps the most important factor in the development of a definite conception of the gods: it laid the foundation of the ideas which subsequently were built up into a theory of the soul: in fact, it was intimately connected with the birth of all those ideals and aspirations which are now included in the conception of religious belief and ritual. A multitude of other trains of thought were started amidst the intellectual ferment of the formulation of the earliest concrete system of biological theory. The idea of the properties and functions of water which had previously sprung up in connexion with the development of agriculture became crystallized into a more definite form as the result of the development of mummification, and this has played an obtrusive part in religion, in philosophy and in medicine ever since. Moreover its influence has become embalmed for all time in many languages and in the ritual of every religion.

But it was a factor in the development not merely of religious beliefs, temples and ritual, but it was also very closely related to the origin of much of the paraphernalia of the gods and of current popular beliefs. The swastika and the thunderbolt, dragons and demons, totemism and the sky-world are all of them conceptions that were more or less closely connected with the matters I have been discussing.

The ideas which grew up in association with the practice of mummification were responsible for the development of the temple and its ritual and for a definite formulation of the conception of deities. But they were also responsible for originating a priesthood. For the resuscitation of the dead king, Osiris, and for the maintenance of his existence it was necessary for his successor, the reigning king, to perform the ritual of animation and the provision of food and drink. The king, therefore, was the first priest, and his functions were not primarily acts of worship but merely the necessary preliminaries for restoring life and consciousness to the dead seer so that he could consult him and secure his advice and help.

It was only when the number of temples became so great and their ritual so complex and elaborate as to make it a physical impossibility for the king to act in this capacity in all of them and on every occasion that he was compelled to delegate some of his priestly functions to others, either members of the royal family or high officials. In course of time certain individuals devoted themselves exclusively to these duties and became professional priests; but it is important to remember that at first it was the exclusive privilege of Horus, the reigning king, to intercede with Osiris, the dead king, on behalf of men, and that the earliest priesthood consisted of those individuals to whom he had delegated some of these duties.

In conclusion I should like to express in words what must be only too apparent to every reader of this statement. It claims to be nothing more than a contribution to the study of some of the most difficult problems in the history of human thought. For one so ill-equipped for a task of such a nature as I am to attempt it calls for a word of explanation. The clear light that recent research has shed upon the earliest literature in the world has done much to destroy the foundations upon which the theories propounded by scholars have been built up. It seemed to be worth while to attempt to read afresh the voluminous mass of old documents with the illumination of this new information.

The other reason for making such an attempt is that almost every modern scholar who has discussed the matters at issue has assumed that the fashionable doctrine of the independent development of human beliefs and practices was a safe basis upon which to construct his theories. At best it is an unproven and reckless speculation. I am convinced it is utterly false. Holding such views I have attempted to read the evidence afresh.

APPENDIX A.

On re-reading the discussion of the significance of the *ka* I realize that, in striving after brevity and conciseness—to keep the size of my statement within the limits of the *Bulletin of the John Rylands Library*, generously elastic though it is—I have left the argument in a rather nebulous form.

It must not be imagined that a concrete-minded people like the ancient Egyptians entertained highly abstract and ethereal ideas about "the soul". They recognized that all the expressions of consciousness and personality could cease during sleep; and at the same time the phenomena of dreams seemed to afford evidence that these absent elements of the individual's being were enjoying real experiences elsewhere. Thus there was an *alter ego*, identified by this matter-of-fact people with the twin (placenta) which was born with the child and was clearly concerned with its physical and intellectual nourishment—for it was obviously connected by its stalk to the embryo like a tree to its roots, and it seemed to be composed of blood, which was regarded as the vehicle of mind. But this intellectual "twin" kept pace in its growth with the physical body. When a statue was made to represent the latter the *ka* could dwell in the real body or the statue.

The identification of the placenta with the moon helped the growth of the conception that this "birth-promoter" could not only bring about a re-birth in the life to come, but also facilitate a transference to the sky-world. The placenta had already been superintending the deceased's welfare upon earth and would continue to do so when he rejoined his *ka* in the sky world.

The complexity of the conception is due to the fact that the simple early belief in "a double" was gradually elaborated, as one new idea after another became added to it, and rationalized to blend with the former complex in an increasingly involved synthesis. It was only when the elaborate scaffolding of material factors was cleared away that a more ethereal conception of " the soul " was sublimated.

APPENDIX B.

I should like to emphasize the fact that my protest (on p. 63) was directed against the claim that the custom of offering food and drink to the dead was inspired *primarily* to prevent them from troubling the living. Its original purpose was to sustain and reanimate the dead; but, of course, when its real meaning was forgotten, it was explained in a great variety of ways by the people who made a practice of presenting offerings to the dead without really knowing why they did so.

Dr. Alan Gardiner himself has made a statement which casual readers (i.e., those who do not discriminate between the motive for the invention of a procedure and the reasons subsequently given for its continuance) might regard as a contradiction of my quotation from his writings on p. 62. Thus he says: " Any god could doubtless attack human beings, but savage and malicious deities, like Seth [Set], the murderer of Osiris, or Sakhmet, [Sekhet], the ' lady of pestilence ' (*nb-t 'idw*), were doubtless most to be feared." [This attitude of the malignant goddesses is revealed in a most obtrusive form in the village deities of the Dravidians of Southern India.] " The dead were specially to be feared; nor was it only those dead who were unhappy or unburied that might torment the living, for the magician sometimes warns them that their tombs are endangered " (Article " Magic (Egyptian)," *Hastings' Encycl. Ethics and Religion*, p. 264).

But it is important to bear in mind, as the same scholar has explained elsewhere [" Life and Death (Egyptian)," *Hastings' Encycl.*, p. 23] : " Nothing could be farther from the truth [than the statement that ' the funerary rites and practices of the Egyptians were in the main precautionary measures serving to protect the living against the dead '] ; it is of fundamental importance to realize that the vast stores of wealth and thought expended by the Egyptians on their tombs—that wealth and that thought which created not only the pyramids, but also the practice of mummification and a very extensive funerary literature—were due to the anxiety of each member of the community with regard to his own individual future welfare, and not to feelings of respect, or fear, or duty felt towards the other dead."

It was only in response to certain binding obligations that the living observed all those costly and troublesome rules which were believed to insure the welfare of the deceased. But this recognition of the primary and real purpose of the food offerings as sustenance for the dead or the gods must not be allowed to blind us to the fact that there is widespread throughout the world a real fear of the dead and ghosts, and that in many places food-offerings are made for the specific purpose " of appeasing the fairies ".

Mr. Donald Mackenzie tells me that offerings of milk and porridge are made at the stone monuments in Scotland, and children carry meal in their pockets to protect themselves from the fairies. For the dead went to Fairyland.

Beliefs of a similar kind can be collected from most parts of the world: but the point I specially want to emphasize is that they are *secondary* rationalizations of a custom which originally had an utterly different significance.

APPENDIX C.

Prof. Barton's statement (*supra*, p. 64) is typical of a widespread misapprehension, resulting from the confusion between sexual relations and the giving of life. At first primitive people did not realize that the manifestations of the sex instinct had anything whatever to do with reproduction. They were aware of the fact that women gave birth to children; and the organ concerned in this process was regarded as the giver of life, the creator. The apotheosis of these powers led to the conception of the first deity. But it was only secondarily that these life-giving attributes were brought into association with the sexual act and the masculine powers of fertilization. Much confusion has been created by those writers who see manifestations of the sexual factor and phallic ideas in every aspect of primitive religion, where in most cases only the power of life-giving plays a part.

Chapter II.

DRAGONS AND RAIN GODS.[1]

AN adequate account of the development of the dragon-legend would represent the history of the expression of mankind's aspirations and fears during the past fifty centuries and more. For the dragon was evolved along with civilization itself. The search for the elixir of life, to turn back the years from old age and confer the boon of immortality, has been the great driving force that compelled men to build up the material and the intellectual fabric of civilization. The dragon-legend is the history of that search which has been preserved by popular tradition : it has grown up and kept pace with the constant struggle to grasp the unattainable goal of men's desires ; and the story has been constantly growing in complexity, as new incidents were drawn within its scope and confused with old incidents whose real meaning was forgotten or distorted. It has passed through all the phases with which the study of the spreading of rumours or the development of dreams has familiarized students of psychology. The simple original stories, which become blended and confused, their meaning distorted and reinterpreted by the rationalizing of incoherent incidents, are given the dramatic form with which the human mind invests all stories that make a strong appeal to its emotions, and then secondarily elaborated with a wealth of circumstantial detail. This is the history of popular legends and the development of rumours. But these phenomena are displayed in their most emphatic form in dreams.[2] In his waking state man restrains his roving fancies and exercises what Freud has called a "censorship" over the stream of his thoughts : but when he falls asleep, the "censor" dozes also ; and free rein is given to his un-

[1] An elaboration of a Lecture delivered in the John Rylands Library on 8 November, 1916.
[2] In his lecture, "Dreams and Primitive Culture," delivered at the John Rylands Library on 10 April, 1918, Dr. Rivers has expounded the principles of dream-development.

DRAGONS AND RAIN GODS

restrained fancies to make a hotch-potch of the most varied and unrelated incidents, and to create a fantastic mosaic built up from fragments of his actual experience, bound together by the cement of his aspirations and fears. The myth resembles the dream because it has developed without any consistent and effective censorship. The individual who tells one particular phase of the story may exert the controlling influence of his mind over the version he narrates : but as it is handed on from man to man and generation to generation the "censorship" also is constantly changing. This lack of unity of control implies that the development of the myth is not unlike the building-up of a dream-story. But the dragon-myth is vastly more complex than any dream, because mankind as a whole has taken a hand in the process of shaping it ; and the number of centuries devoted to this work of elaboration has been far greater than the years spent by the average individual in accumulating the stuff of which most of his dreams have been made. But though the myth is enormously complex, so vast a mass of detailed evidence concerning every phase and every detail of its history has been preserved, both in the literature and the folk-lore of the world, that we are able to submit it to psychological analysis and determine the course of its development and the significance of every incident in its tortuous rambling.

In instituting these comparisons between the development of myths and dreams, I should like to emphasize the fact that the interpretation of the *myth* proposed in these pages is almost diametrically opposed to that suggested by Freud, and pushed to a *reductio ad absurdum* by his more reckless followers, and especially by Yung.

The dragon has been described as "the most venerable symbol employed in ornamental art and the favourite and most highly decorative motif in artistic design". It has been the inspiration of much, if not most, of the world's great literature in every age and clime, and the nucleus around which a wealth of ethical symbolism has accumulated throughout the ages. The dragon-myth represents also the earliest doctrine or systematic theory of astronomy and meteorology.

In the course of its romantic and chequered history the dragon has been identified with all of the gods and all of the demons of every religion. But it is most intimately associated with the earliest stratum of divinities, for it has been homologized with each of the members of the earliest Trinity, the Great Mother, the Water God, and the

Warrior Sun God, both individually and collectively. To add to the complexities of the story, the dragon-slayer is also represented by the same deities, either individually or collectively; and the weapon with which the hero slays the dragon is also homologous both with him and his victim, for it is animated by him who wields it, and its powers of destruction make it a symbol of the same power of evil which it itself destroys.

Such a fantastic paradox of contradictions has supplied the materials with which the fancies of men of every race and land, and every stage of knowledge and ignorance, have been playing for all these centuries. It is not surprising, therefore, that an endless series of variations of the story has been evolved, each decked out with topical allusions and distinctive embellishments. But throughout the complex tissue of this highly embroidered fabric the essential threads of the web and woof of its foundation can be detected with surprising constancy and regularity.

Within the limits of such an account as this it is obvious that I can deal only with the main threads of the argument and leave the interesting details of the local embellishments until some other time.

The fundamental element in the dragon's powers is the control of water. Both in its beneficent and destructive aspects water was regarded as animated by the dragon, who thus assumed the rôle of Osiris or his enemy Set. But when the attributes of the Water God became confused with those of the Great Mother, and her evil avatar, the lioness (Sekhet) form of Hathor in Egypt, or in Babylonia the destructive Tiamat, became the symbol of disorder and chaos, the dragon became identified with her also.

Similarly the third member of the Earliest Trinity also became the dragon. As the son and successor of the dead king Osiris the living king Horus became assimilated with him. When the belief became more and more insistent that the dead king had acquired the boon of immortality and was really alive, the distinction between him and the actually living king Horus became correspondingly minimized. This process of assimilation was advanced a further stage when the king became a god and was thus more closely identified with his father and predecessor. Hence Horus assumed many of the functions of Osiris; and amongst them those which in foreign lands contributed to making a dragon of the Water God. But if the distinction between Horus and Osiris became more and more attenuated with the lapse of time, the identification with his mother Hathor (Isis) was more complete still. For he took her place and assumed many of her attributes in the later versions of the great saga which is the nucleus of all the literature of mythology—I refer to the story of "The Destruction of Mankind".

The attributes of these three members of the Trinity, Hathor, Osiris, and Horus, thus became intimately linked the one with the other; and in Susa, where the earliest pictorial representation of a real dragon developed, it received concrete form (Fig. 1) as a monster compounded of the lioness of Hathor (Sekhet) with the falcon (or eagle) of Horus, but with the human attributes and water-controlling powers which originally belonged to Osiris. In some parts of Africa

FIG. 1.—EARLY REPRESENTATION OF A "DRAGON" COMPOUNDED OF THE FOREPART OF AN EAGLE AND THE HINDPART OF A LION—(from an Archaic Cylinder-seal from Susa, after Jéquier).

FIG. 2.—THE EARLIEST BABYLONIAN CONCEPTION OF THE DRAGON TIAMAT—(from a Cylinder-seal in the British Museum, after L. W. King).

the earliest "dragon" was nothing more than Hathor's cow or the gazelle or antelope of Horus (Osiris) or of Set.

But if the dragon was compounded of all three deities, who was the slayer of the evil dragon?

The story of the dragon-conflict is really a recital of Horus's vendetta against Set, intimately blended and confused with different versions of "The Destruction of Mankind".[1] The commonplace incidents of the originally prosaic stories were distorted into an almost unrecognizable form, then secondarily elaborated without any attention to their original meaning, but with a wealth of circumstantial embellishment, in accordance with the usual methods of the human mind that I have already mentioned. The history of the legend is in fact the most complete, because it is the oldest and the most widespread, illustration of those instinctive tendencies of the human spirit to bridge the

[1] *Vide infra*, p. 109 *et seq.*

gaps in its disjointed experience, and to link together in a kind of mental mosaic the otherwise isolated incidents in the facts of daily life and the rumours and traditions that have been handed down from the story-teller's predecessors.

In the "Destruction of Mankind," which I shall discuss more fully in the following pages (p. 109 *et seq.*), Hathor does the slaying: in the later stories Horus takes his mother's place and earns his spurs as the Warrior Sun-god :[1] hence confusion was inevitably introduced between the enemies of Re, the original victims in the legend, and Horus's traditional enemies, the followers of Set. Against the latter it was Osiris himself who fought originally ; and in many of the non-Egyptian variants of the legend it is the rain-god himself who is the warrior.

Hence all three members of the Trinity were identified, not only with the dragon, but also with the hero who was the dragon-slayer.

But the weapon used by the latter was also animated by the same Trinity, and in fact identified with them. In the Saga of the Winged Disk, Horus assumed the form of the sun equipped with the wings of his own falcon and the fire-spitting uræus serpents. Flying down from heaven in this form he was at the same time the god and the god's weapon. As a fiery bolt from heaven he slew the enemies of Re, who were now identified with his own personal foes, the followers of Set. But in the earlier versions of the myth (i.e. the "Destruction of Mankind"), it was Hathor who was the "Eye of Re" and descended from heaven to destroy mankind with fire; she also was the vulture (Mut) ; and in the earliest version she did the slaughter with a knife or an axe with which she was animistically identified.

But Osiris also was the weapon of destruction, both in the form of the flood (for he was the personification of the river) and the rain-storms from heaven. But he was also an instrument for vanquishing the demon, when the intoxicating beer or the sedative drink (the potency of which was due to the indwelling spirit of the god) was the chosen means of overcoming the dragon.

This, in brief, is the framework of the dragon-story. The early Trinity as the hero, armed with the Trinity as weapon, slays the

[1] Hence soldiers killed in battle and women dying in childbirth receive special consideration in the exclusive heaven of (Osiris's) Horus's Indian and American representatives, Indra and Tlaloc.

Fig. 7.—A Mediæval Picture of a Chinese Dragon upon its cloud
(After the late Professor W. Anderson)

Fig. 8.—A Chinese Dragon
(After de Groot)

Fig. 9.—Dragon from the Ishtar Gate of Babylon

Fig. 10.—Babylonian Weather God

dragon, which again is the same Trinity. With its illimitable possibilities for dramatic development and fantastic embellishment with incident and ethical symbolism, this theme has provided countless thousands of story-tellers with the skeleton which they clothed with the living flesh of their stories, representing not merely the earliest theories of astronomy and meteorology, but all the emotional conflicts of daily life, the struggle between light and darkness, heat and cold, right and wrong, justice and injustice, prosperity and adversity, wealth and poverty. The whole gamut of human strivings and emotions was drawn into the legend until it became the great epic of the human spirit and the main theme that has appealed to the interest of all mankind in every age.

An ancient Chinese philosopher, Wang Fu, writing in the time of the Han Dynasty, enumerates the "nine resemblances" of the dragon. "His horns resemble those of a stag, his head that of a camel, his eyes those of a demon, his neck that of a snake, his belly that of a clam, his scales those of a carp, his claws those of an eagle, his soles those of a tiger, his ears those of a cow."[1] But this list includes only a small minority of the menagerie of diverse creatures which at one time or another have contributed their quota to this truly astounding hotchpotch.

This composite wonder-beast ranges from Western Europe to the Far East of Asia, and as we shall see, also even across the Pacific to America. Although in the different localities a great number of most varied ingredients enter into its composition, in most places where the dragon occurs the substratum of its anatomy consists of a serpent or a crocodile, usually with the scales of a fish for covering, and the feet and wings, and sometimes also the head, of an eagle, falcon, or hawk, and the forelimbs and sometimes the head of a lion. An association of anatomical features of so unnatural and arbitrary a nature can only mean that all dragons are the progeny of the same ultimate ancestors.

But it is not merely a case of structural or anatomical similarity, but also of physiological identity, that clinches the proof of the derivation of this fantastic brood from the same parents. Wherever the dragon is found, it displays a special partiality for water. It controls the rivers or seas, dwells in pools or wells, or in the clouds on the tops

[1] M. W. de Visser, "The Dragon in China and Japan," *Verhandelingen der Koninklijke Akademie van Wetenschappen te Amsterdam*, Afdeeling Letterkunde, Deel XIII, No. 2, 1913, p. 70.

of mountains, regulates the tides, the flow of streams, or the rainfall, and is associated with thunder and lightning. Its home is a mansion at the bottom of the sea, where it guards vast treasures, usually pearls, but also gold and precious stones. In other instances the dwelling is upon the top of a high mountain; and the dragon's breath forms the rain-clouds. It emits thunder and lightning. Eating the dragon's heart enables the diner to acquire the knowledge stored in this " organ of the mind" so that he can understand the language of birds, and in fact of all the creatures that have contributed to the making of a dragon.

It should not be necessary to rebut the numerous attempts that have been made to explain the dragon-myth as a story relating to extinct monsters. Such fantastic claims can be made only by writers devoid of any knowledge of palæontology or of the distinctive features of the dragon and its history. But when the Keeper of the Egyptian and Assyrian Antiquities in the British Museum, in a book that is not intended to be humorous,[1] seriously claims Dr. Andrews' discovery of a gigantic fossil snake as "proof" of the former existence of "the great serpent-devil Āpep," it is time to protest.

Those who attempt to derive the dragon from such living creatures as lizards like *Draco volans* or *Moloch horridus*[2] ignore the evidence of the composite and unnatural features of the monsters.

"Whatever be the origin of the Northern dragon, the myths, when they first became articulate for us, show him to be in all essentials the same as that of the South and East. He is a power of evil, guardian of hoards, the greedy withholder of good things from men; and the slaying of a dragon is the crowning achievement of heroes—of Siegmund, of Beowulf, of Sigurd, of Arthur, of Tristam—even of Lancelot, the *beau ideal* of mediæval chivalry" (*Encyclopædia Britannica*, vol. viii., p. 467). But if in the West the dragon is usually a "power of evil," in the far East he is equally emphatically a symbol of beneficence. He is identified with emperors and kings; he is the son of heaven, the bestower of all bounties, not merely to mankind directly, but also to the earth as well.

Even in our country his symbolism is not always wholly malevolent,

[1] E. A. Wallis Budge, " The Gods of the Egyptians," 1904, vol. i., p. 11.
[2] Gould's " Mythical Monsters," 1886.

DRAGONS AND RAIN GODS

otherwise—if for the moment we shut our eyes to the history of the development of heraldic ornament—dragons would hardly figure as the supporters of the arms of the City of London, and as the symbol of many of our aristocratic families, among which the Royal House of Tudor is included. It is only a few years since the Red Dragon of Cadwallader was added as an additional badge to the achievement of the Prince of Wales. But, " though a common ensign in war, both in the East and the West, as an ecclesiastical emblem his opposite qualities have remained consistently until the present day. Whenever the dragon is represented, it symbolizes the power of evil, the devil and his works. Hell in mediæval art is a dragon with gaping jaws, belching fire."

And in the East the dragon's reputation is not always blameless. For it figures in some disreputable incidents and does not escape the sort of punishment that tradition metes out to his European cousins.

The Dragon in America and Eastern Asia.

In the early centuries of the Christian era, and probably also even for two or three hundred years earlier still, the leaven of the ancient civilizations of the Old World was at work in Mexico, Central America and Peru. The most obtrusive influences that were brought to bear, especially in the area from Yucatan to Mexico, were inspired by the Cambodian and Indonesian modifications of Indian beliefs and practices. The god who was most often depicted upon the ancient Maya and Aztec codices was the Indian rain-god Indra, who in America was provided with the head of the Indian elephant [1] (i.e. seems to have been confused with the Indian Ganesa) and given other attributes more suggestive of the Dravidian Nâga than his enemy, the Aryan deity. In other words the character of the American god, known as *Chac* by the Maya people and as *Tlaloc* by the Aztecs, is an interesting illustration of the effects of such a mixture of cultures as Dr. Rivers has studied in Melanesia.[2] Not only does the elephant-headed god in America represent a blend of the two great Indian rain-gods which in the Old World are mortal enemies, the one of the other (partly for

---

[1] " Precolumbian Representations of the Elephant in America," *Nature*, Nov. 25, 1915, p. 340; Dec. 16, 1915, p. 425; and Jan. 27, 1916, p. 593.
[2] " History of Melanesian Society," Cambridge, 1914.

the political reason that the Dravidians and Aryans were rival and hostile peoples), but all the traits of each deity, even those depicting the old Aryan conception of their deadly combat, are reproduced in America under circumstances which reveal an ignorance on the part of the artists of the significance of the paradoxical contradictions they are representing. But even many incidents in the early history of the Vedic gods, which were due to arbitrary circumstances in the growth of the legends, reappear in America. To cite one instance (out of scores which might be quoted), in the Vedic story Indra assumed many of the attributes of the god Soma. In America the name of the god of rain and thunder, the Mexican Indra, is *Tlaloc*, which is generally translated " pulque of the earth," from *tlal*[*l*]*i*, " earth," and *oc*[*tli*], " pulque, a fermented drink (like the Indian drink *soma*) made from the juice of the agave ".[1]

The so-called " long-nosed god " (the elephant-headed rain-god) has been given the non-committal designation " god B," by Schellhas.[2]

I reproduce here a remarkable drawing (Fig. 11) from the Codex Troano, in which this god, whom the Maya people called *Chac*, is shown pouring the rain out of a water-jar (just as the deities of Babylonia and India are often represented), and putting his foot upon the head of a serpent, who is preventing the rain from reaching the earth. Here we find depicted with childlike simplicity and directness the Vedic conception of Indra overcoming the demon Vritra. Stempell describes this scene as " the elephant-headed god B standing upon the head of a serpent " ;[3] while Seler, who claims that god B is a tortoise, explains it as the serpent forming a footstool for the rain-god.[4] In the

---

[1] H. Beuchat, " Manuel d' Archéologie Americaine," 1912, p. 319.

[2] " Representation of Deities of the Maya Manuscripts," *Papers of the Peabody Museum*, vol. iv., 1904.

[3] *Zeitschrift für Ethnologie*, Bd. 40, 1908, p. 716.

[4] " Die Tierbilder der mexikanischen und der Maya-Handschriften," *Zeitschrift für Ethnologie*, Bd. 42, 1910, pp. 75 and 77. In the remarkable series of drawings from Maya and Aztec sources reproduced by Seler in his articles in the *Zeitschrift für Ethnologie*, the *Peabody Museum Papers*, and his monograph on the *Codex Vaticanus*, not only is practically every episode of the dragon-myth of the Old World graphically depicted, but also every phase and incident of the legends from India (and Babylonia, Egypt and the Ægean) that contributed to the building-up of the myth.

Fig. 11. Reproduction of a picture in the Maya Codex Troano representing the Rain-god *Chac* treading upon the Serpent's head, which is interposed between the earth and the rain the god is pouring out of a bowl. A Rain-goddess stands upon the Serpent's tail.

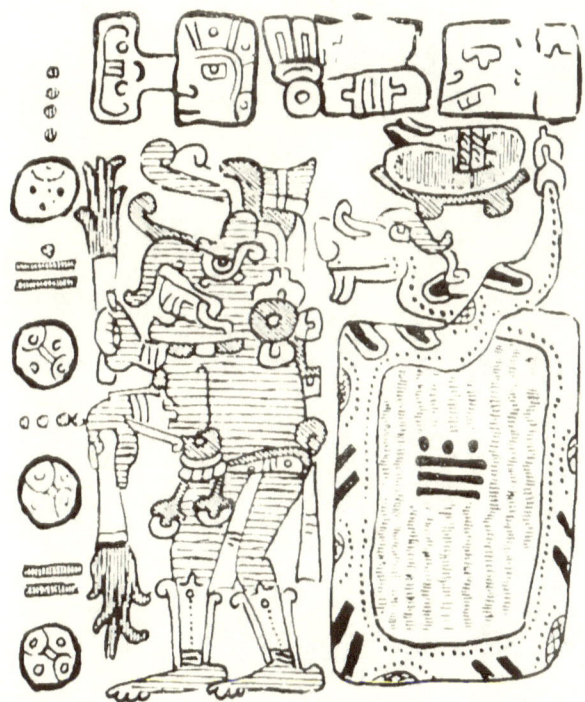

Fig. 12.—Another representation of the Elephant-headed Rain god. He is holding thunderbolts, conventionalised in a hand-like form. The Serpent is converted into a sac, holding up the rain-waters.

Codex Cortes the same theme is depicted in another way, which is truer to the Indian conception of Vritra, as "the restrainer"[1] (Fig. 12).

The serpent (the American rattlesnake) restrains the water by coiling itself into a sac to hold up the rain and so prevent it from reaching the earth. In the various American codices this episode is depicted in as great a variety of forms as the Vedic poets of India described when they sang of the exploits of Indra. The Maya Chac is, in fact, Indra transferred to the other side of the Pacific and there only thinly disguised by a veneer of American stylistic design.

But the Aztec god Tlaloc is merely the Chac of the Maya people transferred to Mexico. Schellhas declares that the "god B," the "most common figure in the codices," is a "universal deity to whom the most varied elements, natural phenomena, and activities are subject". "Many authorities consider God B to represent Kukulkan, the Feathered Serpent, whose Aztec equivalent is Quetzalcoatl. Others identify him with Itzamna, the Serpent God of the East, or with Chac, the Rain God of the four quarters and the equivalent of Tlaloc of the Mexicans."[2]

From the point of view of its Indian analogies these confusions are peculiarly significant, for the same phenomena are found in India. The snake and the dragon can be either the rain-god of the East or the enemy of the rain-god; either the dragon-slayer or the evil dragon who has to be slain. The Indian word *Nâga*, which is applied to the beneficent god or king identified with the cobra, can also mean "elephant," and this double significance probably played a part in the confusion of the deities in America.

In the Dresden Codex the elephant-headed god is represented in one place grasping a serpent, in another issuing from a serpent's mouth, and again as an actual serpent (Fig. 13). Turning next to the attributes of these American gods we find that they reproduce with amazing precision those of Indra. Not only were they the divinities who controlled rain, thunder, lightning, and vegetation, but they also carried axes and thunderbolts (Fig. 13) like their homologues in the Old World. Like Indra, Tlaloc was intimately associated with the East and with the tops of mountains, where he had a special heaven, reserved for

---

[1] Compare Hopkins, "Religions of India," p. 94.
[2] Herbert J. Spinden, "Maya Art," p. 62.

warriors who fell in battle and women who died in childbirth. As a water-god also he presided over the souls of the drowned and those who in life suffered from dropsical affections. Indra also specialized in the same branch of medicine.

In fact, if one compares the account of Tlaloc's attributes and achievements, such as is given in Mr. Joyce's "Mexican Archæology" or Professor Seler's monograph on the "Codex Vaticanus," with Professor Hopkins's summary of Indra's character ("Religions of India") the identity is so exact, even in the most arbitrary traits and confusions with other deities' peculiarities, that it becomes impossible for any serious investigator to refuse to admit that Tlaloc and Chac are merely American forms of Indra. Even so fantastic a practice as the representation of the American rain-god's face as composed of contorted snakes [1] finds its analogy in Siam, where in relatively recent times this curious device was still being used by artists.[2]

"As the god of fertility maize belonged to him [Tlaloc], though not altogether by right, for according to one legend he stole it after it had been discovered by other gods concealed in the heart of a mountain."[3] Indra also obtained soma from the mountain by similar means.[4]

In the ancient civilization of America one of the most prominent deities was called the "Feathered Serpent," in the Maya language, Kukulkan, Quiché Gukumatz, Aztec Quetzalcoatl, the Pueblo "Mother of Waters". Throughout a very extensive part of America the snake, like the Indian Nâga, is the emblem of rain, clouds, thunder and lightning. But it is essentially and pre-eminently the symbol of rain ; and the god who controls the rain, Chac of the Mayas, Tlaloc of the Aztecs, carried the axe and the thunderbolt like his homologues and prototypes in the Old World. In America also we find reproduced in full, not only the legends of the antagonism between the

---

[1] Seler, "Codex Vaticanus," Figs. 299-304.
[2] See, for example, F. W. K. Müller, "Nang," *Int. Arch. f. Ethnolog.*, 1894, Suppl. zu Bd. vii., Taf. vii., where the mask of *Ravana* (a late surrogate of Indra in the *Ramayana*) reveals a survival of the prototype of the Mexican designs.
[3] Joyce, *op. cit.*, p. 37.
[4] For the incident of the stealing of the soma by Garuda, who in this legend is the representative of Indra, see Hopkins, "Religions of India," pp. 360-61.

FIG. 13.—A PAGE (THE 36TH) OF THE DRESDEN MAYA CODEX.

Fig. 13.

A photographic reproduction of the 36th page of the Dresden Maya Codex.

Of the three pictures in the top row one represents the elephant-headed god *Chac* with a snake's body He is pouring out rain. The central picture represents the lightning animal carrying fire down from heaven to earth. On the right *Chac* is shown in human guise carrying thunderweapons in the form of burning torches.

In the second row a goddess sits in the rain: her head is prolonged into that of a bird, holding a fish in its beak. The central picture shows *Chac* in his boat ferrying a woman across the water from the East. The third illustration depicts the familiar conflict between the vulture and serpent.

In the third row *Chac* is seen with his axe: in the central picture he is standing in the water looking up towards a rain-cloud; and on the right he is shown sitting in a hut resting from his labours.

DRAGONS AND RAIN GODS

thunder-bird and the serpent, but also the identification of these two rivals in one composite monster, which, as I have already mentioned, is seen in the winged disks, both in the Old World and the New.[1] Hardly any incident in the history of the Egyptian falcon or the thunder-birds of Babylonia, Greece or India, fails to reappear in America and find pictorial expression in the Maya and Aztec codices.

What makes America such a rich storehouse of historical data is the fact that it is stretched across the world almost from pole to pole; and for many centuries the jetsam and flotsam swept on to this vast strand has made it a museum of the cultural history of the Old World, much of which would have been lost for ever if America had not saved it. But a record preserved in this manner is necessarily in a highly confused state. For essentially the same materials reached America in manifold forms. The original immigrants into America brought from North-Eastern Asia such cultural equipment as had reached the area east of the Yenesei at the time when Europe was in the Neolithic phase of culture. Then when ancient mariners began to coast along the Eastern Asiatic littoral and make their way to America by the Aleutian route there was a further infiltration of new ideas. But when more venturesome sailors began to navigate the open seas and exploit Polynesia, for centuries[2] there was a more or less constant influx of customs and beliefs, which were drawn from Egypt and Babylonia, from the Mediterranean and East Africa, from India and Indonesia, China and Japan, Cambodia and Oceania. One and the same fundamental idea, such as the attributes of the serpent as a water-god, reached America in an infinite variety of guises, Egyptian, Babylonian, Indian, Indonesian, Chinese and Japanese, and from this amazing jumble of confusion the local priesthood of Central America built up a system of beliefs which is distinctively American, though most of the ingredients and the principles of synthetic composition were borrowed from the Old World.

Every possible phase of the early history of the dragon-story and all the ingredients which in the Old World went to the making

[1] "The Influence of Ancient Egyptian Civilization in the East and in America," Bulletin of the John Rylands Library, 1916, Fig. 4, "The Serpent-Bird".
[2] Probably from about 300 B.C. to 700 A.D.

of it have been preserved in American pictures and legends in a bewildering variety of forms and with an amazing luxuriance of complicated symbolism and picturesque ingenuity. In America, as in India and Eastern Asia, the power controlling water was identified both with a serpent (which in the New World, as in the Old, was often equipped with such inappropriate and arbitrary appendages, as wings, horns and crests) and a god, who was either associated or confused with an elephant. Now many of the attributes of these gods, as personifications of the life-giving powers of water, are identical with those of the Babylonian god Ea and the Egyptian Osiris, and their reputations as warriors with the respective sons and representatives, Marduk and Horus. The composite animal of Ea-Marduk, the "sea-goat" (the Capricornus of the Zodiac), was also the vehicle of Varuna in India, whose relationship to Indra was in some respects analogous to that of Ea to Marduk in Babylonia.[1] The Indian "sea-goat" or *Makara* was in fact intimately associated both with Varuna and with Indra. This monster assumed a great variety of forms, such as the crocodile, the dolphin, the sea-serpent or dragon, or combinations of the heads of different animals with a fish's body (Fig. 14). Amongst these we find an elephant-headed form of the *makara*, which was adopted as far east as Indonesia and as far west as Scotland.

I have already called attention[2] to the part played by the *makara* in determining the development of the form of the elephant-headed god in America. Another form of the *makara* is described in the following American legend, which is interesting also as a mutilated version of the original dragon-story of the Old World.

In 1912 Hernández translated and published a Maya manuscript[3] which had been written out in Spanish characters in the early days

---

[1] For information concerning Ea's "Goat-Fish," which can truly be called the "Father of Dragons," as well as the prototype of the Indian *makara*, the mermaid, the "sea-serpent," the "dolphin of Aphrodite," and of most composite sea-monsters, see W. H. Ward's "Seal Cylinders of Western Asia," pp. 382 *et seq.* and 399 *et seq.*; and especially the detailed reports in de Morgan's *Mémoires* (Délégation en Perse).

[2] *Nature, op. cit., supra.*

[3] Juan Martinez Hernández, "La Creación del Mundo segun los Mayas," Páginas Inéditas del MS. De Chumayel, *International Congress of Americanists, Proceedings of the XVIII. Session*, London, 1912, p. 164.

FIG. 14

Fig. 14.

A. The so-called " sea-goat " of Babylonia, a creature compounded of the antelope and fish of Ea.

B. The " sea-goat " as the vehicle of Ea or Marduk.

C to K—a series of varieties of the *makara* from the Buddhist Rails at Buddha Gaya and Mathura, circa 70 B.C.—70 A.D., after Cunningham ("Archæological Survey of India," Vol. III, 1873, Plates IX and XXIX).

L. The *makara* as the vehicle of Varuna, after Sir George Birdwood. It is not difficult to understand how, in the course of the easterly diffusion of culture, such a picture should develop into the Chinese Dragon or the American Elephant-headed God.

of the conquest of the Americas, but had been overlooked until six years ago. It is an account of the creation, and includes the following passages: "All at once came the water [? rain] after the dragon was carried away. The heaven was broken up; it fell upon the earth; and they say that *Cantul-ti-ku* (four gods), the four Baccab, were those who destroyed it. . . . 'The whole world,' said *Ah-uuc-chek-nale* (he who seven times makes fruitful), 'proceeded from the seven bosoms of the earth.' And he descended to make fruitful *Itzam-kab-ain* (the female whale with alligator-feet), when he came down from the central angle of the heavenly region" (p. 171).

Hernández adds that "the old fishermen of Yucatan still call the whale *Itzam*: this explains the name of *Itzaes*, by which the Mayas were known before the founding of Mayapan".

The close analogy to the Indra-story is suggested by the phrase describing the coming of the water "after the dragon was carried away". Moreover, the Indian sea-elephant *makara*, which was confused in the Old World with the dolphin of Aphrodite, and was sometimes also regarded as a crocodile, naturally suggests that the "female whale with the alligator-feet" was only an American version of the old Indian legend.

All this serves, not only to corroborate the inferences drawn from the other sources of information which I have already indicated, but also to suggest that, in addition to borrowing the chief divinities of their pantheon from India, the Maya people's original name was derived from the same mythology.[1]

It is of considerable interest and importance to note that in the earliest dated example of Maya workmanship (from Tuxtla, in the Vera Cruz State of Mexico), for which Spinden assigns a tentative date of 235 B.C., an unmistakable elephant figures among the four hieroglyphs which Spinden reproduces (*op. cit.*, p. 171). A similar hieroglyphic sign is found in the Chinese records of the Early Chow Dynasty (John Ross, "The Origin of the Chinese People," 1916, p. 152).

The use of the numerals four and seven in the narrative translated

---

[1] From the folk-lore of America I have collected many interesting variants of the Indra story and other legends (and artistic designs) of the elephant. I hope to publish these in the near future.

by Hernández, as in so many other American documents, is itself, as Mrs. Zelia Nuttall has so conclusively demonstrated,[1] a most striking and conclusive demonstration of the link with the Old World.

Indra was not the only Indian god who was transferred to America, for all the associated deities, with the characteristic stories of their exploits,[2] are also found depicted with childlike directness of incident, but amazingly luxuriant artistic phantasy, in the Maya and Aztec codices.

We find scattered throughout the islands of the Pacific the familiar stories of the dragon. One mentioned by the Bishop of Wellington refers to a New Zealand dragon with jaws like a crocodile's, which spouted water like a whale. It lived in a fresh-water lake.[3] In the same number of the same *Journal* Sir George Grey gives extracts from a Maori legend of the dragon, which he compares with corresponding passages from Spenser's "Faery Queen". "Their strict verbal and poetical conformity with the New Zealand legends are such as at first to lead to the impression either that Spenser must have stolen his images and language from the New Zealand poets, or that they must have acted unfairly by the English bard" (p. 362). The Maori legend describes the dragon as "in size large as a monstrous whale, in shape like a hideous lizard ; for in its huge head, its limbs, its tail, its scales, its tough skin, its sharp spines, yes, in all these it resembled a lizard" (p. 364).

Now the attributes of the Chinese and Japanese dragon as the controller of rain, thunder and lightning are identical with those of the American elephant-headed god. It also is associated with the East and with the tops of mountains. It is identified with the Indian Nâga, but the conflict involved in this identification is less obtrusive than it is either in America or in India. In Dravidian India the rulers and the gods are identified with the serpent : but among the Aryans, who were hostile to the Dravidians, the rain-god is the enemy of the Nâga. In America the confusion becomes more pronounced because Tlaloc (Chac) represents both Indra and his enemy the serpent. The representation in the codices of his conflict with the serpent is merely a tra-

---

[1] *Peabody Museum Papers*, 1901.
[2] See, for example, Wilfrid Jackson's " Shells as Evidence of the Migration of Early Culture," pp. 50-66.
[3] " Notes on the Maoris, etc.," *Journal of the Ethnological Society*, vol. i., 1869, p. 368.

dition which the Maya and Aztec scribes followed, apparently without understanding its meaning.

In China and Japan the Indra-episode plays a much less prominent part, for the dragon is, like the Indian Nâga, a beneficent creature, which approximates more nearly to the Babylonian Ea or the Egyptian Osiris. It is not only the controller of water, but the impersonation of water and its life-giving powers : it is identified with the emperor, with his standard, with the sky, and with all the powers that give, maintain, and prolong life and guard against all kinds of danger to life. In other words, it is the bringer of good luck, the rejuvenator of mankind, the giver of immortality.

But if the physiological functions of the dragon of the Far East can thus be assimilated to those of the Indian Nâga and the Babylonian and Egyptian Water God, who is also the king, anatomically he is usually represented in a form which can only be regarded as the Babylonian composite monster, as a rule stripped of his wings, though not of his avian feet.

In America we find preserved in the legends of the Indians an accurate and unmistakable description of the Japanese dragon (which is mainly Chinese in origin). Even Spinden, who "does not care to dignify by refutation the numerous empty theories of ethnic connections between Central America" [and in fact America as a whole] "and the Old World," makes the following statement (in the course of a discussion of the myths relating to horned snakes in California) : "a similar monster, possessing antlers, and sometimes wings, is also very common in Algonkin and Iroquois legends, although rare in art. As a rule the horned serpent is a water spirit and an enemy of the thunder bird. Among the Pueblo Indians the horned snake seems to have considerable prestige in religious belief. . . . It lives in the water or in the sky and is connected with rain or lightning."[1]

Thus we find stories of a dragon equipped with those distinctive tokens of Chinese origin, the deer's antlers ; and along with it a snake with less specialized horns suggesting the Cerastes of Egypt and Babylonia. A horned viper distantly akin to the Cerastes of the Old World does occur in California ; but its "horns" are so insignificant as to make it highly improbable that they could have been in any way responsible for the obtrusive role played by horns in these widespread

[1] *Op. cit.*, p. 231.

American stories. But the proof of the foreign origin of these stories is established by the horned serpent's achievements.

It "lives in the water or the sky" like its homologue in the Old World, and it is "a water spirit". Now neither the Cobra nor the Cerastes is actually a water serpent. Their achievements in the myths therefore have no possible relationship with the natural habits of the real snakes. They are purely arbitrary attributes which they have acquired as the result of a peculiar and fortuitous series of historical incidents.

It is therefore utterly inconceivable and in the highest degree improbable that this long chain of chance circumstances should have happened a second time in America, and have been responsible for the creation of the same bizarre story in reference to one of the rarer American snakes of a localized distribution, whose horns are mere vestiges, which no one but a trained morphologist is likely to have noticed or recognized as such.

But the American horned serpent, like its Babylonian and Indian homologues, is also the enemy of the thunder bird. Here is a further corroboration of the transmission to America of ideas which were the chance result of certain historical events in the Old World, which I have mentioned in this lecture.

In the figure on page 94 I reproduce a remarkable drawing of an American dragon. If the Algonkin Indians had not preserved legends of a winged serpent equipped with deer's antlers, no value could be assigned to this sketch: but as we know that this particular tribe retains the legend of just such a wonder-beast, we are justified in treating this drawing as something more than a jest.

"Petroglyphs are reported by Mr. John Criley as occurring near Ava, Jackson County, Illinois. The outlines of the characters observed by him were drawn from memory and submitted to Mr. Charles S. Mason, of Toledo, Ohio, through whom they were furnished to the Bureau of Ethnology. Little reliance can be placed upon the accuracy of such drawing, but from the general appearance of the sketches the originals of which they are copies were probably made by one of the middle Algonquin tribes of Indians.[1]

[1] I quote this and the following paragraphs verbatim from Garrick Mallery, "Picture Writing of the American Indians," 10*th Annual Report*, 1888-89, *Bureau of Ethnology* (*Smithsonian Institute*), p. 78.

DRAGONS AND RAIN GODS

"The 'Piasa' rock, as it is generally designated, was referred to by the missionary explorer Marquette in 1675. Its situation was immediately above the city of Alton, Illinois."

Marquette's remarks are translated by Dr. Francis Parkman as follows:—

"On the flat face of a high rock were painted, in red, black, and green, a pair of monsters, each 'as large as a calf, with horns like a deer, red eyes, a beard like a tiger, and a frightful expression of countenance. The face is something like that of a man, the body covered with scales; and the tail so long that it passes entirely round the body, over the head, and between the legs, ending like that of a fish.'"

Another version, by Davidson and Struve, of the discovery of the petroglyph is as follows:—

"Again they (Joliet and Marquette) were floating on the broad bosom of the unknown stream. Passing the mouth of the Illinois, they soon fell into the shadow of a tall promontory, and with great astonishment beheld the representation of two monsters painted on its lofty limestone front. According to Marquette, each of these frightful figures had the face of a man, the horns of a deer, the beard of a tiger, and the tail of a fish so long that it passed around the body, over the head, and between the legs. It was an object of Indian worship and greatly impressed the mind of the pious missionary with the necessity of substituting for this monstrous idolatry the worship of the true God."

A footnote connected with the foregoing quotation gives the following description of the same rock:—

"Near the mouth of the Piasa creek, on the bluff, there is a smooth rock in a cavernous cleft, under an overhanging cliff, on whose face 50 feet from the base, are painted some ancient pictures or hieroglyphics, of great interest to the curious. They are placed in a horizontal line from east to west, representing men, plants and animals. The paintings, though protected from dampness and storms, are in great part destroyed, marred by portions of the rock becoming detached and falling down."

Mr. McAdams, of Alton, Illinois, says, "The name Piasa is Indian and signifies, in the Illini, the bird which devours men". He furnishes a spirited pen-and-ink sketch, 12 by 15 inches in size and purporting to represent the ancient painting described by Marquette.

On the picture is inscribed the following in ink: "Made by Wm. Dennis, April 3rd, 1825". The date is in both letters and figures. On the top of the picture in large letters are the two words, "FLYING DRAGON". This picture, which has been kept in the old Gilham family of Madison county and bears the evidence of its age, is reproduced as Fig. 3.

He also publishes another representation with the following remarks :—

"One of the most satisfactory pictures of the Piasa we have ever seen is in an old German publication entitled 'The Valley of the Mississippi Illustrated. Eighty illustrations from Nature, by H. Lewis, from the Falls of St. Anthony to the Gulf of Mexico,' published about the year 1839 by Arenz & Co., Dusseldorf, Germany. One of the

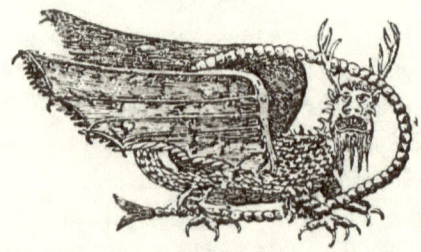

FIG. 3.—WM. DENNIS'S DRAWING OF THE "FLYING DRAGON" DEPICTED ON THE ROCKS AT PIASA, ILLINOIS.

large full-page plates in this work gives a fine view of the bluff at Alton, with the figure of the Piasa on the face of the rock. It is represented to have been taken on the spot by artists from Germany. . . . In the German picture there is shown just behind the rather dim outlines of the second face a ragged crevice, as though of a fracture. Part of the bluff's face might have fallen and thus nearly destroyed one of the monsters, for in later years writers speak of but one figure. The whole face of the bluff was quarried away in 1846-47."

The close agreement of this account with that of the Chinese and Japanese dragon at once arrests attention. The anatomical peculiarities are so extraordinary that if Père Marquette's account is trustworthy there is no longer any room for doubt of the Chinese or Japanese derivation of this composite creature. If the account is not accepted we will be driven, not only to attribute to the pious seventeenth-century missionary serious dishonesty or culpable gullibility, but also to credit him with

DRAGONS AND RAIN GODS

a remarkably precise knowledge of Mongolian archæology. When Algonkin legends are recalled, however, I think we are bound to accept the missionary's account as substantially accurate.

Minns claims that representations of the dragon are unknown in China before the Han dynasty. But the legend of the dragon is much more ancient. The evidence has been given in full by de Visser.[1]

He tells us that the earliest reference is found in the *Yih King*, and shows that the dragon was "a water animal akin to the snake, which [used] to sleep in pools during winter and arises in the spring". "It is the god of thunder, who brings good crops when he appears in the rice fields (as rain) or in the sky (as dark and yellow clouds), in other words when he makes the rain fertilize the ground" (p. 38).

In the *Shu King* there is a reference to the dragon as one of the symbolic figures painted on the upper garment of the emperor Hwang Ti (who according to the Chinese legends, which of course are not above reproach, reigned in the twenty-seventh century B.C.). In this ancient literature there are numerous references to the dragon, and not merely to the legends, *but also to representations* of the benign monster on garments, banners and metal tablets.[2] "The ancient texts ... are short, but sufficient to give us the main conceptions of Old China with regard to the dragon. In those early days [just as at present] he was the god of water, thunder, clouds, and rain, the harbinger of blessings, and the symbol of holy men. As the emperors are the holy beings on earth, the idea of the dragon being the symbol of Imperial power is based upon this ancient conception" (*op. cit.*, p. 42).

In the fifth appendix to the *Yih King*, which has been ascribed to Confucius (i.e. three centuries earlier than the Han dynasty mentioned by Mr. Minns), it is stated that "*K'ien* (Heaven) is a horse, *Kw'un* (Earth) is a cow, *Chen* (*Thunder*) *is a dragon*" (*op. cit.*, p. 37).[3]

The philosopher Hwai Nan Tsze (who died 122 B.C.) declared that the dragon is the origin of all creatures, winged, hairy, scaly, and

---

[1] *Op. cit.*, pp. 35 *et seq.*
[2] See de Visser, p. 41.
[3] There can be no doubt that the Chinese dragon is the descendant of the early Babylonian monster, and that the inspiration to create it probably reached Shensi during the third millennium B.C. by the route indicated in my "Incense and Libations" (*Bull. John Rylands Library*, vol. iv., No. 2, p. 239). Some centuries later the Indian dragon reached the Far East via Indonesia and mingled with his Babylonian cousin in Japan and China.

mailed; and he propounded a scheme of evolution (de Visser, p. 65). He seems to have tried to explain away the fact that he had never actually witnessed the dragon performing some of the remarkable feats attributed to it: "Mankind cannot see the dragons rise: wind and rain assist them to ascend to a great height" (*op. cit.*, p. 65). Confucius also is credited with the frankness of a similar confession: "As to the dragon, we cannot understand his riding on the wind and clouds and his ascending to the sky. To-day I saw Lao Tsze; is he not like the dragon?" (p. 65).

This does not necessarily mean that these learned men were sceptical of the beliefs which tradition had forged in their minds, but that the dragon had the power of hiding itself in a cloak of invisibility, just as clouds (in which the Chinese saw dragons) could be dissipated in the sky. The belief in these powers of the dragon was as sincere as that of learned men of other countries in the beneficent attributes which tradition had taught them to assign to their particular deities. In the passages I have quoted the Chinese scholars were presumably attempting to bridge the gap between the ideas inculcated by faith and the evidence of their senses, in much the same sort of spirit as, for instance, actuated Dean Buckland last century, when he claimed that the glacial deposits of this country afforded evidence in confirmation of the Deluge described in the Book of Genesis.

The tiger and the dragon, the gods of wind and water, are the keystones of the doctrine called *fung shui*, which Professor de Groot has described in detail.[1]

He describes it "as a quasi-scientific system, supposed to teach men where and how to build graves, temples, and dwellings, in order that the dead, the gods, and the living may be located therein exclusively, or as far as possible, under the auspicious influences of Nature". The dragon plays a most important part in this system, being "the chief spirit of water and rain, and at the same time representing one of the four quarters of heaven (i.e. the East, called the Azure Dragon, and the first of the seasons, spring)." The word Dragon comprises the high grounds in general, and the water streams which have their sources therein or wind their way through them.[2]

[1] "Religious System of China," vol. iii., chap. xii., pp. 936-1056.
[2] This paragraph is taken almost verbatim from de Visser, *op. cit.*, pp. 59 and 60.

The attributes thus assigned to the Blue Dragon, his control of water and streams, his dwelling on high mountains whence they spring, and his association with the East, will be seen to reveal his identity with the so-called "god B" of American archæologists, the elephant-headed god *Tlaloc* of the Aztecs, *Chac* of the Mayas, whose more direct parent was Indra.

It is of interest to note that, according to Gerini,[1] the word *Nâga* denotes not only a snake but also an elephant. Both the Chinese dragon and the Mexican elephant-god are thus linked with the Nâga, who is identified both with Indra himself and Indra's enemy Vritra. This is another instance of those remarkable contradictions that one meets at every step in pursuing the dragon. In the confusion resulting from the blending of hostile tribes and diverse cultures the Aryan deity who, both for religious and political reasons, is the enemy of the Nâgas becomes himself identified with a Nâga!

I have already called attention (*Nature*, Jan. 27, 1916) to the fact that the graphic form of representation of the American elephant-headed god was derived from Indonesian pictures of the *makara*. In India itself the *makara* (see Fig. 14) is represented in a great variety of forms, most of which are prototypes of different kinds of dragons. Hence the homology of the elephant-headed god with the other dragons is further established and shown to be genetically related to the evolution of the protean manifestations of the dragon's form.

The dragon in China is "the heavenly giver of fertilizing rain" (*op. cit.*, p. 36). In the *Shu King* "the emblematic figures of the ancients are given as the sun, the moon, the stars, the mountain, the *dragon*, and the variegated animals (pheasants) which are depicted on the upper sacrificial garment of the Emperor" (p. 39). In the *Li Ki* the unicorn, the phœnix, the tortoise, and the dragon are called the four *ling* (p. 39), which de Visser translates "spiritual beings," creatures with enormously strong vital spirit. The dragon possesses the most *ling* of all creatures (p. 64). The tiger is the deadly enemy of the dragon (p. 42).

The dragon sheds a brilliant light at night (p. 44), usually from his glittering eyes. He is the giver of omens (p. 45), good and bad,

---

[1] G. E. Gerini, "Researches on Ptolemy's Geography of Eastern Asia," *Asiatic Society's Monographs*, No. 1, 1909, p. 146.

rains and floods. The dragon-horse is a vital spirit of Heaven and Earth (p. 58) and also of river water: it has the tail of a huge serpent.

The ecclesiastical vestments of the Wu-ist priests are endowed with magical properties which are considered to enable the wearer to control the order of the world, to avert unseasonable and calamitous events, such as drought, untimely and superabundant rainfall, and eclipses. These powers are conferred by the decoration upon the dress. Upon the back of the chief vestment the representation of a range of mountains is embroidered as a symbol of the world: on each side (the right and left) of it a large dragon arises above the billows to represent the fertilizing rain. They are surrounded by gold-thread figures representing clouds and spirals typifying rolling thunder.[1]

A ball, sometimes with a spiral decoration, is commonly represented in front of the Chinese dragon. The Chinese writer Koh Hung tells us that "a spiral denotes the rolling of thunder from which issues a flash of lightning".[2] De Visser discusses this question at some length and refers to Hirth's claim that the Chinese triquetrum, i.e., the well-known three-comma shaped figure, the Japanese *mitsu-tomoe*, the ancient spiral, represents thunder also.[3] Before discussing this question, which involves the consideration of the almost world-wide belief in a thunder-weapon and its relationship to the spiral ornament, the octopus,

---

[1] De Visser, p. 102, and de Groot, vi., p. 1265, Plate XVIII. The reference to "a range of mountains ... as a symbol of the world" recalls the Egyptian representation of the eastern horizon as two hills between which Hathor or her son arises (see Budge, "Gods of the Egyptians," vol. ii., p. 101; and compare Griffith's "Hieroglyphs," p. 30): the same conception was adopted in Mesopotamia (see Ward, "Seal Cylinders of Western Asia," fig. 412, p. 156) and in the Mediterranean (see Evans, "Mycenæan Tree and Pillar Cult," pp. 37 *et seq.*). It is a remarkable fact that Sir Arthur Evans, who, upon p. 64 of his memoir, reproduces two drawings of the Egyptian "horizon" supporting the sun's disk, should have failed to recognize in it the prototype of what he calls "the horns of consecration". Even if the confusion of the "horizon" with a cow's horns was very ancient (for the horns of the Divine Cow supporting the moon made this inevitable), this rationalization should not blind us as to the real origin of the idea, which is preserved in the ancient Egyptian, Babylonian, Cretan and Chinese pictures (see Fig. 26, facing p. 188).

[2] De Visser, p. 103.

[3] P. 104, The Chinese triquetrum has a circle in the centre and five or eight commas.

FIG. 15.—PHOTOGRAPH OF A CHINESE EMBROIDERY IN THE MANCHESTER SCHOOL OF ART REPRESENTING THE DRAGON AND THE PEARL-MOON SYMBOL.

the pearl, the swastika and triskele, let us examine further the problem of the dragon's ball (see Fig. 15).

De Groot regards the dragon as a thunder-god and therefore, like Hirth, assumes that the supposed thunder-ball is being *belched forth* and not being *swallowed* by the dragon. But de Visser, as the result of a conversation with Mr. Kramp and the study of a Chinese picture in Blacker's " Chats on Oriental China " (1908, p. 54), puts forward the suggestion that the ball is the moon or the pearl-moon which the dragon is swallowing, thereby causing the fertilizing rain. The Chinese themselves refer to the ball as the " precious pearl," which, under the influence of Buddhism in China, was identified with " the pearl that grants all desires" and is under the special protection of the Nâga, i.e., the dragon. Arising out of this de Visser puts the conundrum : " Was the ball originally also a pearl, not of Buddhism but of Taoism ? "

In reply to this question I may call attention to the fact that the germs of civilization were first planted in China by people strongly imbued with the belief that the pearl was the quintessence of life-giving and prosperity-conferring powers :[1] it was not only identified with the moon, but also was itself a particle of moon-substance which fell as dew into the gaping oyster. It was the very people who held such views about pearls and gold who, when searching for alluvial gold and freshwater pearls in Turkestan, were responsible for transferring these same life-giving properties to jade ; and the magical value thus attached to jade was the nucleus, so to speak, around which the earliest civilization of China was crystallized.

As we shall see, in the discussion of the thunder-weapon (p. 121), the luminous pearl, which was believed to have fallen from the sky, was homologized with the thunderbolt, with the functions of which its own magical properties were assimilated.

Kramp called de Visser's attention to the fact that the Chinese hieroglyphic character for the dragon's ball is compounded of the signs for *jewel* and *moon*, which is also given in a Japanese lexicon as *divine pearl*, the pearl of the bright moon.

" When the clouds approached and covered the moon, the ancient

---

[1] See on this my paper " The Origin of Early Siberian Civilization," now being published in the *Memoirs and Proceedings of the Manchester Literary and Philosophical Society*.

Chinese may have thought that the dragons had seized and swallowed this pearl, more brilliant than all the pearls of the sea" (de Visser, p. 108).

The difficulty de Visser finds in regarding his own theory as wholly satisfactory is, first, the red colour of the ball, and secondly, the spiral pattern upon it. He explains the colour as possibly an attempt to represent the pearl's lustre. But de Visser seems to have overlooked the fact that red and rose-coloured pearls obtained from the conch-shell were used in China and Japan.[1]

"The spiral is much used in delineating the sacred pearls of Buddhism, so that it might have served also to design those of Taoism; although I must acknowledge that the spiral of the Buddhist pearl goes upward, while the spiral of the dragon is flat" (p. 103).

De Visser sums up the whole argument in these words:—

"These are, however, all mere suppositions. The only facts we know are: the eager attitude of the dragons, ready to grasp and swallow the ball; the ideas of the Chinese themselves as to the ball being the moon or a pearl; the existence of a kind of sacred "moon-pearl"; the red colour of the ball, its emitting flames and its spiral-like form. As the three last facts are in favour of the thunder theory, I should be inclined to prefer the latter. Yet I am convinced that the dragons do not *belch out* the thunder. If their trying to *grasp* or *swallow* the thunder could be explained, I should immediately accept the theory concerning the thunder-spiral, especially on account of the flames it emits. But I do not see the reason why the god of thunder should persecute thunder itself. Therefore, after having given the above facts that the reader may take them into consideration, I feel obliged to say: 'non liquet'" (p. 108).

It does not seem to have occurred to the distinguished Dutch scholar, who has so lucidly put the issue before us, that his demonstration of the fact of the ball being the pearl-moon about to be swallowed by the dragon does not preclude it being also confused with the thunder. Elsewhere in this volume I have referred to the origin of the spiral symbolism and have shown that it became associated with the pearl *before* it became the symbol of thunder. The pearl-association in fact was

---

[1] Wilfrid Jackson, "Shells as Evidence of the Migrations of Early Culture," p. 106.

one of the links in the chain of events which made the pearl and the spirally-coiled arm of the octopus the sign of thunder.[1]

It seems quite clear to me that de Visser's pearl-moon theory is the true interpretation. But when the pearl-ball was provided with the spiral, painted red, and given flames to represent its power of emitting light and shining by night, the fact of the spiral ornamentation and of the pearl being one of the surrogates of the thunder-weapon was rationalized into an identification of the ball with thunder and the light it was emitting as lightning. It is, of course, quite irrational for a thunder-god to swallow his own thunder: but popular interpretations of subtle symbolism, the true explanation of which is deeply buried in the history of the distant past, are rarely logical and almost invariably irrelevant.

In his account of the state of Brahmanism in India after the times of the two earlier Vedas, Professor Hopkins[2] throws light upon the real significance of the ball in the dragon-symbolism. " Old legends are varied. The victory over Vritra is now expounded thus: Indra, who slays Vritra, is the sun. Vritra is the moon, who swims into the sun's mouth on the night of the new moon. The sun rises after swallowing him, and the moon is invisible because he is swallowed. The sun vomits out the moon, and the latter is then seen in the west, and increases again, to serve the sun as food. In another passage it is said that when the moon is invisible he is hiding in plants and waters."

This seems to clear away any doubt as to the significance of the ball. It is the pearl-moon, which is both swallowed and vomited by the dragon.

The snake takes a more obtrusive part in the Japanese than in the Chinese dragon and it frequently manifests itself as a god of the sea. The old Japanese sea-gods were often female water-snakes. The cultural influences which reached Japan from the south by way of Indonesia—many centuries before the coming of Buddhism—naturally emphasized the serpent form of the dragon and its connexion with the ocean.

But the river-gods, or " water-fathers," were real four-footed dragons identified with the dragon-kings of Chinese myth, but at the

---

[1] I shall discuss this more fully in " The Birth of Aphrodite ".
[2] " Religions of India," p. 197.

same time were strictly homologous with the Nâga Rajas or cobra-kings of India.

The Japanese "Sea Lord" or "Sea Snake" was also called "Abundant-Pearl-Prince," who had a magnificent palace at the bottom of the sea. His daughter ("Abundant-Pearl-Princess") married a youth whom she observed, reflected in the well, sitting on a cassia tree near the castle gate. Ashamed at his presence at her lying-in she was changed into a *wani* or crocodile (de Visser, p. 139), elsewhere described as a dragon (*makara*). De Visser gives it as his opinion that the *wani* is "an old Japanese dragon, or serpent-shaped sea-god, and the legend is an ancient Japanese tale, dressed in an Indian garb by later generations" (p. 140). He is arguing that the Japanese dragon existed long before Japan came under Indian influence. But he ignores the fact that at a very early date both India and China were diversely influenced by Babylonia, the great breeding place of dragons; and, secondly, that Japan was influenced by Indonesia, and through it by the West, for many centuries before the arrival of such later Indian legends as those relating to the palace under the sea, the castle gate and the cassia tree. As Aston (quoted by de Visser) remarks, all these incidents and also the well that serves as a mirror, "form a combination not unknown to European folklore".

After de Visser had given his own views, he modified them (on p. 141) when he learned that essentially the same dragon-stories had been recorded in the Kei Islands and Minahassa (Celebes). In the light of this new information he frankly admits that "the resemblance of several features of this myth with the Japanese one is so striking, that we may be sure that the latter is of Indonesian origin." He goes further when he recognizes that "probably the foreign invaders, who in prehistoric times conquered Japan, came from Indonesia, and brought the myth with them" (p. 141). The evidence recently brought together by W. J. Perry in his book "The Megalithic Culture of Indonesia" makes it certain that the people of Indonesia in turn got it from the West.

An old painting reproduced by F. W. K. Müller,[1] who called de Visser's attention to these interesting stories, shows Hohodemi (the

---

[1] "Mythe der Kei-Insulaner und Verwandtes," *Zeitsch. f. Ethnologie*, vol. xxv., 1893, pp. 533 *et seq.*

DRAGONS AND RAIN GODS

youth on the cassia tree who married the princess) returning home mounted on the back of a crocodile, like the Indian Varuna upon the *makara* in a drawing reproduced by the late Sir George Birdwood.[1]

The *wani* or crocodile thus introduced from India, via Indonesia, is really the Chinese and Japanese dragon, as Aston has claimed. Aston refers to Japanese pictures in which the Abundant-Pearl-Prince and his daughter are represented with dragon's heads appearing over their human ones, but in the old Indonesian version they maintain their forms as *wani* or crocodiles.

The dragon's head appearing over a human one is quite an Indian motive, transferred to China and from there to Korea and Japan (de Visser, p. 142), and, I may add, also to America.

[Since the foregoing paragraphs have been printed, the Curator of the Liverpool Museum has kindly called my attention to a remarkable series of Maya remains in the collection under his care, which were obtained in the course of excavations made by Mr. T. W. F. Gann, M.R.C.S., an officer in the Medical Service of British Honduras (see his account of the excavations in Part II. of the 19th Annual Report of the Bureau of Ethnology, Smithsonian Institution of Washington). Among them is a pottery figure of a *wani* or *makara* in the form of an alligator, equipped with diminutive deer's horns (like the dragon of Eastern Asia); and its skin is studded with circular elevations, presumably meant to represent the spots upon the star-spangled "Celestial Stag" of the Aryans (p. 130). As in the Japanese pictures mentioned by Aston, a human head is seen emerging from the creature's throat. It affords a most definite and convincing demonstration of the sources of American culture.]

The jewels of flood and ebb in the Japanese legends consist of the pearls of flood and ebb obtained from the dragon's palace at the bottom of the sea. By their aid storms and floods could be created to destroy enemies or calm to secure safety for friends. Such stories are the logical result of the identification of pearls with the moon, the influence of which upon the tides was probably one of the circumstances which was responsible for bringing the moon into the circle of the great scientific theory of the life-giving powers of water. This in turn played a great, if not decisive, part in originating the earliest belief in a sky world, or heaven.

[1] See Fig. 14.

The Evolution of the Dragon.

The American and Indonesian dragons can be referred back primarily to India, the Chinese and Japanese varieties to India and Babylonia. The dragons of Europe can be traced through Greek channels to the same ultimate source. But the cruder dragons of Africa are derived either from Egypt, from the Ægean, or from India. All dragons that strictly conform to the conventional idea of what such a wonder-beast should be can be shown to be sprung from the fertile imagination of ancient Sumer, the "great breeding place of monsters" (Minns).

But the history of the dragon's evolution and transmission to other countries is full of complexities; and the dragon-myth is made up of many episodes, some of which were not derived from Babylonia.

In Egypt we do not find the characteristic dragon and dragon-story. Yet all of the ingredients out of which both the monster and the legends are compounded have been preserved in Egypt, and in perhaps a more primitive and less altered form than elsewhere. Hence, if Egypt does not provide dragons for us to dissect, it does supply us with the evidence without which the dragon's evolution would be quite unintelligible.

Egyptian literature affords a clearer insight into the development of the Great Mother, the Water God, and the Warrior Sun God than we can obtain from any other writings of the origin of this fundamental stratum of deities. And in the three legends: The Destruction of Mankind, The Story of the Winged Disk, and The Conflict between Horus and Set, it has preserved the germs of the great Dragon Saga. Babylonian literature has shown us how this raw material was worked up into the definite and familiar story, as well as how the features of a variety of animals were blended to form the composite monster. India and Greece, as well as more distant parts of Africa, Europe, and Asia, and even America have preserved many details that have been lost in the real home of the monster.

In the earliest literature that has come down to us from antiquity a clear account is given of the original attributes of Osiris. "Horus comes, he recognizes his father in thee [Osiris], youthful in thy name of 'Fresh Water'." "Thou art indeed the Nile, great on the fields at the beginning of the seasons; gods and men live by the moisture that is in thee." He is also identified with the inundation of the river. "It is Unis [the dead king identified with Osiris] who inundates the land." He also brings the wind and guides it. It is the breath of life which raises the king from the dead as an Osiris. The wine-press god comes to Osiris bearing wine-juice and the great god becomes "Lord of the overflowing wine": he is also identified with barley and with the beer made from it. Certain trees also are personifications of the god.

But Osiris was regarded not only as the waters upon earth, the rivers and streams, the moisture in the soil and in the bodies of animals and plants, but also as "the waters of life that are in the sky".

"As Osiris was identified with the waters of earth and sky, he may even become the sea and the ocean itself. We find him addressed thus: 'Thou art great, thou art green, in thy name of Great Green (Sea); lo, thou art round as the Great Circle (Okeanos); lo, thou art turned about, thou art round as the circle that encircles the Haunebu (Ægeans).''

This series of interesting extracts from Professor Breasted's "Religion and Thought in Ancient Egypt" (pp. 18-26) gives the earliest Egyptians' own ideas of the attributes of Osiris. The Babylonians regarded Ea in almost precisely the same light and endowed him with identical powers. But there is an important and significant difference between Osiris and Ea. The former was usually represented as a man, that is, as a dead king, whereas Ea was represented as a man wearing a fish-skin, as a fish, or as the composite monster with a fish's body and tail, which was the prototype of the Indian *makara* and "the father of dragons".

In attempting to understand the creation of the dragon it is important to remember that, although Osiris and Ea were regarded primarily as personifications of the beneficent life-giving powers of water, as the bringers of fertility to the soil and the givers of life and immortality to living creatures, they were also identified with the destructive forces of water, by which men were drowned or their welfare affected in various ways by storms of sea and wind.

Thus Osiris or the fish-god Ea could destroy mankind. In other words the fish-dragon, or the composite monster formed of a fish and an antelope, could represent the destructive forces of wind and water. Thus even the malignant dragon can be the homologue of the usually beneficent gods Osiris and Ea, and their Aryan surrogates Mazdah and Varuna.

By a somewhat analogous process of archaic rationalization the sons respectively of Osiris and Ea, the sun-gods Horus and Marduk, acquired a similarly confused reputation. Although their outstanding achievements were the overcoming of the powers of evil, and, as the givers of light, conquering darkness, their character as warriors made them also powers of destruction. The falcon of Horus thus became also a symbol of chaos, and as the thunder-bird became the most obtrusive feature in the weird anatomy of the composite Mesopotamian dragon and his more modern bird-footed brood, which ranges from Western Europe to the Far East of Asia and America.

That the sun-god derived his functions directly or indirectly from Osiris and Hathor is shown by his most primitive attributes, for in " the earliest sun-temples at Abusir, he appears as the source of life and increase". " Men said of him : 'Thou hast driven away the storm, and hast expelled the rain, and hast broken up the clouds'."[1] Horus was in fact the son of Osiris and Hathor, from whom he derived his attributes. The invention of the sun-god was not, as most scholars pretend, an attempt to give direct expression to the fact that the sun is the source of fertility. That is a discovery of modern science. The sun-god acquired his attributes secondarily (and for definite historical reasons) from his parents, who were responsible for his birth.

The quotation from the Pyramid Texts is of special interest as an illustration of one of the results of the assimilation of the idea of Osiris as the controller of water with that of a sky-heaven and a sun-god. The sun-god's powers are rationalized so as to bring them into conformity with the earliest conception of a god as a power controlling water.

Breasted attempts to interpret the statements concerning the storm and rain-clouds as references to the enemies of the sun, who steal the sky-god's eye, i.e., obscure the sun or moon. The incident of Horus's loss of an eye, which looms so large in Egyptian legends, is possibly more closely related to the earliest attempts at explaining eclipses of the sun and moon, the " eyes " of the sky. The obscuring of the sun and moon by clouds is a matter of little significance to the Egyptian : but the modern Egyptian *fellah*, and no doubt his predecessors also,

[1] Breasted, *op. cit.*, p. 11.

regard eclipses with much concern. Such events excite great alarm, for the peasants consider them as actual combats between the powers of good and evil.

In other countries where rain is a blessing and not, as in Egypt, merely an unwelcome inconvenience, the clouds play a much more prominent part in the popular beliefs. In the Rig-Veda the power that holds up the clouds is evil: as an elaboration of the ancient Egyptian conception of the sky as a Divine Cow, the Great Mother, the Aryan Indians regarded the clouds as a herd of cattle which the Vedic warrior-god Indra (who in this respect is the homologue of the Egyptian warrior Horus) stole from the powers of evil and bestowed upon mankind. In other words, like Horus, he broke up the clouds and brought rain.

The antithesis between the two aspects of the character of these ancient deities is most pronounced in the case of the other member of this most primitive Trinity, the Great Mother. She was the great beneficent giver of life, but also the controller of life, which implies that she was the death-dealer. But this evil aspect of her character developed only under the stress of a peculiar dilemma in which she was placed. On a famous occasion in the very remote past the great Giver of Life was summoned to rejuvenate the ageing king. The only elixir of life that was known to the pharmacopœia of the times was human blood: but to obtain this life-blood the Giver of Life was compelled to slaughter mankind. She thus became the destroyer of mankind in her lioness *avatar* as Sekhet.

The earliest known pictorial representation of the dragon (Fig. 1) consists of the forepart of the sun-god's falcon or eagle united with the hindpart of the mother-goddess's lioness. The student of modern heraldry would not regard this as a dragon at all, but merely a gryphon or griffin. A recent writer on heraldry has complained that, " in spite of frequent corrections, this creature is persistently confused in the popular mind with the *dragon*, which is even more purely imaginary ".[1] But the investigator of the early history of these wonder-beasts is compelled, even at the risk of incurring the herald's censure, to regard the gryphon as one of the earliest known tentative efforts at dragon-making. But though the fish, the falcon or eagle, and the composite eagle-lion

[1] G. W. Eve, " Decorative Heraldry," 1897, p. 35.

monster are early known pictorial representations of the dragon, good or bad, the serpent is probably more ancient still (Fig. 2).

The earliest form assumed by the power of evil was the serpent: but it is important to remember that, as each of the primary deities can be a power of either good or evil, any of the animals representing them can symbolize either aspect. Though Hathor in her cow manifestation is usually benevolent and as a lioness a power of destruction, the cow may become a demon in certain cases and the lioness a kindly creature. The falcon of Horus (or its representatives, eagle, hawk, woodpecker, dove, redbreast, etc.) may be either good or bad: so also the gazelle (antelope or deer), the crocodile, the fish, or any of the menagerie of creatures that enter into the composition of good or bad demons.

"The Nâgas are semi-divine serpents which very often assume human shapes and whose kings live with their retinues in the utmost luxury in their magnificent abodes at the bottom of the sea or in rivers or lakes. When leaving the Nâga world they are in constant danger of being grasped and killed by the gigantic semi-divine birds, the Garudas, which also change themselves into men" (de Visser, p. 7).

"The Nâgas are depicted in three forms: common snakes, guarding jewels; human beings with four snakes in their necks; and winged sea-dragons, the upper part of the body human, but with a horned, ox-like head, the lower part of the body that of a coiling-dragon. Here we find a link between the snake of ancient India and the four-legged Chinese dragon" (p. 6), hidden in the clouds, which the dragon himself emitted, like a modern battleship, for the purpose of rendering himself invisible. In other words, the rain clouds were the dragon's breath. The fertilizing rain was thus in fact the vital essence of the dragon, being both water and the breath of life.

"We find the Nâga king not only in the possession of numberless jewels and beautiful girls, but also of mighty charms, bestowing supernatural vision and hearing. The palaces of the Nâga kings are always described as extremely splendid, abounding with gold and silver and precious stones, and the Nâga women, when appearing in human shape, were beautiful beyond description" (p. 9).

De Visser records the story of an evil Nâga protecting a big tree that grew in a pond, who failed to emit clouds and thunder when the tree was cut down, because he was neither despised nor wounded: for his body became the support of the stūpa and the tree became a beam of the stūpa (p. 16). This aspect of the Nâga as a tree-demon is rare in India, but common in China and Japan. It seems to be identical with the Mediterranean conception of the pillar of wood or stone, which is both a representative of the Great Mother and the chief support of a temple.[1]

In the magnificent city that king Yaçahketu saw, when he dived into the sea, "wishing trees that granted every desire" were among the objects that met his vision. There were also palaces of precious stones and gardens and tanks, and, of course, beautiful maidens (de Visser, p. 20).

In the Far Eastern stories it is interesting to note the antagonism of the dragon to the tiger, when we recall that the lioness-form of Hathor was the prototype of the earliest malevolent dragon.

There are five sorts of dragons: serpent-dragons; lizard-dragons; fish-dragons; elephant-dragons; and toad-dragons (de Visser, p. 23).

"According to de Groot, the blue colour is chosen in China because this is the colour of the East, from where the rain must come; this quarter is represented by the Azure Dragon, the highest in rank among all the dragons. We have seen, however, that the original sūtra already prescribed to use the blue colour and to face the East. . . . Indra, the rain-god, is the patron of the East, and Indra-colour is *nila*, dark blue or rather blue-black, the regular epithet of the rain clouds. If the priest had not to face the East but the West, this would agree with the fact that the Nâgas were said to live in the western quarter and that in India the West corresponds with the blue colour. Facing the East, however, seems to point to an old rain ceremony in which Indra was invoked to raise the blue-black clouds" (de Visser, pp. 30 and 31).

The Dragon Myth.

The most important and fundamental legend in the whole history of mythology is the story of the "Destruction of Mankind". "It was discovered, translated, and commented upon by Naville ("La Destruction des hommes par les Dieux," in the *Transactions of the Society of Biblical Archæology*, vol. iv., pp. 1-19, reproducing Hay's copies made at the beginning of [the nineteenth] century; and

---

[1] Arthur J. Evans, "Mycenæan Tree and Pillar Cult," pp. 88 *et seq.*

"L'Inscription de la Destruction des hommes dans le tombeau de Ramsès III," in the *Transactions*, vol. viii., pp. 412-20); afterwards published anew by Herr von Bergmann (*Hieroglyphische Inscriften*, pls. lxxv.-lxxxii., and pp. 55, 56); completely translated by Brugsch (*Die neue Weltordnung nach Vernichtung des sündigen Menschengeschlechts nach einer Altägyptischen Ueberlieferung*, 1881); and partly translated by Lauth (*Aus Ægyptens Vorzeit*, pp. 70-81) and by Lefébure ("Une chapitre de la chronique solaire," in the *Zeitschrift für Ægyptische Sprache*, 1883, pp. 32, 33) ".[1]

Important commentaries upon this story have been published also by Brugsch and Gauthier.[2]

As the really important features of the story consist of the incoherent and contradictory details, and it would take up too much space to reproduce the whole legend here, I must refer the reader to Maspero's account of it (*op. cit.*), or to the versions given by Erman in his " Life in Ancient Egypt" (p. 267, from which I quote) or Budge in " The Gods of the Egyptians," vol. i., p. 388.

Although the story as we know it was not written down until the time of Seti I (*circa* 1300 B.C.), it is very old and had been circulating as a popular legend for more than twenty centuries before that time. The narrative itself tells its own story because it is composed of many contradictory interpretations of the same incidents flung together in a highly confused and incoherent form.

The other legends to which I shall have constantly to refer are " The Saga of the Winged Disk," " The Feud between Horus and Set," " The Stealing of Re's Name by Isis," and a series of later variants and confusions of these stories.[3]

---

[1] G. Maspero, "The Dawn of Civilization," p. 164.

[2] H. Brugsch, "Die Alraune als altägyptische Zauberpflanze," *Zeit. f. Ægypt. Sprache*, Bd. 29, 1891, pp. 31-3; and Henri Gauthier, "Le nom hiéroglyphique de l'argile rouge d'Éléphantine," *Revue Égyptologique*, t. xie, Nos. i.-ii., 1904, p. 1.

[3] These legends will be found in the works by Maspero, Erman and Budge, to which I have already referred. A very useful digest will be found in Donald A. Mackenzie's " Egyptian Myth and Legend ". Mr. Mackenzie does not claim to have any first-hand knowledge of the subject, but his exceptionally wide and intimate knowledge of Scottish folk-lore, which has preserved a surprisingly large part of the same legends, has enabled him to present the Egyptian stories with exceptional clearness and

The Egyptian legends cannot be fully appreciated unless they are studied in conjunction with those of Babylonia and Assyria,[1] the mythology of Greece,[2] Persia,[3] India,[4] China,[5] Indonesia,[6] and America.[7]

For it will be found that essentially the same stream of legends was flowing in all these countries, and that the scribes and painters have caught and preserved certain definite phases of this verbal currency. The legends which have thus been preserved are not to be regarded as having been directly derived the one from the other but as collateral phases of a variety of waves of story spreading out from one centre. Thus the comparison of the whole range of homologous legends is peculiarly instructive and useful; because the gaps in the Egyptian series, for example, can be filled in by necessary phases which are missing in Egypt itself, but are preserved in Babylonia or Greece, Persia or India, China or Britain, or even Oceania and America.

The incidents in the Destruction of Mankind may be briefly summarized:—

As Re grows old "the men who were begotten of his eye"[8] show signs of rebellion. Re calls a council of the gods and they advise him

sympathetic insight. But I refer to his book specially because he is one of the few modern writers who has made the attempt to compare the legends of Egypt, Babylonia, Crete, India and Western Europe. Hence the reader who is not familiar with the mythology of these countries will find his books particularly useful as works of reference in following the story I have to unfold: "Teutonic Myth and Legend," "Egyptian Myth and Legend," "Indian Myth and Legend," "Myths of Babylonia and Assyria" and "Myths of Crete and Pre-Hellenic Europe".

[1] See Leonard W. King, "Babylonian Religion," 1899.
[2] For a useful collection of data see A. B. Cook, "Zeus".
[3] Albert J. Carnoy, "Iranian Views of Origins in connexion with Similar Babylonian Beliefs," *Journal of the American Oriental Society*, vol. xxxvi., 1916, pp. 300-20; and "The Moral Deities of Iran and India and their Origins," *The American Journal of Theology*, vol. xxi., No. i., January, 1917.
[4] Hopkins, "Religions of India".
[5] De Groot, "The Religious System of China".
[6] Perry, "The Megalithic Culture of Indonesia," Manchester, 1918.
[7] H. Beuchat, "Manuel d' Archéologie Américaine," Paris, 1912; T. A. Joyce, "Mexican Archæology," and especially the memoir by Seler on the "Codex Vaticanus" and his articles in the *Zeitschrift für Ethnologie* and elsewhere.
[8] I.e. the offspring of the Great Mother of gods and men, Hathor, the "Eye of Re".

to "shoot forth his Eye¹ that it may slay the evil conspirators. . . . Let the goddess Hathor descend [from heaven] and slay the men on the mountains [to which they had fled in fear]." As the goddess complied she remarked: "it will be good for me when I subject mankind," and Re replied, "I shall subject them and slay them". Hence the goddess received the additional name of *Sekhmet* from the word "to subject". The destructive Sekhmet² *avatar* of Hathor is represented as a fierce lion-headed goddess of war wading in blood. For the goddess set to work slaughtering mankind and the land was flooded with blood.³ Re became alarmed and determined to save at least some remnant of mankind. For this purpose he sent messengers to Elephantine to obtain a substance called *d'd'* in the Egyptian text, which he gave to the god Sektet of Heliopolis to grind up in a mortar. When the slaves had crushed barley to make beer the powdered *d'd'* was mixed with it so as to make it red like human blood. Enough of this blood-coloured beer was made to fill 7000 jars. At nighttime this was poured out upon the fields, so that when the goddess came to resume her task of destruction in the morning she found the fields inundated and her face was mirrored in the fluid. She drank of the fluid and became intoxicated so that she no longer recognized mankind.⁴

Thus Re saved a remnant of mankind from the bloodthirsty, terrible Hathor. But the god was weary of life on earth and withdrew to heaven upon the back of the Divine Cow.

There can be no doubt as to the meaning of this legend, highly confused as it is. The king who was responsible for introducing irriga-

[1] That is, Hathor, who as the moon is the "Eye of Re".

[2] Elsewhere in these pages I have used the more generally adopted spelling "*Sekhet*".

[3] Mr. F. Ll. Griffith tells me that the translation "flooding the land" is erroneous and misleading. Comparison of the whole series of stories, however, suggests that the amount of blood shed rapidly increased in the development of the narrative: at first the blood of a single victim; then the blood of mankind; then 7000 jars of a substitute for blood; then the red inundation of the Nile.

[4] This verson I have quoted mainly from Erman, *op. cit.*, pp. 267-9, but with certain alterations which I shall mention later. In another version of the legend wine replaces the beer and is made out of "the blood of those who formerly fought against the gods," *cf.* Plutarch, De Iside (ed. Parthey) 6.

DRAGONS AND RAIN GODS

tion came to be himself identified with the life-giving power of water. He was the river : his own vitality was the source of all fertility and prosperity. Hence when he showed signs that his vital powers were failing it became a logical necessity that he should be killed to safeguard the welfare of his country and people.[1]

The time came when a king, rich in power and the enjoyment of life, refused to comply with this custom. When he realized that his virility was failing he consulted the Great Mother, as the source and giver of life, to obtain an elixir which would rejuvenate him and obviate the necessity of being killed. The only medicine in the pharmacopœia of those times that was believed to be useful in minimizing danger to life was human blood. Wounds that gave rise to severe hæmorrhage were known to produce unconsciousness and death. If the escape of

---

[1] It is still the custom in many places, and among them especially the regions near the headwaters of the Nile itself, to regard the king or rain-maker as the impersonation of the life-giving properties of water and the source of all fertility. When his own vitality shows signs of failing he is killed, so as not to endanger the fruitfulness of the community by allowing one who is weak in life-giving powers to control its destinies. Much of the evidence relating to these matters has been collected by Sir James Frazer in " The Dying God," 1911, who quotes from Dr. Seligman the following account of the Dinka " Osiris " :

" While the mighty spirit Lerpiu is supposed to be embodied in the rain-maker, it is also thought to inhabit a certain hut which serves as a shrine. In front of the hut stands a post to which are fastened the horns of many bullocks that have been sacrificed to Lerpiu ; and in the hut is kept a very sacred spear which bears the name of Lerpiu and is said to have fallen from heaven six generations ago. As fallen stars are also called Lerpiu, we may suspect that an intimate connexion is supposed to exist between meteorites and the spirit which animates the rain-maker " (Frazer, *op. cit.*, p. 32). Here then we have a house of the dead inhabited by Lerpiu, who can also enter the body of the rain-maker and animate him, as well as the ancient spear and the falling stars, which are also animate forms of the same god, who obviously is the homologue of Osiris, and is identified with the spear and the falling stars.

In spring when the April moon is a few days old bullocks are sacrificed to Lerpiu. " Two bullocks are led twice round the shrine and afterwards tied by the rain-maker to the post in front of it. Then the drums beat and the people, old and young, men and women, dance round the shrine and sing, while the beasts are being sacrificed, ' Lerpiu, our ancestor, we have brought you a sacrifice. Be pleased to cause rain to fall.' The blood of the bullocks is collected in a gourd, boiled in a pot on the fire, and eaten by the old and important people of the clan. The horns of the animals are attached to the post in front of the shrine " (pp. 32 and 33).

the blood of life could produce these results it was not altogether illogical to assume that the exhibition of human blood could also add to the vitality of living men and so "turn back the years from their old age," as the Pyramid Texts express it.

Thus the Great Mother, the giver of life to all mankind, was faced with the dilemma that, to provide the king with the elixir to restore his youth, she had to slay mankind, to take the life she herself had given to her own children. Thus she acquired an evil reputation which was to stick to her throughout her career. She was not only the beneficent creator of all things and the bestower of all blessings : but she was also a demon of destruction who did not hesitate to slaughter even her own children.

In course of time the practice of human sacrifice was abandoned and substitutes were adopted in place of the blood of mankind. Either the blood of cattle,[1] who by means of appropriate ceremonies could be transformed into human beings (for the Great Mother herself was the Divine Cow and her offspring cattle), was employed in its stead ; or red ochre was used to colour a liquid which was used ritually to replace the blood of sacrifice. When this phase of culture was reached the goddess provided for the king an elixir of life consisting of beer stained red by means of red ochre, so as to simulate human blood.

But such a mixture was doubly potent, for the barley from which the beer was made and the drink itself was supposed to be imbued with the life-giving powers of Osiris, and the blood-colour reinforced its therapeutic usefulness. The legend now begins to become involved and confused. For the goddess is making the rejuvenator for the king, who in the meantime has died and become deified as Osiris ; and the beer, which is the vehicle of the life-giving powers of Osiris, is now being used to rejuvenate his son and successor, the living king Horus, who in the version that has come down to us is replaced by the sun-god Re.

---

[1] In Northern Nigeria an official who bore the title of Killer of the Elephant throttled the king "as soon as he showed signs of failing health or growing infirmity". The king-elect was afterwards conducted to the centre of the town, called Head of the Elephant, where he was made to lie down on a bed. Then a black ox was slaughtered and its blood allowed to pour all over his body. Next the ox was flayed, and the remains of the dead king, which had been disembowelled and smoked for seven days over a slow fire, were wrapped up in the hide and dragged along to the place of burial, where they were interred in a circular pit " (Frazer, *op. cit.*, p. 35).

DRAGONS AND RAIN GODS

It is Re who is king and is growing old: he asks Hathor, the Great Mother, to provide him with the elixir of life. But comparison with some of the legends of other countries suggests that Re has usurped the place previously occupied by Horus and originally by Osiris, who as the real personification of the life-giving power of water is obviously the appropriate person to be slain when his virility begins to fail. Dr. C. G. Seligman's account of the Dinka rain-maker Lerpiu, which I have already quoted (p. 113) from Sir James Frazer's "Dying God," suggests that the slain king or god was originally Osiris.

The introduction of Re into the story marks the beginning of the belief in the sky-world or heaven. Hathor was originally nothing more than an amulet to enhance fertility and vitality. Then she was personified as a woman and identified with a cow. But when the view developed that the moon controlled the powers of life-giving in women and exercised a direct influence upon their life-blood, the Great Mother was identified with the moon. But how was such a conception to be brought into harmony with the view that she was also a cow? The human mind displays an irresistible tendency to unify its experience and to bridge the gaps that necessarily exist in its broken series of scraps of knowledge and ideas. No break is too great to be bridged by this instinctive impulse to rationalize the products of diverse experience. Hence, early man, having identified the Great Mother both with a cow and the moon, had no compunction in making "the cow jump over the moon" to become the sky. The moon then became the "Eye" of the sky and the sun necessarily became its other "Eye". But, as the sun was clearly the more important "Eye," seeing that it determined the day and gave warmth and light for man's daily work, it was the more important deity. Therefore Re, at first the Brother-Eye of Hathor, and afterwards her husband, became the supreme sky-deity, and Hathor merely one of his Eyes.

When this stage of theological evolution was reached, the story of the "Destruction of Mankind" was re-edited, and Hathor was called the "Eye of Re". In the earlier versions she was called into consultation solely as the giver of life and, to obtain the life-blood, she cut men's throats with a knife.

But as the Eye of Re she was identified with the fire-spitting uræus-serpent which the king or god wore on his forehead. She was both the moon and the fiery bolt which shot down from the sky to slay the enemies of Re. For the men who were originally slaughtered to provide the blood for an elixir now became the enemies of Re. The reason for this was that, human sacrifice having been abandoned and substitutes provided to replace the human blood, the story-teller was at a loss to know why the goddess killed mankind. A reason had to be found—and the rationalization adopted was that men had rebelled against the gods and had to be killed. This interpretation was probably the result of a confusion with the old legend of the fight between Horus and Set, the rulers of the two kingdoms of Egypt. The possibility also suggests itself that a pun made by some priestly jester may have been the real factor that led to this mingling of two originally separate stories. In the "Destruction of Mankind" the story runs, according to Budge,[1] that Re, referring to his enemies, said: *mā-ten set uār er set*, "Behold ye them (*set*) fleeing into the mountain (*set*)". The enemies were thus identified with the mountain or stone and with Set, the enemy of the gods.[2]

In Egyptian hieroglyphics the symbol for stone is used as the determinative for Set. When the "Eye of Re" destroyed mankind and the rebels were thus identified with the followers of Set, they were regarded as creatures of "stone". In other words the Medusa-eye petrified the enemies. From this feeble pun on the part of some ancient Egyptian scribe has arisen the world-wide stories of the influence of the "Evil Eye" and the petrification of the enemies of the gods.[3] As the name for Isis in Egyptian is "*Set*," it is possible that the confusion of the Power of Evil with the Great Mother may also have been facilitated by an extension of the same pun.

It is important to recognize that the legend of Hathor descending from the moon or the sky in the form of destroying fire had nothing whatever to do, in the first instance, with the phenomena of lightning

---

[1] "Gods of the Egyptians," vol. i., p. 392.

[2] The eye of the sun-god, which was subsequently called the eye of Horus and identified with the Uræus-snake on the forehead of Re and of the Pharaohs, the earthly representatives of Re, finally becoming synonymous with the crown of Lower Egypt, was a mighty goddess, Uto or Buto by name" (Alan Gardiner, Article "Magic (Egyptian)" in Hastings' *Encyclopædia of Religion and Ethics*, p. 268, quoting Sethe.

[3] For an account of the distribution of this story see E. Sidney Hartland, "The Legend of Perseus"; also W. J. Perry, "The Megalithic Culture of Indonesia".

and meteorites. It was the result of verbal quibbling after the destructive goddess came to be identified with the moon, the sky and the "Eye of Re". But once the evolution of the story on these lines prepared the way, it was inevitable that in later times the powers of destruction exerted by the fire from the sky should have been identified with the lightning and meteorites.

When the destructive force of the heavens was attributed to the "Eye of Re" and the god's enemies were identified with the followers of Set, it was natural that the traditional enemy of Set who was also the more potent other "Eye of Re" should assume his mother's rôle of punishing rebellious mankind. That Horus did in fact take the place at first occupied by Hathor in the story is revealed by the series of trivial episodes from the "Destruction of Mankind" that reappear in the "Saga of the Winged Disk". The king of Lower Egypt (Horus) was identified with a falcon, as Hathor was with the vulture (Mut): like her, he entered the sun-god's boat[1] and sailed up the river with him: he then mounted up to heaven as a winged disk, i.e. the sun of Re equipped with his own falcon's wings. The destructive force displayed by Hathor as the Eye of Re was symbolized by her identification with Tefnut, the fire-spitting uræus-snake. When Horus assumed the form of the winged disk he added to his insignia two fire-spitting serpents to destroy Re's enemies. The winged disk was at once the instrument of destruction and the god himself. It swooped (or flew) down from heaven like a bolt of destroying fire and killed the enemies of Re. By a confusion with Horus's other fight against the

[1] The original "boat of the sky" was the crescent moon, which, from its likeness to the earliest form of Nile boat, was regarded as the vessel in which the moon (seen as a faint object upon the crescent), or the goddess who was supposed to be personified in the moon, travelled across the waters of the heavens. But as this "boat" was obviously part of the moon itself, it also was regarded as an animate form of the goddess, the "Eye of Re". When the Sun, as the other "Eye," assumed the chief rôle, Re was supposed to traverse the heavens in his own "boat," which was also brought into relationship with the actual boat used in the Osirian burial ritual.

The custom of employing the name "dragon" in reference to a boat is found in places as far apart as Scandinavia and China. It is the direct outcome of these identifications of the sun and moon with a boat animated by the respective deities. In India the *Makara*, the prototype of the dragon, was sometimes represented as a boat which was looked upon as the fish-*avatar* of Vishnu, Buddha or some other deity.

followers of Set, the enemies of Re become identified with Set's army and they are transformed into crocodiles, hippopotami and all the other kinds of creatures whose shapes the enemies of Osiris assume.

In the course of the development of these legends a multitude of other factors played a part and gave rise to transformations of the meaning of the incidents.

The goddess originally slaughtered mankind, or perhaps it would be truer to say, made *a* human sacrifice, to obtain blood to rejuvenate the king. But, as we have seen already, when the sacrifice was no longer a necessary part of the programme, the incident of the slaughter was not dropped out of the story, but a new explanation of it was framed. Instead of simply making a human sacrifice, mankind as a whole was destroyed for rebelling against the gods, the act of rebellion being murmuring about the king's old age and loss of virility. The elixir soon became something more than a rejuvenator: it was transformed into the food of the gods, the ambrosia that gave them their immortality, and distinguished them from mere mortals. Now when the development of the story led to the replacement of the single victim by the whole of mankind, the blood produced by the wholesale slaughter was so abundant that the fields were flooded by the life-giving elixir. By the sacrifice of men the soil was renewed and refertilized. When the blood-coloured beer was substituted for the actual blood the conception was brought into still closer harmony with Egyptian ideas, because the beer was animated with the life-giving powers of Osiris. But Osiris was the Nile. The blood-coloured fertilizing fluid was then identified with the annual inundation of the red-coloured waters of the Nile. Now the Nile waters were supposed to come from the First Cataract at Elephantine. Hence by a familiar psychological process the previous phase of the legend was recast, and by confusion the red ochre (which was used to colour the beer red) was said to have come from Elephantine.[1]

[1] This is an instance of the well-known tendency of the human mind to blend numbers of different incidents into one story. An episode of one experience, having been transferred to an earlier one, becomes rationalized in adaptation to its different environment. This process of psychological transference is the explanation of the reference to Elephantine as the source of the *d'd'*, and has no relation to actuality. The naïve efforts of Brugsch and Gauthier to study the natural products of Elephantine for the purpose of identifying *d'd'* were therefore wholly misplaced.

DRAGONS AND RAIN GODS

Thus we have arrived at the stage where, by a distortion of a series of phases, the new incident emerges that by means of a human sacrifice the Nile flood can be produced. By a further confusion the goddess, who originally did the slaughter, becomes the victim. Hence the story assumed the form that by means of the sacrifice of a beautiful and attractive maiden the annual inundation can be produced. As the most potent symbol of life-giving it is essential that the victim should be sexually attractive, i.e. that she should be a virgin and the most beautiful and desirable in the land. When the practice of human sacrifice was abandoned a figure or an animal was substituted for the maiden in ritual practice, and in legends the hero rescued the maiden, as Andromeda was saved from the dragon.[1] The dragon is the personification of the monsters that dwell in the waters as well as the destructive forces of the flood itself. But the monsters were no other than the followers of Set; they were the victims of the slaughter who became identified with the god's other traditional enemies, the followers of Set. Thus the monster from whom Andromeda is rescued is merely another representative of herself!

But the destructive forces of the flood now enter into the programme. In the phases we have so far discussed it was the slaughter of mankind which caused the inundation: but in the next phase it is the flood itself which causes the destruction, as in the later Egyptian and the borrowed Sumerian, Babylonian, Hebrew—and in fact the world-wide—versions. Re's boat becomes the ark; the winged disk which was despatched by Re from the boat becomes the dove and the other birds sent out to spy the land, as the winged Horus spied the enemies of Re.

Thus the new weapon of the gods—we have already noted Hathor's knife and Horus's winged disk, which is the fire from heaven, the lightning and the thunderbolt—is the flood. Like the others it can be either a beneficent giver of life or a force of destruction.

But the flood also becomes a weapon of another kind. One of the earlier incidents of the story represents Hathor in opposition to Re. The goddess becomes so maddened with the zest of killing that the god becomes alarmed and asks her to desist and spare some representatives of the race. But she is deaf to entreaties. Hence the god is

[1] In Hartland's "Legend of Perseus" a collection of variants of this story will be found.

said to have sent to Elephantine for the red ochre to make a sedative draught to overcome her destructive zeal. We have already seen that this incident had an entirely different meaning—it was merely intended to explain the obtaining of the colouring matter wherewith to redden the sacred beer so as to make it resemble blood as an elixir for the god. It was brought from Elephantine, because the red waters of inundation of the Nile were supposed by the Egyptians to come from Elephantine.

But according to the story inscribed in Seti Ist's tomb, the red ochre was an essential ingredient of the sedative mixture (prepared under the direction of Re by the Sekti[1] of Heliopolis) to calm Hathor's murderous spirit.

It has been claimed that the story simply means that the goddess became intoxicated with beer and that she became genially inoffensive solely as the effect of such inebriation. But the incident in the Egyptian story closely resembles the legends of other countries in which some herb is used specifically as a sedative. In most books on Egyptian mythology the word ($d'd'$) for the substance put into the drink to colour it is translated "mandragora," from its resemblance to the Hebrew word *dudaim* in the Old Testament, which is often translated "mandrakes" or "love-apples". But Gauthier has clearly demonstrated that the Egyptian word does not refer to a vegetable but to a mineral substance, which he translates "red clay"[2]. Mr. F. Ll. Griffith tells me, however, that it is "red ochre". In any case, mandrake is not found at Elephantine (which, however, for the reasons I have already given, is a point of no importance so far as the identification of the substance is concerned), nor in fact anywhere in Egypt.

But if some foreign story of the action of a sedative drug had become blended with and incorporated in the highly complex and composite Egyptian legend the narrative would be more intelligible. The mandrake is such a sedative as might have been employed to calm the murderous frenzy of a maniacal woman. In fact it is closely allied to hyoscyamus, whose active principle, hyoscin, is used in modern medicine precisely for such purposes. I venture to suggest that a folk-tale describing the effect of opium or some other "drowsy syrup" has been absorbed into the legend of the Destruction of Mankind, and has provided the starting point of all those incidents in the dragon-story in which poison or some

[1] In the version I have quoted from Erman he refers to "the god Sektet".
[2] *Op. cit., supra.*

sleep-producing drug plays a part. For when Hathor defies Re and continues the destruction, she is playing the part of her Babylonian representative Tiamat, and is a dragon who has to be vanquished by the drink which the god provides.

The red earth which was pounded in the mortar to make the elixir of life and the fertilizer of the soil also came to be regarded as the material out of which the new race of men was made to replace those who were destroyed.

The god fashioned mankind of this earth and, instead of the red ochre being merely the material to give the blood-colour to the draught of immortality, the story became confused: actual blood was presented to the clay images to give them life and consciousness.

In a later elaboration the remains of the former race of mankind were ground up to provide the material out of which their successors were created. This version is a favourite story in Northern Europe, and has obviously been influenced by an intermediate variant which finds expression in the Indian legend of the Churning of the Ocean of Milk. Instead of the material for the elixir of the gods being pounded by the Sekti of Heliopolis and incidentally becoming a sedative for Hathor, it is the milk of the Divine Cow herself which is churned to provide the *amrita*.

The Thunder-Weapon.[1]

In the development of the dragon-story we have seen that the instruments of destruction were of a most varied kind. Each of the three primary deities, Hathor, Osiris and Horus can be a destructive power as well as a giver of life and of all kinds of boons. Every homologue or surrogate of these three deities can become a weapon for dragon-destroying, such as the moon or the lotus of Hathor, the water

---

[1] The history of the thunder-weapon cannot wholly be ignored in discussing the dragon-myth because it forms an integral part of the story. It was animated both by the dragon and the dragon-slayer. But an adequate account of the weapon would be so highly involved and complex as to be unintelligible without a very large series of illustrations. Hence I am referring here only to certain aspects of the subject. Pending the preparation of a monograph upon the thunder-weapon, I may refer the reader to the works of Blinkenberg, d'Alviella, Ward, Evans and A. B. Cook (to which frequent reference is made in these pages) for material, especially in the form of illustrations, to supplement my brief and unavoidably involved summary.

or the beer of Osiris, the sun or the falcon of Horus. Originally Hathor used a flint knife or axe: then she did the execution as "the Eye of Re," the moon, the fiery bolt from heaven: Osiris sent the destroying flood and the intoxicating beer, each of which, like the knife, axe and moon of Hathor, were animated by the deity. Then Horus came as the winged disk, the falcon, the sun, the lightning and the thunderbolt. As the dragon-story was spread abroad in the world any one of these "weapons" was confused with any of (or all) the rest. The Eye of Re was the fire-spitting uræus-serpent; and foreign people, like the Greeks, Indians and others, gave the Egyptian verbal simile literal expression and converted it into an actual Cyclopean eye planted in the forehead, which shot out the destroying fire.

The warrior god of Babylonia is called the bright one,[1] the sword or lightning of Ishtar, who was herself called both the sword or lightning of heaven.

In the Ægean area also the sons of Zeus and the progeny of heaven may be axes, stone implements, meteoric stones and thunderbolts. In a Swahili tale the hero's weapon is "a sword like a flash of lightning".

According to Bergaigne,[2] the myth of the celestial drink *soma*, brought down from heaven by a bird ordinarily called *çyena*, "eagle," is parallel to that of Agni, the celestial fire brought by Mâtariçvan. This parallelism is even expressly stated in the Rig Veda, verse 6 of hymn 1 to Agni and Soma. Mâtariçvan brought the one from heaven, the eagle brought the other from the celestial mountain.

Kuhn admits that the eagle represents Indra; and Lehmann regards the eagle who takes the fire as Agni himself. It is patent that both Indra and Agni are in fact merely specialized forms of Horus of the Winged Disk Saga, in one of which the warrior sun-god is represented, in the other the living fire. The elixir of life of the Egyptian story is represented by the *soma*, which by confusion is associated with the eagle: in other words, the god Soma is the homologue not only of Osiris, but also of Horus.

Other incidents in the same original version are confused in the Greek story of Prometheus. He stole the fire from heaven and brought

---

[1] As in Egypt Osiris is described as "a ray of light" which issued from the moon (Hathor), *i.e.* was born of the Great Mother.

[2] "Religion védique," i., p. 173, quoted by S. Reinach, "Ætos Prometheus," *Revue archéologique*, 4ᶦᵉ série, tome x., 1917, p. 72.

it to earth : but, in place of the episode of the elixir, which is adopted in the Indian story just mentioned, the creation of men from clay is accredited by the Greeks to the "flaming one," the "fire eagle" Prometheus.

The double axe was the homologue of the winged disk which fell, or rather flew, from heaven as the tangible form of the god. This fire from heaven inevitably came to be identified with the lightning. According to Blinkenberg (*op. cit.*, p. 19) "many points go to prove that the double-axe is a representation of the lightning (see Usener, p. 20)". He refers to the design on the famous gold ring from Mycenæ where "the sun, the moon, a double curved line presumably representing the rainbow, and the double-axe, i.e. the lightning" : but "the latter is placed lower than the others, probably because it descends from heaven to earth," like Horus when he assumed the form of the winged disk and flew down to earth as a fiery bolt to destroy the enemies of Re.

The recognition of the homology of the winged disk with the double axe solves a host of problems which have puzzled classical scholars within recent years. The form of the double axe on the Mycenæan ring [1] and the painted sarcophagus from Hagia Triada in Crete (and especially the oblique markings upon the axe) is probably a suggestion of the double series of feathers and the outlines of the individual feathers respectively on the wings. The position of the axe upon a symbolic tree is not intended, as Blinkenberg claims (*op. cit.*, p. 21), as "a ritual representation of the trees struck by lightning" : but is the familiar scene of the Mesopotamian culture-area, the tree of life surmounted by the winged disk.[2]

The bird poised upon the axe in the Cretan picture is the homologue of the falcon of Horus : it is in fact a second representation of the winged disk itself. This interpretation is not affected by the consideration that the falcon may be replaced by the eagle, pigeon, woodpecker or raven, for these substitutions were repeatedly made by the ancient priesthoods in flagrant defiance of the proprieties of ornithological homologies. The same phenomenon is displayed even more obtrusively in Central America and Mexico, where the ancient sculptors

---

[1] Evans, *op. cit.*, Fig. 4, p. 10.
[2] William Hayes Ward, "The Seal Cylinders of Western Asia," chapter xxxviii.

and painters represented the bird perched upon the tree of life as a falcon, an eagle, a vulture, a macaw or even a turkey.[1]

The incident of the winged disk descending to effect the sun-god's purposes upon earth probably represents the earliest record of the recognition of thunder and lightning and the phenomena of rain as manifestations of the god's powers. All gods of thunder, lightning, rain and clouds derive their attributes, and the arbitrary graphic representation of them, from the legend which the Egyptian scribe has preserved for us in the Saga of the Winged Disk.

The sacred axe of Crete is represented elsewhere as a sword which became the visible impersonation of the deity.[2] There is a Hittite story of a sword-handle coming to life. Hose and McDougall refer to the same incident in certain Sarawak legends; and the story is true to the original in the fact that the sword fell from the sun.[3]

Sir Arthur Evans describes as "the aniconic image of the god" a stone pillar on which crude pictures of a double axe have been scratched. These representations of the axe in fact serve the same purpose as the winged disk in Egypt, and, as we shall see subsequently, there was an actual confusion between the Egyptian symbol and the Cretan axe.

The obelisk at Abusir was the aniconic representative of the sun-god Re, or rather, the support of the pyramidal apex, the gilded surface of which reflected the sun's rays and so made manifest the god's presence in the stone.

The Hittites seem to have substituted the winged disk as a representation of the sun: for in a design copied from a seal[4] we find the Egyptian symbol borne upon the apex of a cone.

The transition from this to the great double axe from Hagia Triada in the Candia Museum[5] is a relatively easy one, which was materially helped, as we shall see, by the fact that the winged disk was actually homologized with an axe or knife as alternative weapons used by the sun-god for the destruction of mankind.

In Dr. Seligman's account of the Dinka rain-maker (*supra*, p. 113)

---

[1] Seler, "Codex Vaticanus, No. 3773," vol. i., p. 77 *et seq.*
[2] Evans, *op. cit.*, p. 8.
[3] "The Pagan Tribes of Borneo," 1912, vol. ii., p. 137.
[4] Evans, *op. cit.*, Fig. 8, *c*, p. 17.
[5] There is an excellent photograph of this in Donald McKenzie's "Myths of Crete and Pre-Hellenic Europe," facing p. 160.

we have already seen that the Soudanese Osiris was identified with a spear and falling stars.

According to Dr. Budge[1] the Egyptian hieroglyph used as the determinative of the word *neter*, meaning god or spirit, is the axe with a handle. Mr. Griffith, however, interprets it as a roll of yellow cloth ("Hieroglyphics," p. 46). On Hittite seals the axe sometimes takes the place of the god Teshub.[2]

Sir Arthur Evans endeavours to explain these conceptions by a vague appeal to certain natural phenomena (*op. cit.*, pp. 20 and 21); but the identical traditions of widespread peoples are much too arbitrary and specific to be interpreted by any such speculations.

Sanchoniathon's story of Baetylos being the son of Ouranos is merely a poetical way of saying that the sun-god fell to earth in the form of a stone or a weapon, as a Zeus Kappôtas or a Horus in the form of a winged disk, flying down from heaven to destroy the enemies of Re.

"The idea of their [the weapons] flying through the air or falling from heaven, and their supposed power of burning with inner fire or shining in the nighttime," was not primarily suggested, as Sir Arthur Evans claims (*op. cit.*, p. 21), "by the phenomena associated with meteoric stones," but was a rationalization of the events described in the early Egyptian and Babylonian stories.

They "shine at night" because the original weapon of destruction was the moon as the Eye of Re. They "burn with inward fire," like the Babylonian Marduk, when in the fight with the dragon Tiamat "he filled his body with burning flame" (King, *op. cit.*, p. 71), because they *were* fire, the fire of the sun and of lightning, the fire spat out by the Eye of Re.

Further evidence in corroboration of these views is provided by the fact that in the Ægean area the double-axe replaces the moon between the cow's horns (Evans, *op. cit.*, Fig. 3, p. 9).

In King's "Babylonian Religion" (pp. 70 and 71) we are told how the gods provided Marduk with an invincible weapon in preparation for the combat with the dragon: and the ancient scribe himself sets forth a series of its homologues:—

---

[1] "The Gods of the Egyptians," vol. i., pp. 63 *et seq.*
[2] See, for example, Ward, *op. cit.*, p. 411.

> He made ready his bow . . .
> He slung a spear . . .
> The bow and quiver . . .
> He set the lightning in front of him,
> With burning flame he filled his body.

An ancient Egyptian writer has put on record further identifications of weapons. In the 95th Chapter of the Book of the Dead, the deceased is reported to have said: "I am he who sendeth forth terror into the powers of rain and thunder. . . . I have made to flourish my knife which is in the hand of Thoth in the powers of rain and thunder" (Budge, "Gods of the Egyptians," vol. i., p. 414).

The identification of the winged disk with the thunderbolt which emerges so definitely from these homologies is not altogether new, for it was suggested some years ago by Count d'Alviella[1] in these words:—

"On seeing some representations of the Thunderbolt which recall in a remarkable manner the outlines of the Winged Globe, it may be asked if it was not owing to this latter symbol that the Greeks transformed into a winged spindle the Double Trident derived from Assyria. At any rate the transition, or, if it be preferred, the combination of the two symbols is met with in those coins from Northern Africa where Greek art was most deeply impregnated with Phœnician types. Thus on coins of Bocchus II, King of Mauretania, figures are found which M. Lajard connected with the Winged Globe, and M. L. Müller calls Thunderbolts, but which are really the result of crossing between these two emblems".

The thunderbolt, however, is not always, or even commonly, the direct representative of the winged disk. It is more often derived from lightning or some floral design.[2]

According to Count d'Alviella[3] "the Trident of Siva at times exhibits the form of a lotus calyx depicted in the Egyptian manner".

"Perhaps other transformations of the *trisula* might still be found at Boro-Budur [in Java]. . . . The same Disk which, when transformed into a most complicated ornament, is sometimes crowned by a Trident, is also met with between two serpents—which brings us back to the origin of the Winged Circle—the Globe of Egypt with the

---

[1] "The Migration of Symbols," pp. 220 and 221.
[2] Blinkenberg, *op. cit.*, p. 53. [3] *Op. cit.*, p. 256.

uræi" (see d'Alviella's Fig. 158). "Moreover this ornament, between which and certain forms of the *trisula* the transition is easily traced, commonly surmounts the entrance to the pagodas depicted in the bas-reliefs—in exactly the same manner as the Winged Globe adorns the lintel of the temples in Egypt and Phœnicia."

Thus we find traces of a blending of the two homologous designs, derived independently from the lotus and the winged disk, which acquired the same symbolic significance.

The weapon of Poseidon, the so-called "Trident of Neptune," is "sometimes crowned with a trilobate lotus flower, or with three lotus buds; in other cases it is depicted in a shape that may well represent a fishing spear" (Blinkenberg, *op. cit.*, pp. 53 and 54).

"Even if Jacobsthal's interpretation of the flower as a common Greek symbol for fire be not accepted, the conventionalization of the trident as a lotus blossom is quite analogous to the change, on Greek soil, of the Assyrian thunderweapon to two flowers pointing in opposite directions" (p. 54).

But the conception of a flower as a symbol of fire cannot thus summarily be dismissed. For Sir Arthur Evans has collected all the stages in the transformation of Egyptian palmette pillars into the rayed pillars of Cyprus, in which the leaflets of the palmette become converted (in the Cypro-Mycenæan derivatives) into the rays which he calls "the natural concomitant of divinities of light".[1]

The underlying motive which makes such a transference easy is the Egyptian conception of Hathor as a sacred lotus from which the sun-god Horus is born. The god of light is identified with the water-plant, whether lotus, iris or lily; and the lotus form of Horus can be correlated with its Hellenic surrogate, Apollo Hyakinthos. "The fleur-de-lys type now takes its place beside the sacred lotus" (*op. cit.*, p. 50). The trident and the fleur-de-lys are thunderweapons because they represent forms of Horus or his mother.

The classical keraunos is still preserved in Tibet as the *dorje*, which is identified with Indra's thunderbolt, the *vajra*.[2] This word is also applied to the diamond, the "king of stones," which in turn acquired many of the attributes of the pearl, another of the Great

---

[1] "Mycenæan Tree and Pillar Cult," pp. 51 and 52.
[2] See Blinkenberg, *op. cit.*, pp. 45-8.

Mother's surrogates, which is reputed to have fallen from heaven like the thunderbolt.[1]

The Tibetan *dorje*, like its Greek original, is obviously a conventionalized flower, the leaf-design about the base of the corona being quite clearly defined.

The influence of the Winged-Disk Saga is clearly revealed in such Greek myths as that relating to Ixion. "Euripides is represented by Aristophanes as declaring that *Aithér* at the creation devised

> The eye to mimic the wheel of the sun."[1]

When we read of Zeus in anger binding Ixion to a winged wheel made of fire, and sending him spinning through the air, we are merely dealing with a Greek variant of the Egyptian myth in which Re despatched Horus as a winged disk to slay his enemies. In the Hellenic version the sky-god is angry with the father of the centaurs for his ill-treatment of his father-in-law and his behaviour towards Hera and her cloud-manifestation: but though distorted all the incidents reveal their original inspiration in the Egyptian story and its early Aryan variants.

It is remarkable that Mr. A. B. Cook, who compared the wheel of Ixion with the Egyptian winged disk (pp. 205-10), did not look deeper for a common origin of the two myths, especially when he got so far as to identify Ixion with the sun-god (p. 211).

Blinkenberg sums up the development of the thunder-weapon thus: "From the old Babylonian representation of the lightning, i.e. two or three zigzag lines representing flames, a tripartite thunder-weapon was evolved and carried east and west from the ancient seat of civilization.

---

[1] I must defer consideration of the part played by certain of the Great Mother's surrogates in the development of the thunder-weapon's symbolism and the associated folk-lore. I have in mind especially the influence of the octopus and the cow. The former was responsible in part for the use of the spiral as a thunder-symbol; and the latter for the beliefs in the special protective power of thunderstones over cows (see Blinkenberg, *op. cit.*). The thunderstone was placed over the lintel of the cow-shed for the same purpose as the winged disk over the door of an Egyptian temple. Until the relations of the octopus to the dragon have been set forth it is impossible adequately to discuss the question of the seven-headed dragon, which ranges from Scotland to Japan and from Scandinavia to the Zambesi. In "The Birth of Aphrodite" I shall call attention to the basal factors in its evolution.

[2] A. B. Cook, "Zeus," vol. i., p. 198.

Together with the axe (in Western Asia Minor the double-edged, and towards the centre of Asia the single-edged, axe) it became a regular attribute of the Asiatic thunder-gods. . . . The Indian trisula and the Greek triaina are both its descendants" (p. 57).

Discussing the relationship of the sun-god to thunder, Dr. Rendel Harris refers to the fact that Apollo's "arrows are said to be lightnings," and he quotes Pausanias, Apollodorus and Mr. A. B. Cook in substantiation of his statements.[1] Both sons of Zeus, Dionysus and Apollo, are "concerned with the production of fire".

According to Hyginus, Typhon was the son of Tartarus and the Earth: he made war against Jupiter for dominion, and, being struck by lightning, was thrown flaming to the earth, where Mount Ætna was placed upon him.[2]

In this curious variant of the story of the winged disk, the conflict of Horus with Set is merged with the Destruction, for the son of Tartarus [Osiris] and the Earth [Isis] here is not Horus but his hostile brother Set. Instead of fighting for Jupiter (Re) as Horus did, he is against him. The lightning (which is Horus in the form of the winged disk) strikes Typhon and throws him flaming to earth. The episode of Mount Ætna is the antithesis of the incident in the Indian legend of the churning of the ocean: Mount Meru is placed in the sea upon the tortoise *avatar* of Vishnu and is used to churn the food of immortality for the gods. In the Egyptian story the red ochre brought from Elephantine is pounded with the barley.

The story told by Hyginus leads up to the vision in Revelations (xii., 7 *et seq*.): "There was war in heaven; Michael and his angels fought against the dragon; and the dragon fought, and his angels, and prevailed not, neither was their place found any more in heaven. And the great dragon was cast out, that old serpent called the Devil and Satan, which deceiveth the whole world: he was cast into the earth, and his angels were cast out with him."

---

[1] "The Ascent of Olympus," p. 32.
[2] Tartarus ex Terra procreavit Typhonem, immani magnitudine, specieque portentosa, cui centum capita draconum ex humeris enata erant. Hic Jovem provocavit, si vellet secum de regno centare. Jovis fulmine ardenti pectus ejus percussit. Cui cum flagraret, montem Ætnam, qui est in Sicilia, super eum imposuit; qui ex eo adhuc ardere dicitur" (Hyginus, fab. 152).

In the later variants the original significance of the Destruction of Mankind seems to have been lost sight of. The life-giving Great Mother tends to drop out of the story and her son Horus takes her place. He becomes the warrior-god, but he not only assumes his mother's rôle but he also adopts her tactics. Just as she attacked Re's enemies in the capacity of the sky-god's "Eye," so Horus as the other "Eye," the sun, to which he gave his own falcon's wings, attacked in the form of the winged disk. The winged disk, like the other "Eye of Re," was not merely the sky weapon which shot down to destroy mankind, but also was the god Horus himself. This early conception involved the belief that the thunderbolt and lightning represented not merely the fiery weapon but the actual god.

The winged disk thus exhibits the same confusion of attributes as we have already noticed in Osiris and Hathor. It is the commonest symbol of life-giving and beneficent protective power: yet it is the weapon used to slaughter mankind. It is in fact the healing caduceus as well as the baneful thunder-weapon.

The Deer.

One of the most surprising features of the dragon in China, Japan and America, is the equipment of deer's horns.

In Babylonia both Ea and Marduk are intimately associated with the antelope or gazelle, and the combination of the head of the antelope (or in other cases the goat) with the body of a fish is the most characteristic manifestation of either god. In Egypt both Osiris and Horus are at times brought into relationship with the gazelle or antelope, but more often it represents their enemy Set. Hence, in some parts of Africa, especially in the west, the antelope plays the part of the dragon in Asiatic stories.[1] The cow[2] of Hathor (Tiamat) may represent the dragon also. In East Africa the antelope assumes the rôle of the hero,[3] and is the representative of Horus. In the Ægean area, Asia Minor

[1] Frobenius, "The Voice of Africa," vol. ii., p. 467 *inter alia*.
[2] *Op. cit.*, p. 468.
[3] J. F. Campbell, "The Celtic Dragon Myth," with the "Geste of Fraoch and the Dragon," translated with Introduction by George Henderson, Edinburgh, 1911, p. 136.

DRAGONS AND RAIN GODS

and Europe the antelope, gazelle or the deer, may be associated with the Great Mother.

In India the god Soma's chariot is drawn by an antelope. I have already suggested that Soma is only a specialized form of the Babylonian Ea, whose evil *avatar* is the dragon: there is thus suggested another link between the antelope and the latter. The Ea-element explains the fish-scales and the antelope provides the horns. I shall return to the discussion of this point later.

Vayu or Pavana, the Indian god of the winds, who afterwards became merged with Indra, rides upon an antelope like the Egyptian Horus. Soma's attributes also were in large measure taken over by Indra. Hence in this complex tissue of contradictions we once more find the dragon-slayer acquiring the insignia, in this case the antelope, of his mortal enemy.

I have already referred to the fact that the early Babylonian deities could also be demons. Tiamat, the dragon whom Marduk fought, was merely the malevolent *avatar* of the Great Mother. The dragon acquired his covering of fish-scales from an evil form of Ea.

In his Hibbert Lectures Professor Sayce claimed that the name of Ea was expressed by an ideograph which signifies literally " the antelope " (p. 280). " Ea was called ' the antelope of the deep,' ' the antelope the creator,' ' the lusty antelope '. We should have expected the animal of Ea to have been the fish: the fact that it is not so points to the conclusion that the culture-god of Southern Babylonia was an amalgamation of two earlier deities, one the divine antelope and the other the divine fish." Ea was " originally the god of the river and was also associated with the snake ". Nina was also both the fish-goddess and the divinity whose name is interchanged with that of the deep. Professor Sayce then refers to " the curious process of development which transformed the old serpent-goddess, ' the lady Nina,' into the embodiment of all that was hostile to the powers of heaven ; but after all, Nina had sprung from the fish-god of the deep [who also was

---

For example the red deer occupies the place usually taken by the goddess's lions upon a Cretan gem (Evans, " Mycenæan Tree and Pillar Cult," Fig. 32, p. 56): on the bronze plate from Heddemheim (A. B. Cook, " Zeus," vol. i., pl. xxxiv., and p. 620) Isis is represented standing on a hind: Artemis, another *avatar* of the same Great Mother, was intimately associated with deer.

both antelope and serpent as well, see p. 282], and Tiamat is herself 'the deep' in Semitic dress" (p. 283).

"At times Ea was regarded as a gazelle rather than as an antelope." The position of the name in the list of animals shows what species of animal must be meant. *Lulim*, "a stag," seems to be a re-duplicated form of the same word. Both *lulim* and *elim* are said to be equivalent to *sarru*, king (p. 284).

Certain Assyriologists, from whom I asked for enlightenment upon these philological matters, express some doubt as to the antiquity or to the reality of the association of the names of Ea and the word for an antelope, gazelle or stag. But whatever the value of the linguistic evidence, the archæological, at any rate as early as the time of Nebuchadnezzar I, brings both Ea and Marduk into close association with a strange creature equipped with the horns of an antelope or gazelle. The association with the antelope of the homologous deities in India and Egypt leaves the reality of the connexion in no doubt. I had hoped that Professor Sayce's evidence would have provided some explanation of the strange association of the antelope. But whether or not the philological data justify the inferences which Professor Sayce drew from them, there can be no doubt concerning the correctness of his statement that Ea was represented both by fish and antelope, for in the course of his excavations at Susa M. J. de Morgan brought to light representations of Ea's animal consisting of an antelope's head on the body of a fish.[1] He also makes the statement that the ideogram of Ea, *turahu-apsu*, means "antelope of the sea". I have already (p. 88) referred to the fact that this "antelope of the sea," the so-called "goat-fish," is identical with the prototype of the dragon.

If his claim that the names of Ea meant both a "fish" and an "antelope" were well founded, the pun would have solved this problem, as it has done in the case of many other puzzles in the history of early civilization. But if this is not the case, the question is still open for solution. As Set was held to be personified in all the desert animals, the gazelle was identified with the demon of evil for this reason. In her important treatise on "The Asiatic Dionysos" Miss Gladys Davis tells us that "in his aspect of Moon 'the lord of stars'

[1] J. de Morgan, article on "Koudourrous," *Mem. Del. en Perse*, t. 7, 1905. Figures on p. 143 and p. 148 : see also an earlier article on the same subject in tome i. of the same series.

Soma has in this character the antelope as his symbol. In fact, one of the names given to the moon by the early Indians was 'mṛiga-piplu' or marked like an antelope" (p. 202). Further she adds: "The Sanskrit name for the lunar mansion over which Soma presides is 'mṛiga-śiras' or the deer-headed." If it be admitted that Soma is merely the Aryan specialization of Ea and Osiris, as I have claimed, Sayce's association of Ea with the antelope is corroborated, even if it is not explained.

In China the dragon was sometimes called "the celestial stag" (de Groot, *op. cit.*, p. 1143). In Mexico the deer has the same intimate celestial relations as it has in the Old World (see Seler, *Zeit. f. Ethnologie*, Bd. 41, p. 414). I have already referred to the remarkable Maya deer-crocodile *makara* in the Liverpool Museum (p. 103).

The systematic zoology of the ancients was lacking in the precision of modern times ; and there are reasons for supposing that the antelope and gazelle could exchange places the one with the other in their divine rôles ; the deer and the rabbit were also their surrogates. In India a spotted rabbit can take the place of the antelope in playing the part of what we call "the man in the moon". This interpretation is common, not only in India, but also in China, and is repeatedly found in the ancient Mexican codices (Seler, *op. cit.*). In the spread of the ideas we have just been considering from Babylonia towards the north we find that the deer takes the place of the antelope.

In view of the close resemblance between the Indian god Soma and the Phrygian Dionysus, which has been demonstrated by Miss Gladys Davis, it is of interest to note that in the service of the Greek god a man was disguised as a stag, slain and eaten.[1]

Artemis also, one of the many *avatars* of the Great Mother, who was also related to the moon, was closely associated with the deer.

I have already referred to the fact that in Africa the dragon rôle of the female antelope may be assumed by the cow or buffalo. In the case of the gods Soma and Dionysus their association with the antelope or deer may be extended to the bull. Miss Davis (*op. cit.*) states that in the Homa Yasht the deer-headed lunar mansion over which the god presides is spoken of as "leading the Paurvas," i.e. Pleiades : " Mazda brought to thee (Homa) the star-studded spirit-fashioned girdle (the belt of Orion) leading the Paurvas. Now the Bull-Dionysus

[1] A. B. Cook, " Zeus," vol. i., p. 674.

was especially associated with the Pleiades on ancient gems and in classical mythology—which form part of the sign Taurus." The bull is a sign of Haoma (Homa) or Soma. The belt of the thunder-god Thor corroborates the fact of the diffusion of these Babylonian ideas as far as Northern Europe.

THE RAM.

The close association of the ram with the thunder-god is probably related with the fact that the sun-god Amon in Egypt was represented by the ram with a distinctive spiral horn. This spiral became a distinctive feature of the god of thunder throughout the Hellenic and Phœnician worlds and in those parts of Africa which were affected by their influence or directly by Egypt.

An account of the widespread influence of the ram-headed god of thunder in the Soudan and West Africa has been given by Frobenius.[1]

But the ram also became associated with Agni, the Indian fire-god, and the spiral as a head-appendage became the symbol of thunder throughout China and Japan, and from Asia spread to America where such deities as Tlaloc still retain this distinctive token of their origin from the Old World.

In Europe this association of the ram and its spiral horn played an even more obtrusive part.

The octopus as a surrogate of the Great Mother was primarily responsible for the development of the life-giving attributes of the spiral motif. But the close connexion of the Great Mother with the dragon and the thunder-weapon prepared the way for the special association of the spiral with thunder, which was confirmed when the ram with its spiral horn became the God of Thunder.

THE PIG.

The relationship of the pig to the dragon is on the whole analogous to that of the cow and the stag, for it can play either a beneficent or a malevolent part. But the nature of the special circumstances which gave the pig a peculiar notoriety as an unclean animal are so intimately associated with the "Birth of Aphrodite" that I shall defer the discussion of them for my lecture on the history of the goddess.

[1] *Op. cit.*, vol. i., pp. 212-27.

DRAGONS AND RAIN GODS

Certain Incidents in the Dragon Myth.

Throughout the greater part of the area which tradition has peopled with dragons, iron is regarded as peculiarly lethal to the monsters. This seems to be due to the part played by the "smiths" who forged iron weapons with which Horus overcame Set and his followers,[1] or in the earlier versions of the legend the metal weapons by means of which the people of Upper Egypt secured their historic victory over the Lower Egyptians. But the association of meteoric iron with the thunderbolt, the traditional weapon for destroying dragons, gave added force to the ancient legend and made it peculiarly apt as an incident in the story.

But though the dragon is afraid of iron, he likes precious gems and *k'ung-ts'ing* ("The Stone of Darkness") and is fond of roasted swallows.

The partiality of dragons for swallows was due to the transmission of a very ancient story of the Great Mother, who in the form of Isis was identified with the swallow. In China, so ravenous is the monster for this delicacy, that anyone who has eaten of swallows should avoid crossing the water, lest the dragon whose home is in the deep should devour the traveller to secure the dainty morsel of swallow. But those who pray for rain use swallows to attract the beneficent deity. Even in England swallows flying low are believed to be omens of coming rain —a tale which is about as reliable as the Chinese variant of the same ancient legend.

"The beautiful gems remind us of the Indian dragons; the pearls of the sea were, of course, in India as well as China and Japan, considered to be in the special possession of the dragon-shaped sea-gods" (de Visser, p. 69). The cultural drift from West to East along the southern coast of India was effected mainly by sailors who were searching for pearls. Sharks constituted the special dangers the divers had to incur in exploiting pearl-beds to obtain the precious "giver of life". But at the time these great enterprises were first undertaken in the Indian Ocean the people dwelling in the neighbourhood of the chief pearl-beds regarded the sea as the great source of all life-giving virtues and the god who exercised these powers was incarnated in a fish. The sharks therefore had to be brought into harmony with this scheme, and

[1] Budge, "Gods of the Egyptians," vol. i., p. 476.

they were rationalized as the guardians of the storehouse of life-giving pearls at the bottom of the sea.

I do not propose to discuss at present the diffusion to the East of the beliefs concerning the shark and the modifications which they underwent in the course of these migrations in Melanesia and elsewhere; but in my lecture upon "the Birth of Aphrodite" I shall have occasion to refer to its spread to the West and explain how the shark's rôle was transferred to the dog-fish in the Mediterranean. The dog-fish then assumed a terrestrial form and became simply the dog who plays such a strange part in the magical ceremony of digging up the mandrake.

At present we are concerned merely with the shark as the guardian of the stores of pearls at the bottom of the sea. He became identified with the Nâga and the dragon, and the store of pearls became a vast treasure-house which it became one of the chief functions of the dragon to guard. This episode in the wonder-beast's varied career has a place in most of the legends ranging from Western Europe to Farthest Asia. Sometimes the dragon carries a pearl under his tongue or in his chin as a reserve of life-giving substance.

Mr. Donald Mackenzie has called attention[1] to the remarkable influence upon the development of the Dragon Myth of the familiar Egyptian representation of the child Horus with a finger touching his lips. On some pretence or other, many of the European dragon-slaying heroes, such as Sigurd and the Highland Finn, place their fingers in their mouths. This action is usually rationalized by the statement that the hero burnt his fingers while cooking the slain monster.

The Ethical Aspect.

So far in this discussion I have been dealing mainly with the problems of the dragon's evolution, the attainment of his or her distinctive anatomical features and physiological attributes. But during this process of development a moral and ethical aspect of the dragon's character was also emerging.

Now that we have realized the fact of the dragon's homology with the moon-god it is important to remember that one of the primary functions of this deity, which later became specialized in the Egyptian

[1] "Egyptian Myth and Legend," pp. 340 *et seq.*

FIG. 16.—THE GOD OF THUNDER
(From a Chinese drawing (? 17th Century) in the John Rylands Library)

Fig. 17.—From Joannes de Turrecremata's "Meditationes seu Contemplationes". *Rome: Ulrich Han*, 1467

god Thoth, was the measuring of time and the keeping of records. The moon, in fact, was the controller of accuracy, of truth, and order, and therefore the enemy of falsehood and chaos. The identification of the moon with Osiris, who from a dead king eventually developed into a king of the dead, conferred upon the great Father of Waters the power to exact from men respect for truth and order. For even if at first these ideas were only vaguely adumbrated and not expressed in set phrases, it must have been an incentive to good discipline when men remembered that the record-keeper and the guardian of law and order was also the deity upon whose tender mercies they would have to rely in the life after death. Set, the enemy of Osiris, who is the real prototype of the evil dragon, was the antithesis of the god of justice : he was the father of falsehood and the symbol of chaos. He was the prototype of Satan, as Osiris was the first definite representative of the Deity of which any record has been preserved.

The history of the evil dragon is not merely the evolution of the devil, but it also affords the explanation of his traditional peculiarities, his bird-like features, his horns, his red colour, his wings and cloven hoofs, and his tail. They are all of them the dragon's distinctive features ; and from time to time in the history of past ages we catch glimpses of the reality of these identifications. In one of the earliest woodcuts (Pl. VI.) found in a printed book Satan is depicted as a monk with the bird's feet of the dragon. A most interesting intermediate phase is seen in a Chinese water-colour in the John Rylands Library, in which the thunder-dragon is represented in a form almost exactly reproducing that of the devil of European tradition (Pl. VII.).

Early in the Christian era, when ancient beliefs in Egypt became disguised under a thin veneer of Christianity, the story of the conflict between Horus and Set was converted into a conflict between Christ and Satan. M. Clermont-Ganneau has described an interesting bas-relief in the Louvre in which a hawk-headed St. George, clad in Roman military uniform and mounted on a horse, is slaying a dragon which is represented by Set's crocodile. But the Biblical references to Satan leave no doubt as to his identity with the dragon, who is

---

[1] " Horus et St. George d'après un bas-relief inedit du Louvre," *Revue Archéologique*, Nouvelle Série, t. xxxii., 1876, p. 196, pl. xviii. It is right to explain that M. Clermont-Ganneau's interpretation of this relief has not been accepted by all scholars.

specifically mentioned in the Book of Revelations as "the old serpent, which is the Devil and Satan" (xx. 2).

The devil Set was symbolic of disorder and darkness, while the god Osiris was the maintainer of order and the giver of light. Although the moon-god, in the form of Osiris, Thoth and other deities, thus came to acquire the moral attributes of a just judge, who regulated the movements of the celestial bodies, controlled the waters upon the earth, and was responsible for the maintenance of order in the Universe, the ethical aspect of his functions was in large measure disguised by the material importance of his duties. In Babylonia similar views were held with respect to the beneficent water-god Ea, who was the giver of civilization, order and justice, and Sin, the moon-god, who "had attained a high position in the Babylonian pantheon," as "the guide of the stars and the planets, the overseer of the world at night". "From that conception a god of high moral character soon developed." "He is an extremely beneficent deity, he is a king, he is the ruler of men, he produces order and stability, like Shamash and like the Indian Varuna and Mitra, but besides that, he is also a judge, he loosens the bonds of the imprisoned, like Varuna. His light, like that of Varuna, is the symbol of righteousness. . . . Like the Indian Varuna and the Iranian Mazdâh, he is a god of wisdom."

When these Egyptian and Babylonian ideas were borrowed by the Aryans, and the Iranian Mazdâh and the Indian Varuna assumed the rôle of the beneficent deity of the former more ancient civilizations, the material aspect of the functions of the moon-god became less obtrusive; and there gradually emerged the conception, to which Zarathushtra first gave concrete expression, of the beneficent god Ahura Mazdâh as "an omniscient protector of morality and creator of marvellous power and knowledge". "He is the most-knowing one, and the most-seeing one. No one can deceive him. He watches with radiant eyes everything that is done in open or in secret." "Although he has a strong personality he has no anthropomorphic features." He has shed the material aspects which loomed so large in his Egyptian, Babylonian and earlier Aryan prototypes, and a more ethereal conception of a God of the highest ethical qualities has emerged.

The whole of this process of transformation has been described with deep insight and lucid exposition by Professor Cumont, from whose important and convincing memoir I have quoted so freely in the foregoing paragraphs.[1]

The creation of a beneficent Deity of such moral grandeur inevitably emphasized the baseness and the malevolence of the "Power of Evil". No longer are the gods merely glorified human beings who can work good or evil as they will; but there is now an all-powerful God controlling the morals of the universe, and in opposition to Him "the dragon, the old serpent, which is the Devil and Satan".

[1] Albert J. Carnoy, "The Moral Deities of Iran and India and their Origins," *The American Journal of Theology*, vol. xxi., No. 1, Jan. 1917, p. 58.

Chapter III.

THE BIRTH OF APHRODITE.[1]

IT may seem ungallant to discuss the birth of Aphrodite as part of the story of the evolution of the dragon. But the other chapters of this book, in which frequent references have been made to the early history of the Great Mother, have revealed how vital a part she played in the development of the dragon. The earliest real dragon was Tiamat, one of the forms assumed by the Great Mother; and an even earlier prototype was the lioness (Sekhet) manifestation of Hathor.

Thus it becomes necessary to enquire more fully (than has been done in the other chapters) into the circumstances of the Great Mother's birth and development, and to investigate certain aspects of her ontogeny to which only scant attention has been paid in the preceding pages.

Several reasons have led me to select Aphrodite from the vast legion of Great Mothers for special consideration. In spite of her high specialization in certain directions the Greek goddess of love retains in greater measure than any of her sisters some of the most primitive associations of her original parent. Like vestigial structures in biology, these traits afford invaluable evidence, not only of Aphrodite's own ancestry and early history, but also of that of the whole family of goddesses of which she is only a specialized type. For Aphrodite's connexion with shells is a survival of the circumstances which called into existence the first Great Mother and made her not only the Creator of mankind and the universe, but also the parent of all deities, as she was historically the first to be created by human inventiveness. In this lecture I propose to deal with the more general aspects of the evolution of all these daughters of the Great Mother:

[1] An elaboration of a lecture delivered at the John Rylands Library, on 14 November, 1917.

THE BIRTH OF APHRODITE 141

but I have used Aphrodite's name in the title because her shell-associations can be demonstrated more clearly and definitely than those of any of her sisters.

In the past a vast array of learning has been brought to bear upon the problems of Aphrodite's origin; but this effort has, for the most part, been characterized by a narrowness of vision and a lack of adequate appreciation of the more vital factors in her embryological history. In the search for the deep human motives that found specific expression in the great goddess of love, too little attention has been paid to primitive man's psychology, and his persistent striving for an elixir of life to avert the risk of death, to renew youth and secure a continuance of existence after death. On the other hand, the possibility of obtaining any real explanation has been dashed aside by most scholars, who have been content simply to juggle with certain stereotyped catch-phrases and baseless assumptions, simply because the traditions of classical scholarship have made these devices the pawns in a rather aimless game.

It is unnecessary to cite specific illustrations in support of this statement. Reference to any of the standard works on classical archæology, such as Roscher's "Lexikon," will testify to the truth of my accusation. In her "Prolegomena to the Study of Greek Religion" Miss Jane Harrison devotes a chapter (VI) to "The Making of a Goddess," and discusses "The Birth of Aphrodite". But she strictly observes the traditions of the classical method; and assumes that the meaning of the myth of Aphrodite's birth from the sea—the germs of which are at least fifty centuries old—can be decided by the omission of any representation of the sea in the decoration of a pot made in the fifth century B.C.!

But apart from this general criticism, the lack of resourcefulness and open mindedness, certain more specific factors have deflected classical scholars from the true path. In the search for the ancestry of Aphrodite, they have concentrated their attention too exclusively upon the Mediterranean area and Western Asia, and so ignored the most ancient of the historic Great Mothers, the African Hathor, with whom (as Sir Arthur Evans[1] clearly demonstrated more than fifteen years ago) the Cypriote goddess has much closer affinities than with

---

[1] "Mycenæan Tree and Pillar Cult," p. 52. Compare also A. E. W. Budge, "The Gods of the Egyptians," Vol. I, p. 435.

any of her Asiatic sisters. Yet no scholar, either on the Greek or Egyptian side, has seriously attempted to follow up this clue and really investigate the nature of the connexions between Aphrodite and Hathor, and the history of the development of their respective specializations of functions.[1]

But some explanation must be given for my temerity in venturing to invade the intensively cultivated domains of Aphrodite " with a mind undebauched by classical learning ". I have already explained how the study of Libations and Dragons brought me face to face with the problems of the Great Mother's attributes. At that stage of the enquiry two circumstances directed my attention specifically to Aphrodite. Mr. Wilfrid Jackson was collecting the data relating to the cultural uses of shells, which he has since incorporated in a book.[2] As the results of his search accumulated, the fact soon emerged that

[1] With a strange disregard of Sir Arthur Evans's " Mycenæan Tree and Pillar Cult," Mr. H. R. Hall makes the following remarks in his " Ægean Archæology " (p. 150) : " The origin of the goddess Aphrodite has long been taken for granted. It has been regarded as a settled fact that she was Semitic, and came to Greece from Phœnicia or Cyprus. But the new discoveries have thrown this, like other received ideas, into the melting-pot, for the Minoans undoubtedly worshipped an Aphrodite. We see her, naked and with her doves, on gold plaques from one of the Mycenæan shaft-graves (Schuchhardt, *Schliemann*, Figs. 180, 181), which must be as old as the First Late Minoan period (*c.* 1600-1500 B.C.), and—not rising from the foam, but sailing over it—in a boat, naked, on the lost gold ring from Mochlos. It is evident now that she was not only a Canaanitish-Syrian goddess, but was common to all the people of the Levant. She is Aphrodite-Paphia in Cyprus, Ashtaroth-Astarte in Canaan, Atargatis in Syria, Derketo in Philistria, Hathor in Egypt ; what the Minoans called her we do not know, unless she was Britomartis. She must take her place by the side of Rhea-Diktynna in the Minoan pantheon."

It is not without interest to note that on the Mochlos ring the goddess is sailing in a papyrus float of Egyptian type, like the moon-goddess in her crescent moon.

The association of this early representative of Aphrodite with doves is of special interest in view of Highnard's attempt (" Le Mythe de Venus," *Annales du Musée Guimet*, T. 1, 1880, p. 23) to derive the name of " la déesse à la colombe " from the Chaldean and Phœnician *phrit* or *phrut* meaning " a dove ".

Mr. Hall might have extended his list of homologues to Mesopotamia, Iran, and India, to Europe and Further Asia, to America, and, in fact, every part of the world that harbours goddesses.

[2] " Shells as Evidence of the Migration of Early Culture."

THE BIRTH OF APHRODITE

the original Great Mother was nothing more than a cowry-shell used as a life-giving amulet ; and that Aphrodite's shell-associations were a survival of the earliest phase in the Great Mother's history. At this psychological moment Dr. Rendel Harris[1] claimed that Aphrodite was a personification of the mandrake. But the magical attributes of the mandrake, which he claimed to have been responsible for converting the amulet into a goddess, were identical with those which Jackson's investigations had previously led me to regard as the reasons for deriving Aphrodite from the cowry. The mandrake was clearly a surrogate of the shell or vice versa.[2] The problem to be solved was to decide which amulet was responsible for suggesting the process of life-giving. The goddess Aphrodite was closely related to Cyprus ; the mandrake was a magical plant there ; and the cowry is so intimately associated with the island as to be called *Cypræa*. So far as is known, however, the shell-amulet is vastly more ancient than the magical reputation of the plant. Moreover, we know why the cowry was regarded as feminine and accredited with life-giving attributes. There are no such reasons for assigning life-giving powers or the female sex to the mandrake. The claim that its magical properties are due to the fancied resemblance of its root to a human being is wholly untenable.[3] The roots of many plants are at least as manlike ; and, even if this character was the exclusive property of the mandrake, how does it help to explain the remarkable repetory of quite arbitrary and fantastic properties and the female sex assigned to the plant ? Sir James Frazer's claim[4] that " such beliefs and practices illustrate the primitive tendency to personify nature " is a gratuitous and quite irrelevant assumption, which offers no explanation whatsoever of the specific and arbitrary nature of the form assumed by the personification. But when we investigate the historical development of the peculiar

---

[1] " The Ascent of Olympus."

[2] A striking confirmation of the fact that the mandrake is really a surrogate of the cowry is afforded by the practice in modern Greece of using the mandrake carried in a leather bag in the same way (and for the same magical purpose as a love philtre) as the Baganda of East Africa use the cowry (in a leather bag) at the present time.

[3] Old Gerade was frank enough to admit that he " never could perceive shape of man or woman " (quoted by Rendel Harris, *op. cit.*, p. 110).

[4] " Jacob and the Mandrakes," *Proceedings of the British Academy*, Vol. VIII, p. 22.

attributes of the cowry-shell, and appreciate why and how they were acquired, any doubt as to the source from which the mandrake obtained its "magic" is removed; and with it the fallacy of Sir James Frazer's wholly unwarranted claims is also exposed.

If we ignore Sir James Frazer's naïve speculations we can make use of the compilations of evidence which he makes with such remarkable assiduity. But it is more profitable to turn to the study of the remarkable lectures which Dr. Rendel Harris has been delivering in this room[1] during the last few years. Our genial friend has been cultivating his garden on the slopes of Olympus,[2] and has been plucking the rich fruits of his ripe scholarship and nimble wit. At the same time, with rougher implements and cruder methods, I have been burrowing in the depths of the earth, trying to recover information concerning the habits and thoughts of mankind many centuries before Dionysus and Apollo, and Artemis and Aphrodite, were dreamt of.

In the course of these subterranean gropings no one was more surprised than I was to discover that I was getting entangled in the roots of the same plants whose golden fruit Dr. Rendel Harris was gathering from his Olympian heights. But the contrast in our respective points of view was perhaps responsible for the different appearance the growths assumed.

To drop the metaphor, while he was searching for the origins of the deities a few centuries before the Christian era began, I was finding their more or less larval forms flourishing more than twenty centuries before the commencement of his story. For the gods and goddesses of his narrative were only the thinly disguised representatives of much more ancient deities decked out in the sumptuous habiliments of Greek culture.

In his lecture on Aphrodite, Dr. Rendel Harris claimed that the goddess was a personification of the mandrake; and I think he made out a good prima facie case in support of his thesis. But other scholars have set forth equally valid reasons for associating Aphrodite with the argonaut, the octopus, the purpura, and a variety of other shells, both univalves and bivalves.[3]

The goddess has also been regarded as a personification of water,

---

[1] The John Rylands Library. [2] "The Ascent of Olympus."
[3] See the memoirs by Tümpel, Jahn, Houssay, and Jackson, to which reference is made elsewhere in these pages.

THE BIRTH OF APHRODITE

the ocean, or its foam.[1] Then again she is closely linked with pigs, cows, lions, deer, goats, rams, dolphins, and a host of other creatures, not forgetting the dove, the swallow, the partridge, the sparling, the goose, and the swan.[2]

The mandrake theory does not explain, or give adequate recognition to, any of these facts. Nor does Dr. Rendel Harris suggest why it is so dangerous an operation to dig up the mandrake which he identifies with the goddess, or why it is essential to secure the assistance of a dog[3] in the process. The explanation of this fantastic fable gives an important clue to Aphrodite's antecedents.

THE SEARCH FOR THE ELIXIR OF LIFE. BLOOD AS LIFE.

In delving into the remotely distant history of our species we cannot fail to be impressed with the persistence with which, throughout the whole of his career, man (of the species *sapiens*) has been seeking[4] for an elixir of life, to give added "vitality" to the dead (whose existence was not consciously regarded as ended), to prolong the days of active life to the living, to restore youth, and to protect his own life from all assaults, not merely of time, but also of circumstance. In other words, the elixir he sought was something that would bring "good luck" in all the events of his life and its continuation. Most of the amulets, even of modern times, the lucky trinkets, the averters of the "Evil Eye," the practices and devices for securing good luck in love and sport, in curing bodily ills or mental distress, in attaining material prosperity, or a continuation of existence after death, are survivals of this ancient and persistent striving after those objects which our earliest forefathers called collectively the "givers of life".

From statements in the earliest literature[5] that has come down to us from antiquity, no less than from the views that still prevail among

---

[1] The well-known circumstantial story told in Hesiod's theogony.

[2] See the article "Aphrodite" in Roscher's "Lexikon".

[3] Sir James Frazer's claim that the incident of the ass in a late Jewish story of Jacob and the mandrakes (*op. cit.*, p. 20) "helps us to understand the function of the dog," is quite unsupported. The learned guardian of the Golden Bough does not explain *how* it helps us to understand.

[4] In response to the prompting of the most fundamental of all instincts, that of the preservation of life.

[5] See Alan Gardiner, *Journal of Egyptian Archæology*, Vol. IV, Parts II-III, April-July, 1917, p. 205. Compare also the Babylonian story of Gilgamesh.

the relatively more primitive peoples of the present day, it is clear that originally man did not consciously formulate a belief in immortality.

It was rather the result of a defect of thinking, or as the modern psychologist would express it, an instinctive repression of the unpleasant idea that death would come to him personally, that primitive man refused to contemplate or to entertain the possibility of life coming to an end. So intense was his instinctive love of life and dread of such physical damage as would destroy his body that man unconsciously avoided thinking of the chance of his own death : hence his belief in the continuance of life cannot be regarded as the outcome of an active process of constructive thought.

This may seem altogether paradoxical and incredible.

How, it may be asked, can man be said to repress the idea of death, if he instinctively refused to admit its possibility ? How did he escape the inevitable process of applying to himself the analogy he might have been supposed to make from other men's experience and recognize that he must die ?

Man appreciated the fact that he could kill an animal or another man by inflicting certain physical injuries on him. But at first he seems to have believed that if he could avoid such direct assaults upon himself, his life would flow on unchecked. When death does occur and the onlookers recognize the reality, it is still the practice among certain relatively primitive people to search for the man who has inflicted death on his fellow.

It would, of course, be absurd to pretend that any people could fail to recognize the reality of death in the great majority of cases. The mere fact of burial is an indication of this. But the point of difference between the views of these early men and ourselves, was the tacit assumption on the part of the former, that in spite of the obvious changes in his body (which made inhumation or some other procedure necessary) the deceased was still continuing an existence not unlike that which he enjoyed previously, only somewhat duller, less eventful and more precarious. He still needed food and drink, as he did before, and all the paraphernalia of his mortal life, but he was dependent upon his relatives for the maintenance of his existence.

Such views were difficult of acceptance by a thoughtful people, once they appreciated the fact of the disintegration of the corpse in the grave ; and in course of time it was regarded as essential for continued

THE BIRTH OF APHRODITE 147

existence that the body should be preserved. The idea developed, that so long as the body of the deceased was preserved and there were restored to it all the elements of vitality which it had lost at death, the continuance of existence was theoretically possible and worthy of acceptance as an article of faith.

Let us consider for a moment what were considered to be elements of vitality by the earliest members of our species.[1]

From the remotest times man seems to have been aware of the fact that he could kill animals or his fellow men by means of certain physical injuries. He associated these results with the effusion of blood. The loss of blood could cause unconsciousness and death. Blood, therefore, must be the vehicle of consciousness and life, the material whose escape from the body could bring life to an end.[2]

The first pictures painted by man, with which we are at present acquainted, are found upon the walls and roofs of certain caves in Southern France and Spain. They were the work of the earliest known representatives of our own species, *Homo sapiens*, in the phase of culture now distinguished by the name " Aurignacian ".

The animals man was in the habit of hunting for food are depicted.[3] In some of them arrows are shown implanted in the animal's flank near the region of the heart ; and in others the heart itself is represented.

This implies that at this distant time in the history of our species, it was already realized how vital a spot in the animal's anatomy the heart was. But even long before man began to speculate about the functions of the heart, he must have learned to associate the loss of blood on the part of man or animals with death, and to regard the pouring out of blood as the escape of its vitality. Many factors must have contributed to the new advance in physiology which made the heart the centre or the chief habitation of vitality, volition, feeling, and knowledge.

Not merely the empirical fact, acquired by experience in hunting, of the peculiarly vulnerable nature of the heart, but perhaps also the knowledge that the heart contained life-giving blood, helped in

[1] Some of these have been discussed in Chapter I (" Incense and Libations ") and will not be further considered here.
[2] " The life which is the blood thereof " (Gen. ix. 4).
[3] See, for example, Sollas, " Ancient Hunters," 2nd Edition, 1915, pp. 326 (fig. 163), 333 (fig. 171), and 36 (fig. 189).

developing the ideas about its functions as the bestower of life and consciousness.

The palpitation of the heart after severe exertion or under the influence of intense emotion would impress the early physiologist with the relationship of the heart to the feelings, and afford confirmation of his earlier ideas of its functions.

But whatever the explanation, it is known from the folk-lore of even the most unsophisticated peoples that the heart was originally regarded as the seat of life, feeling, volition, and knowledge, and that the blood was the life-stream. The Aurignacian pictures in the caves of Western Europe suggest that these beliefs were extremely ancient.

The evidence at our disposal seems to indicate that not only were such ideas of physiology current in Aurignacian times, but also certain cultural applications of them had been inaugurated even then. The remarkable method of blood-letting by chopping off part of a finger seems to have been practised even in Aurignacian times.[1]

If it is legitimate to attempt to guess at the meaning these early people attached to so singular a procedure, we may be guided by the ideas associated with this act in outlying corners of the world at the present time. On these grounds we may surmise that the motive underlying this, and other later methods of blood-letting, such as circumcision, piercing the ears, lips, and tongue, gashing the limbs and body, et cetera, was the offering of the life-giving fluid.

Once it was recognized that the state of unconsciousness or death was due to the loss of blood it was a not illogical or irrational procedure to imagine that offerings of blood might restore consciousness and life to the dead.[2] If the blood was seriously believed to be the vehicle of feeling and knowledge, the exchange of blood or the offering of blood to the community was a reasonable method for initiating anyone into the wider knowledge of and sympathy with his fellow-men.

Blood-letting, therefore, played a part in a great variety of ceremonies, of burial and of initiation, and also those of a therapeutic[3] and, later, of a religious significance.

---

[1] Sollas, *op. cit.*, pp. 347 *et seq.*

[2] The "redeeming blood," Φαρμακον ἀθανασίας.

[3] The practice of blood-letting for therapeutic purposes was probably first suggested by a confused rationalization. The act of blood-letting was a means of healing; and the victim himself supplied the vitalizing fluid!

THE BIRTH OF APHRODITE

But from Aurignacian times onwards, it seems to have been admitted that substitutes for blood might be endowed with a similar potency.

The extensive use of red ochre or other red materials for packing around the bodies of the dead was presumably inspired by the idea that materials simulating blood-stained earth, were endowed with the same life-giving properties as actual blood poured out upon the ground in similar vitalizing ceremonies.

As the shedding of blood produced unconsciousness, the offering of blood or red ochre was, therefore, a logical and practical means of restoring consciousness and reinforcing the element of vitality which was diminished or lost in the corpse.

The common statement that primitive man was a fantastically irrational child is based upon a fallacy. He was probably as well endowed mentally as his modern successors; and was as logical and rational as they are; but many of his premises were wrong, and he hadn't the necessary body of accumulated wisdom to help him to correct his false assumptions.

If primitive man regarded the dead as still existing, but with a reduced vitality, it was a not irrational procedure on the part of the people of the Reindeer Epoch in Europe to pack the dead in red ochre (which they regarded as a surrogate of the life-giving fluid) to make good the lack of vitality in the corpse.

If blood was the vehicle of consciousness and knowledge, the exchange of blood was clearly a logical procedure for establishing communion of thought and feeling and so enabling an initiate to assimilate the traditions of his people.

If red carnelian was a surrogate of blood the wearing of bracelets or necklaces of this life-giving material was a proper means of warding off danger to life and of securing good luck.

If red paint or the colour red brought these magical results, it was clearly justifiable to resort to its use.

All these procedures are logical. It is only the premises that were erroneous.

The persistence of such customs in Ancient Egypt makes it possible for us to obtain literary evidence to support the inferences drawn from archæological data of a more remote age. For instance, the red jasper amulet sometimes called the " girdle-tie of Isis," was supposed to represent the blood of the goddess and was applied to the mummy " to stimulate the functions of his blood " ;[1] or perhaps it would be more accurate to say that it was intended to add to the vital substance, which was so obviously lacking in the corpse.

The Cowry as a Giver of Life.

Blood and its substitutes, however, were not the only materials that had acquired a reputation for vitalizing qualities in the Reindeer Epoch. For there is a good deal of evidence to suggest that shells also were regarded, even in that remote time, as life-giving amulets.

If the loss of blood was at first the only recognized cause of death, the act of birth was clearly the only process of life-giving. The portal by which a child entered the world was regarded, therefore, not only as the channel of birth, but also as the actual giver of life.[2] The large Red Sea cowry-shell, which closely simulates this " giver of life," then came to be endowed by popular imagination with the same powers. Hence the shell was used in the same way as red ochre or carnelian: it was placed in the grave to confer vitality on the dead, and worn on bracelets and necklaces to secure good luck by using the " giver of life " to avert the risk of danger to life. Thus the general life-giving properties of blood, blood substitutes, and shells, came to be assimilated the one with the other.[3]

At first it was probably its more general power of averting death or giving vitality to the dead that played the more obtrusive part in the magical use of the shell. But the circumstances which led to the

---

[1] Davies and Gardiner, " The Tomb of Amenemhet," p. 112.

[2] As it is still called in the Semitic languages. In the Egyptian Pyramid Texts there is a reference to a new being formed " by the vulva of Tefnut " (Breasted).

[3] Many customs and beliefs of primitive peoples suggest that this correlation of the attributes of blood and shells went much deeper than the similarity of their use in burial ceremonies and for making necklaces and bracelets. The fact that the monthly effusion of blood in women ceased during pregnancy seems to have given rise to the theory, that the new life of the child was actually formed from the blood thus retained. The beliefs that grew up in explanation of the placenta form part of the system of interpretation of these phenomena: for the placenta was regarded as a mass of clotted blood (intimately related to the child which was supposed to be derived from part of the same material) which harboured certain elements of the child's mentality (because blood was the substance of consciousness).

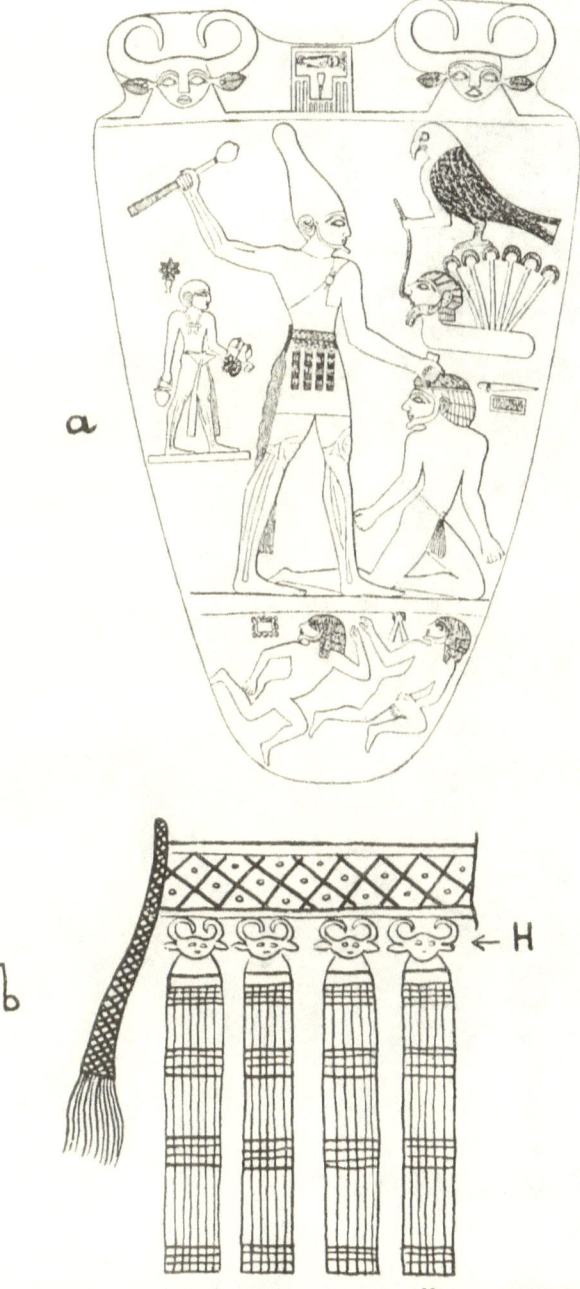

Fig. 18.—(a) The Archaic Egyptian slate palette of Narmer showing, perhaps, the earliest design of Hathor (at the upper corners of the palette) as a woman with cow's horns and ears (compare Flinders Petrie, "The Royal Tombs of the First Dynasty," Part I, 1900, Plate XXVII, Fig. 71). The Pharaoh is wearing a belt from which are suspended four cow-headed Hathor figures in place of the cowry-amulets of more primitive peoples. This affords corroboration of the view that Hathor assumed the functions originally attributed to the cowry-shell.
(b) The king's *sporran*, where Hathor-heads (H) take the place of the cowries of the primitive girdle.

Fig. 19.—The front of Stela B (famous for the realistic representations of the Indian elephant at its upper corners), one of the ancient Maya monuments at Copan, Central America (after Maudslay's photograph and diagram).

The girdle of the chief figure is decorated both with shells (*Oliva* or *Conus*) and amulets representing human faces corresponding to the Hathor-heads on the Narmer palette (Fig. 18).

THE BIRTH OF APHRODITE

development of the shell's symbolism naturally and inevitably conferred upon the cowry special power over women. It was the surrogate of the life-giving organ. It became an amulet to increase the fertility of women and to help them in childbirth. It was, therefore, worn by girls suspended from a girdle, so as to be as near as possible to the organ it was supposed to simulate and whose potency it was believed to be able to reinforce and intensify. Just as bracelets and necklaces of carnelian were used to confer on either sex the vitalizing virtues of blood, which it was supposed to simulate, so also cowries, or imitations of them made of metal or stone, were worn as bracelets, necklaces, or hair-ornaments, to confer health and good luck in both sexes. But these ideas received a much further extension.

As the giver of life, the cowry came to have attributed to it by some people definite powers of creation. It was not merely an amulet to increase fertility: it was itself the actual parent of mankind, the creator of all living things; and the next step was to give these maternal functions material expression, and personify the cowry as an actual woman in the form of a statuette with the distinctly feminine characters grossly exaggerated;[1] and in the domain of belief to create the image of a Great Mother, who was the parent of the universe.

Thus gradually there developed out of the cowry-amulet the conception of a creator, the giver of life, health, and good luck. This Great Mother, at first with only vaguely defined traits, was probably the first deity that the wit of man devised to console him with her watchful care over his welfare in this life and to give him assurance as to his fate in the future.

At this stage I should like to emphasize the fact that these beliefs had taken shape long before any definite ideas had been formulated as to the physiology of animal reproduction and before agriculture was practised.

Man had not yet come to appreciate the importance of vegetable fertility, nor had he yet begun to frame theories of the fertilizing powers of water, or give specific expression to them by creating the god Osiris in his own image.

Nor had he begun to take anything more than the most casual

---

[1] See S. Reinach, "Les Déesses Nues dans l'Art Oriental et dans l'Art Grec," *Revue Archéol.*, T. XXVI, 1895, p. 367. Compare also the figurines of the so-called Upper Palæolithic Period in Europe.

interest in the sun, the moon, and the stars. He had not yet devised a sky-world nor created a heaven. When, for reasons that I have already discussed,[1] the theory of the fertilizing and the animating power of water was formulated, the beliefs concerning this element were assimilated with those which many ages previously had grown up in explanation of the potency of blood and shells. In addition to fertilizing the earth, water could also animate the dead. The rivers and the seas were in fact a vast reservoir of this animating substance. The powers of the cowry, as a product of the sea, were rationalized into an expression of the great creative force of the water.

A bowl of water became the symbol of the fruitfulness of woman. Such symbolism implied that woman, or her uterus, was a receptacle into which the seminal fluid was poured and from which a new being emerged in a flood of amniotic fluid.

The burial of shells with the dead is an extremely ancient practice, for cowries have been found upon human skeletons of the so-called "Upper Palæolithic Age" of Southern Europe.

At Laugerie-Basse (Dordogne) Mediterranean cowries were found arranged in pairs upon the body ; two pairs on the forehead, one near each arm, four in the region of the thighs and knees, and two upon each foot. Others were found in the Mentone caves, and are peculiarly important, because, upon the same stratum as the skeleton with which they were associated, was found part of a *Cassis rufa*, a shell whose habitat does not extend any nearer than the Indian Ocean.[2]

These facts are very important. In the first place they reveal the great antiquity of the practice of burying shells with the dead, presumably for the purpose of "life-giving". Secondly, they suggest the possibility that their magical value as givers of life may be more ancient than their specific use as intensifiers of the fertility of women. Thirdly, the association of these practices with the use of the shell *Cassis rufa* indicates a very early cultural contact between the people living upon the North-Western shores of the Mediterranean in the Reindeer Age and the dwellers on the coasts of the Indian Ocean ; and the proba-

---

[1] Chapter I.
[2] The literature relating to these important discoveries has been summarized by Wilfrid Jackson in his "Shells as Evidence of the Migrations of Early Culture," pp. 135-7.

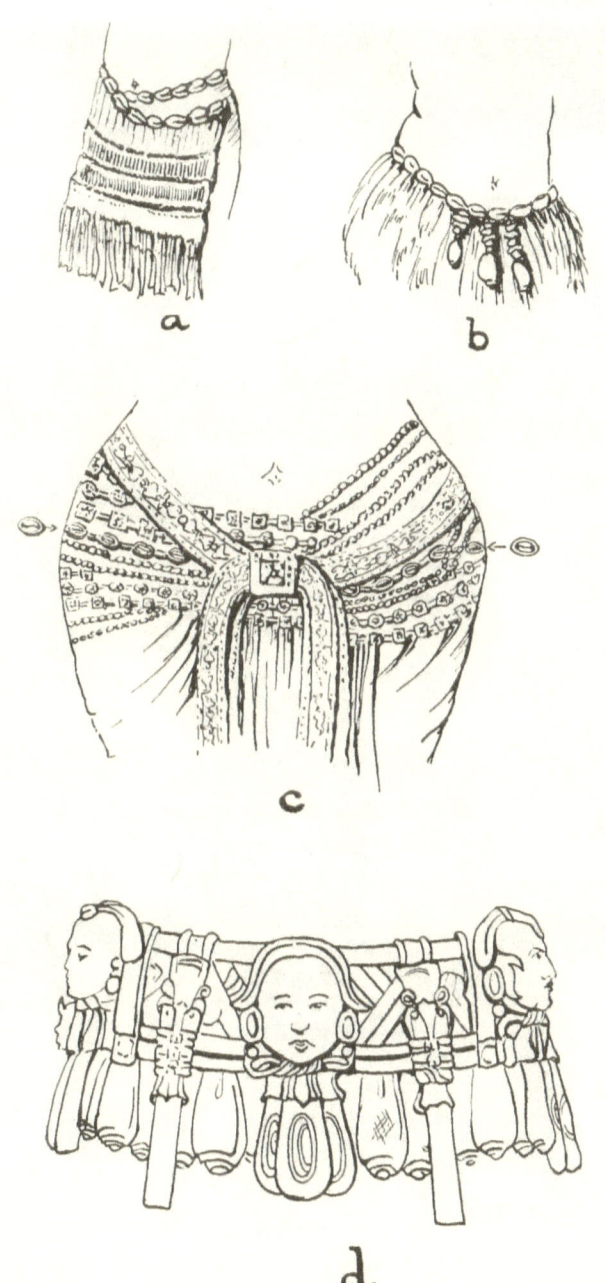

FIG. 20.—DIAGRAMS ILLUSTRATING THE FORM OF COWRY-BELTS WORN IN (*a*) EAST AFRICA AND (*b*) OCEANIA RESPECTIVELY.
(*c*) ANCIENT INDIAN GIRDLE (FROM THE FIGURE OF SIRIMA DEVATA ON THE BHARAT TOPE), CONSISTING OF STRINGS OF PEARLS AND PRECIOUS STONES, AND WHAT SEEM TO BE (FOURTH ROW FROM THE TOP) MODELS OF COWRIES.
(*d*) THE COPAN GIRDLE (FROM FIG. 19) IN WHICH BOTH SHELLS AND HEADS OF DEITIES ARE REPRESENTED. THE TWO OBJECTS SUSPENDED FROM THE BELT BETWEEN THE HEADS RECALL HATHOR'S SISTRA.

THE BIRTH OF APHRODITE 153

bility that these special uses of shells by the former were inspired by the latter.

This hint assumes a special significance when we first get a clear view of the more fully-developed shell-cults of the Eastern Mediterranean many centuries later.[1] For then we find definite indications that the cultural uses of shells were obviously borrowed from the Erythræan area.

Long before the shell-amulet became personified as a woman the Mediterranean people had definitely adopted the belief in the cowry's ability to give life and birth.

The Origin of Clothing.

The cowry and its surrogates were supposed to be potent to confer fertility on maidens; and it became the practice for growing girls to wear a girdle on which to suspend the shells as near as possible to the organ their magic was supposed to stimulate. Among many peoples[2] this girdle was discarded as soon as the girls reached maturity.

This practice probably represents the beginning of the history of clothing; but it had other far-reaching effects in the domain of belief.

It has often been claimed that the feeling of modesty was not the reason for the invention of clothing, but that the clothes begat modesty.[3] This doctrine contains a certain element of truth, but is by no means the whole explanation. For true modesty is displayed by people who have never worn clothes.

Before mankind could appreciate the psychological fact that the wearing of clothing might add to an individual's allurement and enhance her sexual attractiveness, some other circumstances must have been responsible for suggesting the experiments out of which this empirical knowledge emerged. The use of a girdle (*a*) as a protection against danger to life, and (*b*) as a means of conferring fecundity on

---

[1] Cowries were obtained in Neolithic sites at Hissarlik and Spain (Siret, *op. cit.*, p. 18).

[2] See Jackson, *op. cit.*, pp. 139 *et seq.*

[3] For a discussion of this subject see the chapter on "The Psychology of Modesty and Clothing," in William I. Thomas's "Sex and Society," Chicago, 1907; also S. Reinach, "Cults, Myths, and Religions," p. 177; and Paton, "The Pharmakoi and the Story of the Fall," *Revue Archéol.*, Série IV, T. IX, 1907, p. 51.

girls[1] provided the circumstances which enabled men to discover that the sexual attractiveness of maidens, which in a state of nature was originally associated with modesty and coyness, was profoundly intensified by the artifices of clothing and adornment.

Among people (such as those of East Africa and Southern Arabia) in which it was customary for unmarried girls to adorn themselves with a girdle, it is easy to understand how the meaning of the practice underwent a change, and developed into a device for enhancing their charms and stimulating the imaginations of their suitors.

Out of such experience developed the idea of the magical girdle as an allurement and a love-provoking charm or philtre. Thus Aphrodite's girdle acquired the reputation of being able to *compel* love. When Ishtar removed her girdle in the under-world reproduction ceased in the world. The Teutonic Brunhild's great strength lay in her girdle. In fact magic virtues were conferred upon most goddesses in every part of the world by means of a cestus of some sort.[2] But the outstanding

---

[1] It is important to remember that shell-girdles were used by both sexes for general life-giving and luck-bringing purposes, in the funerary ritual of both sexes, in animating the dead or statues of the dead, to attain success in hunting, fishing, and head-hunting, as well as in games. Thus men also at times wore shells upon their belts or aprons, and upon their implements and fishing nets, and adorned their trophies of war and the chase with them. Such customs are found in all the continents of the Old World and also in America, as, for example, in the girdles of *Conus-* and *Oliva*-shells worn by the figures sculptured upon the Copan stelæ. See, for example, Maudslay's pictures of stele N, Plate 82 (Biologia Centrali-Americana; Archæology) *inter alia*. But they were much more widely used by women, not merely by maidens, but also by brides and married women, to heighten their fertility and cure sterility, and by pregnant women to ensure safe delivery in child-birth. It was their wider employment by women that gives these shells their peculiar cultural significance.

[2] Witness the importance of the girdle in early Indian and American sculptures: in the literature of Egypt, Babylonia, Western Europe, and the Mediterranean area. For important Indian analogies and Egyptian parallels see Moret, " Mystères Égyptiens," p. 91, especially note 3. The magic girdle assumed a great variety of forms as the number of surrogates of the cowry increased. The mugwort (Artemisia) of Artemis was worn in the girdle on St. John's Eve (Rendel Harris, *op. cit.*, p. 91): the people of Zante use vervain in the same way; the people of France (Creuse et Corrères) rye-stalks; Eve's fig-leaves; in Vedic India the initiate wore the " cincture of Munga's herbs "; and Kali had her girdle of hands. Breasted, (" Religion and Thought in Ancient Egypt," p. 29) says: " In the oldest fragments we hear of Isis the great, who *fastened on the girdle* in Khemmis, when she brought her [censer] and burned incense before her son Horus ".

feature of Aphrodite's character as a goddess of love is intimately bound up with these conceptions which developed from the wearing of a girdle of cowries.

In the Biblical narrative, after Adam and Eve had eaten the forbidden fruit, " the eyes of them both were opened, and they knew that they were naked ; and they sewed fig leaves together and made themselves aprons," or, as the Revised Version expresses it, " girdles ". The girdle of fig-leaves, however, was originally a surrogate of the

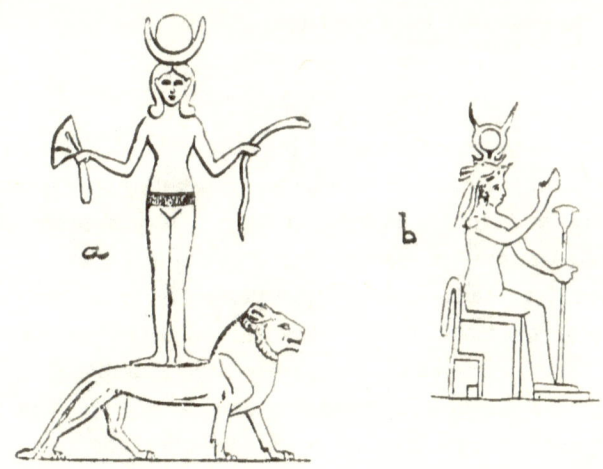

FIG. 4.—TWO REPRESENTATIONS OF ASTARTE (QETESH).

(a) The mother-goddess standing upon a lioness (which is her Sekhet form) : she is wearing her girdle, and upon her head is the moon and the cow's horns, conventionalized so as to simulate the crescent moon. Her hair is represented in the conventional form which is sometimes used as Hathor's symbol. In her hands are the serpent and the lotus, which again are merely forms of the goddess herself.

(b) Another picture of Astarte (from Roscher's " Lexikon ") holding the papyrus sceptre which at times is regarded as an animate form of the mother-goddess herself and as such a thunder weapon.

girdle of cowries : it was an amulet to give fertility. The consciousness of nakedness was part of the knowledge acquired as *the result* of the wearing of such girdles (and the clothing into which they developed), and was not originally the motive that impelled our remote ancestors to clothe themselves.

The use of fig-leaves for the girdle in Palestine is an interesting connecting link between the employment of the cowry and the mandrake for similar purposes in the neighbourhood of the Red Sea and in Cyprus and Syria respectively (*vide infra*).

In Greece and Italy, the sweet basil has a reputation for magical properties analogous to those of the cowry. Maidens collect the plant and wear bunches of it upon their body or upon their girdles ; while married women fix basil upon their heads.[1] It is believed that the odour of the plant will attract admirers : hence in Italy it is called *Bacia-nicola*, " Kiss me, Nicholas ".[2]

In Crete it is a sign of mourning presumably because its life-prolonging attributes, as a means of conferring continued existence to the dead, have been so rationalized in explanation of its use at funerals.

On New Year's day in Athens boys carry a boat and people remark, " St. Basil is come from Cæsarea ".

Pearls.

During the chequered history of the Great Mother the attributes of the original shell-amulet from which the goddess was sprung were also changing and being elaborated to fit into a more complex scheme. The magical properties of the cowry came to be acquired by other Red Sea shells, such as *Pterocera*, the pearl oyster, conch shells, and others. Each of these became intimately associated with the moon.[3] The pearls found in the oysters were supposed to be little moons, drops of the moon-substance (or dew) which fell from the sky into the gaping oyster. Hence pearls acquired the reputation of " shining by night," like the moon from which they were believed to have come : and every surrogate of the Great Mother, whether plant, animal, mineral or mythical instrument, came to be endowed with the power of " shining by night ". But pearls were also regarded as the quintessence of the shell's life-giving properties, which were considered to be all the more potent because they were sky-given emanations of the moon-goddess herself. Hence pearls acquired the reputation of

---

[1] This distinction between the significance of the amulet when worn on the girdle and on the head (in the hair), or as a necklace or bracelet, is very widespread. On the girdle it *usually* has the significance of stimulating the individual's fertility : worn elsewhere it was intended to ward off danger to life, *i.e.* to give good luck. An interesting surrogate of Hathor's distinctive emblem is the necklace of golden apples worn by a priestess of Apollo (Rendel Harris, *op. cit.*, p. 42).

[2] De Gubernatis, " Mythologie des Plantes," Vol. II, p. 35.

[3] For the details see Jackson, *op. cit.*, pp. 57-69. Both the shells and the moon were identified with the Great Mother. Hence they were homologized the one with the other.

THE BIRTH OF APHRODITE

being the "givers of life" *par excellence*, an idea which found literal expression in the ancient Persian word *margan* (from *mar*, "giver" and *gan*, "life"). This word has been borrowed in all the Turanian languages (ranging from Hungary to Kamskatckha), but also in the non-Turanian speech of Western Asia, thence through Greek and Latin (*margarita*) to European languages.[1] The same life-giving attributes were also acquired by the other pearl-bearing shells; and at some subsequent period, when it was discovered that some of these shells could be used as trumpets, the sound produced was also believed to be life-giving or the voice of the great Giver of Life. The blast of the trumpet was also supposed to be able to animate the deity and restore his consciousness, so that he could attend to the appeals of supplicants. In other words the noise woke up the god from his sleep. Hence the shell-trumpet attained an important significance in early religious ceremonials for the ritual purpose of summoning the deity, especially in Crete and India, and ultimately in widely distant parts of the world.[2] Long before these shells are known to have been used as trumpets, they were employed like the other Red Sea shells as "givers of life" to the dead in Egypt. Their use as trumpets was secondary.

And when it was discovered that purple dye could be obtained from certain of the trumpet-shells, the colouring-matter acquired the same life-giving powers as had already been conferred upon the trumpet and the pearls: thus it became regarded as a divine substance and as the exclusive property of gods and kings.

Long before, the colour red had acquired magic potency as a surrogate of life-giving blood; and this colour-symbolism undoubtedly helped in the development of the similar beliefs concerning purple.

Sharks and Dragons.

When the life-giving attributes of water were confused with the same properties with which shells had independently been credited

---

[1] Dr. Mingana has given me the following note: "It is very probable that the Græco-Latin *margarita*, the Aramæo-Syriac *margarita*, the Arabic *margan*, and the Turanian *margan* are derived from the Persian *mar-gân*, meaning both 'pearl' and 'life,' or etymologically 'giver, owner, or possessor, of life'. The word *gân*, in Zend *yân*, is thoroughly Persian and is undoubtedly the original form of this expression."

[2] See Chapter II of Jackson's book, *op. cit.*

long before, the shell's reputation was rationalized as an expression of the vital powers of the ocean in which the mollusc was born. But the same explanation was also extended to include fishes, and other denizens of the water, as manifestations of similar divine powers. In the lecture on "Dragons and Rain Gods" I referred to the identification of Ea, the Babylonian Osiris, with a fish (p. 105). When the value of the pearl as the giver of life impelled men to incur any risks to obtain so precious an amulet, the chief dangers that threatened pearl-fishers were due to sharks. These came to be regarded as demons guarding the treasure-houses at the bottom of the sea. Out of these crude materials the imaginations of the early pearl-fishers created the picture of wonderful submarine palaces of Nâga kings in which vast wealth, not merely of pearls, but also of gold, precious stones, and beautiful maidens (all of them "givers of life," *vide infra*, p. 224), were placed under the protection of shark-dragons.[1] The conception of the pearl (which is a surrogate of the life-giving Great Mother) guarded by dragons is linked by many bonds of affinity with early Erythræan and Mediterranean beliefs. The more usual form of the story, both in Southern Arabian legend and in Minoan and Mycenæan art, represents the Mother Goddess incarnate in a sacred tree or pillar with its protecting dragons in the form of serpents or lions, or a variety of dragon-surrogates, either real animals, such as deer or cattle, or composite monsters (Fig. 26).[2]

[1] In Eastern Asia (see, for example, Shinji Nishimura, "The Hisago-Bune," Tokio, 1918, published by the Tokio Society of Naval Architects, p. 18, where the dragon is identified with the *wani*, which can be either a crocodile or a shark); in Oceania (L. Frobenius, "Das Zeitalter des Sonnengottes," Bd. I., 1904, and C. E. Fox and F. H. Drew, "Beliefs and Tales of San Cristoval," *Journal of the Royal Anthropological Institute*, Vol. XLV, 1915, p. 140); and in America (see Thomas Gann, "Mounds in Northern Honduras," *Nineteenth Annual Report of the Bureau of American Ethnology*, 1897-8, Part II, p. 661) the dragon assumes the form of a shark, a crocodile, or a variety of other animals.

[2] Sir Arthur Evans, "Mycenæan Tree and Pillar Cult," *op. cit. supra*: W. Hayes Ward, "The Seal Cylinders of Western Asia," *op. cit.*: and Robertson Smith, "The Religion of the Semites," p. 133: "In Hadramant it is still dangerous to touch the sensitive mimosa, because the spirit that resides in the plant will avenge the injury". When men interfere with the incense trees it is reported: "the demons of the place flew away with doleful cries in the shape of white serpents, and the intruders died soon afterwards".

THE BIRTH OF APHRODITE

There are reasons for believing that these stories were first invented somewhere on the shores of the Erythræan Sea, probably in Southern Arabia. The animation of the incense-tree by the Great Mother, for the reasons which I have already expounded,[1] formed the link of her identification with the pearl, which probably acquired its magical reputation in the same region.

"In the Persian myth, the white Haoma is a divine tree, growing in the lake Vourukasha : the fish Khar-mâhi circles protectingly around it and defends it against the toad Ahriman. It gives eternal life, children to women, husbands to girls, and horses to men. In the Minôkhired the tree is called 'the preparer of the corpse" (Spiegel, "Eran. Altertumskunde," II, 115—quoted by Jung, "Psychology of the Unconscious," p. 532). The idea of guarding the divine tree [2] by dragons was probably the result of the transference to that particular surrogate of the Great Mother of the shark-stories which originated from the experiences of the seekers after pearls, her other representatives.

There are many other bits of corroborative evidence to suggest

---

[1] *Vide supra*, p. 38.

[2] In Western mythology the dragon guarding the fruit-bearing tree of life is also identified with the Mother of Mankind (Campbell, "Celtic Dragon Myth," pp. xli and 18). Thus the tree and its defender are both surrogates of the Great Mother. When Eve ate the apple from the tree of Paradise she was committing an act of cannibalism, for the plant was only another form of herself. Her "sin" consisted in aspiring to attain the immortality which was the exclusive privilege of the gods. This incident is analogous to that found in the Indian tales where mortals steal the *amrita*. By Eve's sin "death came into the world" for the paradoxical reason that she had eaten the food of the gods which gives immortality. The punishment meted out to her by the Almighty seems to have been to inhibit the life-giving and birth-facilitating action of the fruit of immortality, so that she and all her progeny were doomed to be mortal and to suffer the pangs of child-bearing.

There was a widespread belief among the ancients that ceremonies in connexion with the gods must (to be efficacious) be done in the reverse of the usual human way (Hopkins, "Religions of India," p. 201). So also an act which gives immortality to the gods, brings death to man.

The full realization of the fact that man was mortal imposed upon the early theologians the necessity of explaining the immortality of the gods. The elixir of life was the food of the gods that conferred eternal life upon them. By one of those paradoxes so dear to the maker of myths this same elixir brought death to man.

that these shell-cults and the legends derived from them were actually transmitted from the Red Sea to the Eastern Mediterranean. Nor is it surprising that this should have happened, when it is recalled that Egyptian sailors were trafficking in both seas long before the Pyramid Age, and no doubt carried the beliefs and the legends of one region to the other. I have already referred to the adoption in the Mediterranean area of the idea of the dragon-protectors of the tree- and pillar-forms of the Great Mother, and suggested that this was merely a garbled version of the pearl-fisher's experience of the dangers of attacks by sharks. But the same legends also reached the Levant in a less modified form, and then underwent another kind of transformation (and confusion with the tree-version) in Cyprus or Syria.

As the shark would be a not wholly appropriate actor in the Mediterranean, its rôle is taken by its smaller Selachian relative, the dog-fish. In the notes on Pliny's Natural History, Dr. Bostock and Mr. H. T. Riley [1] refer to the habits of dog-fishes ("Canes marini"), and quote from Procopius ("De Bell. Pers." B. I, c. 4) the following "wonderful story in relation to this subject": "Sea-dogs are wonderful admirers of the pearl-fish, and follow them out to sea. . . . A certain fisherman, having watched for the moment when the shell-fish was deprived of the attention of its attendant sea-dog, . . . seized the shell-fish and made for the shore. The sea-dog, however, was soon aware of the theft, and making straight for the fisherman, seized him. Finding himself thus caught, he made a last effort, and threw the pearl-fish on shore, immediately on which he was torn to pieces by its protector." [2]

Though the written record of this story is relatively modern the incident thus described probably goes back to much more ancient times. It is only a very slightly modified version of an ancient narrative of a shark's attack upon a pearl-diver.

For reasons which I shall discuss in the following pages, the rôle of the cowry and pearl as representatives of the Great Mother was in the Levant assumed by the mandrake, just as we have already seen the Southern Arabian conception of her as a tree adopted in Mycenæan lands. Having replaced the sea-shell by a land plant it became neces-

[1] Bohn's Edition, 1855, Vol. II, p. 433.
[2] A Cretan scene depicts a man attacking a dog-headed sea-monster (Mackenzie, *op. cit.*, "Myths of Crete," p. 139).

THE BIRTH OF APHRODITE 161

sary, in adapting the legend, to substitute for the "sea-dog" some land animal. Not unnaturally it became a dog. Thus the story of the dangers incurred in the process of digging up a mandrake assumed the well-known form.[1] The attempt to dig up the mandrake was said to be fraught with great danger. The traditional means of circumventing these risks has been described by many writers, ancient and modern, and preserved in the folk-lore of most European and western Asiatic countries. The story as told by Josephus is as follows: "They dig a trench round it till the hidden part of the root is very small, then they tie a dog to it, and when the dog tries hard to follow him that tied him, this root is easily plucked up, but the dog dies immediately, as it were, instead of the man that would take the plant away".[2] Thus the dog takes the place of the dog-fish when the mandrake becomes the pearl's surrogate. The only discrepancy between the two stories is the point to which Josephus calls specific attention. For instead of the dog killing the thief, as the shark (dog-fish) kills the stealer of pearls, the dog becomes the victim as a substitute for the man. As Josephus remarks, "the dog dies immediately, as it were, instead of the man that would take the plant away". This distortion of the story is true to the traditions of legend-making. The dog-incident is so twisted as to be transformed into a device for plucking the dangerous plant without risk.

It is quite possible that earlier associations of the dog with the Great Mother may have played some part in this transference of meaning, if only by creating confusion which made such rationalization necessary. I refer to the part played by Anubis in helping Isis to collect the fragments of Osiris; and the rôle played by Anubis, and his Greek *avatar* Cerberus, in the world of the dead. Whether the association of the dog-star Sirius with Hathor had anything to do with the confusion is uncertain.[3]

There was an intimate association of the dog with the goddess of

---

[1] A number of versions of this widespread fable have been collected by Dr. Rendel Harris (*op. cit.*) and Sir James Frazer (*op. cit.*). I quote here from the former (p. 118).

[2] Josephus, "Bell. Jud.," VII, 6, 3, quoted by Rendel Harris, *op. cit.*, p. 118.

[3] The dog-star became associated with Hathor for reasons which are explained on p. 209. It was "the opener of the way" for the birth of the sun and the New Year.

the underworld (Hecate) and the ritual of rebirth of the dead.[1] Perhaps the development of the story of the underworld-goddess Aphrodite's dog and the mandrake may have been helped by this survival of the association of Isis with Anubis, even if there is not a more definite causal relationship between the dog-incidents in the various legends.

The divine dog Anubis is frequently represented in connexion with the ritual of rebirth,[2] where it is shown upon a standard in association with the placenta. The hieroglyphic sign for the Egyptian word *mes*, " to give birth," consists of the skins of three dogs (or jackals, or foxes). The three-headed dog Cerberus that guarded the portal of Hades may possibly be a distorted survival of this ancient symbolism of the three-fold dog-skin as the graphic sign for the act of emergence from the portal of birth. Elsewhere (p. 223) in this lecture I have referred to Charon's *obolus* as a surrogate of the life-giving pearl or cowry placed in the mouth of the dead to provide " vital substance ". Rohde[3] regards Charon as the second Cerberus, corresponding to the Egyptian dog-faced god Anubis : just as Charon received his *obolus*, so in Attic custom the dead were provided with μελιτοῦτια, the object of which is usually said to be to pacify the dog of hell.

What seems to link all these fantastic beliefs and customs with the story of the dog and the mandrake is the fact that they are closely bound up with the conception of the dog as the guardian of hidden treasure.

The mandrake story may have arisen out of a mingling of these two streams of legend—the shark (dog-fish) protecting the treasures at the bottom of the sea, and the ancient Egyptian beliefs concerning the dog-headed god who presides at the embalmer's operations and superintends the process of rebirth.

The dog of the story is a representative of the dragon guarding the goddess in the form of the mandrake, just as the lions over the gate at Mycenæ heraldically support her pillar-form, or the serpents in Southern Arabia protect her as an incense tree. Dog, Lion, and

---

[1] When Artemis acquired the reputation as a huntress and her deer became her quarry the dog was rationalized into the new scheme.

[2] See, for example, Moret's " Mystères Égyptiens," pp. 77-80.

[3] " Psyche," p. 244.

THE BIRTH OF APHRODITE 163

Serpent in these legends are all representatives of the goddess herself, *i.e.* merely her own *avatars* (Fig. 26).

At one time I imagined that the rôle of Anubis as a god of embalming and the restorer of the dead was merely an ingenuous device on the part of the early Egyptians to console themselves for the depredations of jackals in their cemeteries. For if the jackal were converted into a life-giving god it would be a comforting thought to believe that the dead man, even though devoured, was "in the bosom of his god" and thereby had attained a rebirth in the hereafter. In ancient Persia corpses were thrown out for the dogs to devour. There was also the custom of leading a dog to the bed of a dying man who presented him with food, just as Cerberus was given honey-cakes by Hercules in his journey to hell. But I have not been able to obtain any corroboration of this supposition. It is a remarkable coincidence that the Great Mother has been identified with the necrophilic vulture as Mut; and it has been claimed by some writers [1] that, just as the jackal was regarded as a symbol of rebirth in Egypt and the dead were exposed for dogs to devour in Persia, so the vulture's corpse-devouring habits may have been primarily responsible for suggesting its identification with the Great Mother and for the motive behind the Indian practice of leaving the corpses of the dead for the vultures to dispose of.[2] It is not uncommon to find, even in English cathedrals, recumbent statues of bishops with dogs as footstools. Petronius ("Sat.," c. 71) makes the following statement: "valde te rogo, ut secundum pedes statuae meae catellam pingas—ut mihi contingat tuo beneficio post mortem vivere".[3] The belief in the dog's service as a guide to the dead ranges from Western Europe to Peru.

To return to the story of the dog and the mandrake: no doubt the demand will be made for further evidence that the mandrake actually assumed the rôle of the pearl in these stories. If the remark-

---

[1] See, for example, Jung, *op. cit.*, p. 268.
[2] Nekhebit, the Egyptian Vulture goddess, was identified by the Greeks with Eileithyia, the goddess of birth (Wiedemann, "Religion of the Ancient Egyptians," p. 141). She was usually represented as a vulture hovering over the king. Her place can be taken by the falcon of Horus or in the Babylonian story of Etana by the eagle. In the Indian Mahābhārata the Garuda is described as "the bird of life . . . destroyer of all, creator of all".
[3] Quoted by Jung, *op. cit.*, p. 530.

able repertory of magical properties assigned to the mandrake [1] be compared with those which developed in connexion with the cowry and the pearl,[2] it will be found that the two series are identical. The mandrake also is the giver of life, of fertility to women, of safety in childbirth; and like the cowry and the pearl it exerts these magical influences only if it be worn in contact with the wearer's skin.[3] But the most definite indication of the mandrake's homology with the pearl is provided by the legend that "it shines by night". Some scholars,[4] both ancient and modern, have attempted to rationalize this tradition by interpreting it as a reference to the glow-worms that settle on the plant! But it is only one of many attributes borrowed by the mandrake from the pearl, which was credited with this remarkable reputation only when early scientists conceived the hypothesis that the gem was a bit of moon substance.

As the memory of the real history of these beliefs grew dim, confusion was rapidly introduced into the stories. I have already explained how the diving for pearls started the story of the great palace of treasures under the waters which was guarded by dragons. As the pearl had the reputation of shining by night, it is not surprising that it or some of its surrogates should in course of time come to be credited with the power of "revealing hidden treasures," the treasures which in the original story were the pearls themselves. Thus the magic fern-seed and other treasure-disclosing vegetables [5] are surrogates of the mandrake, and like it derive their magical properties directly or indirectly from the pearl.

---

[1] See Rendel Harris (*op. cit.*) and Sir James Frazer (*op. cit.*).

[2] Jackson, *op. cit.*

[3] An interesting rationalization (of which Mr. T. H. Pear has kindly reminded me) of this ancient Oriental belief is still alive amongst British women. It is maintained that pearls "lose their lustre" unless they are worn in contact with the skin. This of course is a pure myth, but also an illuminating survival.

[4] See Frazer, *op. cit.*, p. 16, especially the references to the "devil's candle" and "the lamp of the elves".

[5] Rendel Harris, *op. cit.*, p. 113: Other factors played a part in the development of this legend of opening up treasure-houses. Both Artemis and Hecate are associated with a magical plant capable of opening locks and helping the process of birth. Artemis is a goddess of the portal and her life-giving symbol in a multitude of varied forms is found appropriately placed above the lintel of doors.

Fig. 21.—(a) A SLATE TRIAD FOUND BY PROFESSOR G. A. REISNER IN THE TEMPLE OF THE THIRD PYRAMID AT GIZA. IT SHOWS THE PHARAOH MYCERINUS SUPPORTED ON HIS RIGHT SIDE BY THE GODDESS HATHOR, REPRESENTED AS A WOMAN WITH THE MOON AND THE COW'S HORNS UPON HER HEAD, AND ON THE LEFT SIDE BY A NOME GODDESS, BEARING UPON HER HEAD THE JACKAL-SYMBOL OF HER NOME.
(b) THE ECUADOR APHRODITE. BAS-RELIEF FROM CERRO JABONCILLO (AFTER SAVILLE, "ANTIQUITIES OF MANABI, ECUADOR." PRELIMINARY REPORT, 1907, PLATE XXXVIII). A GROTESQUE COMPOSITE MONSTER INTENDED TO REPRESENT A WOMAN (COMPARE SAVILLE'S PLATES XXXV, XXXVI, AND XXXIX), WHOSE HEAD IS A CONVENTIONALIZED OCTOPUS, WHOSE BODY IS A *LOLIGO*, AND WHOSE LIMBS ARE HUMAN.

THE BIRTH OF APHRODITE

The fantastic story of the dog and the mandrake provides the most definite evidence of the derivation of the mandrake-beliefs from the shell-cults of the Erythræan Sea. There are many other scraps of evidence to corroborate this. I shall refer here only to one of these. " The discovery of the art of purple-dyeing has been attributed to the Tyrian tutelary deity Melkart, who is identified with Baal by many writers. According to Julius Pollux ('Onomasticon,' I, iv.) and Nonnus (' Dionys.,' XL, 306) Hercules (Melkart) was walking on the seashore accompanied by his dog and a Tyrian nymph, of whom he was enamoured. The dog having found a *Murex* with its head protruding from its shell, devoured it, and thus its mouth became stained with purple. The nymph, on seeing the beautiful colour, bargained with Hercules to provide her with a robe of like splendour."[1] This seems to be another variant of the same story.

THE OCTOPUS.

Aphrodite was associated not only with the cowry, the pearl, and the mandrake, but also with the octopus, the argonaut, and other cephalopods. Tümpel seems to imagine that the identification of the goddess with the argonaut and the octopus necessarily excludes her association with molluscs; and Dr. Rendel Harris attributes an equally exclusive importance to the mandrake. But in such methods of argument due recognition is not given to the outstanding fact in the history of primitive beliefs. The early philosophers built up their great generalizations in the same way as their modern successors. They were searching for some explanation of, or a working hypothesis to include, most diverse natural phenomena within a concise scheme. The very essence of such attempts was the institution of a series of homologies and fancied analogies between dissimilar objects. Aphrodite was at one and the same time the personification of the cowry, the conch shell, the purple shell, the pearl, the lotus, and the lily, the mandrake and the bryony, the incense tree and the cedar, the octopus and the argonaut, the pig, and the cow.

Every one of these identifications is the result of a long and chequered history, in which fancied resemblances and confusion of meaning play a very large part. But I cannot too strongly repudiate the claim made by Sir James Frazer that such events are merely so

[1] Jackson, *op. cit.*, p. 195.

many evidences of the innate human tendency to personify nature. The history of the arbitrary circumstances that were responsible for the development of each one of these homologies is entirely fatal to this wholly unwarranted speculation.[1] Tümpel claims [2] the Aphrodite was associated more especially with " a species of *Sepia* ". He refers to the attempts to associate the goddess of love with amulets of univalvular shells "in virtue of a certain peculiar and obscene symbolism".[3] Naturalists, however, designate with the term *Venus Cytherea* certain gaping bivalve molluscs.

But, according to Tümpel (p. 386), neither univalvular nor bivalve shells can be regarded as a real part of the goddess's cultural equipment. There is no representation of Aphrodite coming in a shell from across the sea.[4] The truly sacred Aphrodite-shell was entirely different, so Tümpel believes : it was obviously difficult to preserve, but for that reason more worthy of notice, for the small χοιρίναι (pectines), virginalia marina (Apuleius de mag. 34, 35, and in reference thereto, Isidor. origg. 9, 5, 24) or spuria (σπόρια) were only the commoner and more readily obtained surrogates : the univalvular shells

---

[1] Sir James Frazer, " Jacob and the Mandrakes," *Proc. Brit. Academy*.

[2] K. Tümpel, " Die ' Muschel der Aphrodite,' " *Philologus, Zeitschrift für das Classische Alterthum*, Bd. 51, 1892, p. 385 : compare also, with reference to the " Muschel der Aphrodite," O. Jahn, *SB. d. k. Sächs. G. d. W.*, VII, 1853, p. 16 ff. ; also IX, 1855, p. 80 ; and Stephani, *Compte rendu pour l'an* 1870-71, p. 17 ff.

[3] See Jahn, *op. cit.*, 1855, T. V, 6, and T. IV, 8 : figures of the so-called Χοιρίναι (from Χοῖρος in the double sense as " pig " and " the female pudendum ") : Aristophanes, Eq. 1147 ; Vesp. 332 ; Pollux, 8, 16 ; Hesch. s.v.

[4] The fact that no graphic representation of this event has been found is surely a wholly inadequate reason for refusing to credit the story. Very few episodes in the sacred history of the gods received concrete expression in pictures or sculptures until relatively late. A Hellenistic representation of the goddess emerging from a bivalve was found in Southern Russia (Minns, " Scythians and Greeks," p. 345).

Tümpel cites the following statements : " te (Venus) ex concha natam esse autumant : cave tu harum conchas spernas! " Tibull. 3, 3, 24 : " et faveas concha, Cypria, vecta tua " ; Statius Silv. 1, 2, 117 : Venus to Violentilla, " haec et caeruleis mecum consurgere digna fluctibus et nostra potuit considere concha " ; Fulgent. myth. 2, 4 " concha etiam marina pingitur (Venus) portari (I. HS :—am portare) " ; Paulus Diacon. p. 52, " M. Cytherea Venus ab urbe Cythera, in quam primum devecta esse dicitur concha, cum in mari esset concepta cet ".

THE BIRTH OF APHRODITE

(μονόθυρα of Aristotle), such as those just mentioned, and the other ὄστρεα of Aphrodite, the Nerites (periwinkles, etc.), the purple shell and the Echineïs were also real Veneriae conchae. Among the Nerites Aelian enumerates (N.A. 14, 28): Ἀφροδίτην δὲ συνδιαιτωμένην ἐν τῇ θαλάττῃ ἡσθῆναί τε τῷ Νηρίτῃ τῷδε καὶ ἔχειν αὐτὸν φίλον. On account of their supposed medicinal value in cases of abortion and especially as a prophylactic for pregnant women the Ἐχενηΐς (pure Latin re[mi]mora) was called ὠδινολύτη[1] (Pliny, 32, 1, 5: pisciculus!). According to Mutianus (Pliny, 9, 25 (41), 79 f.), it was a species of purple shell, but larger than the true *Murex purpura*. From this the sanctity of the Echineïs to the Cnidian Aphrodite is demonstrated: "quibus (conchis) inhaerentibus plenam ventis stetisse navem portantem Periandro, ut castrarentur nobilis pueros, conchasque, quae id praestiterint, apud Cnidiorum Venerem coli" (Pliny).

Tümpel then (p. 387) accuses Stephani of being mistaken in his interpretation of Martial's Cytheriacae (Epign. II, 47, 1 = purple shells) as the amulets of Aphrodite, and claims that Jahn has given the correct solution of the following passages from Pliny (N.H., 9, 33 [52], 103, compare 32, 11 [53]): "navigant ex his (conchis) veneriae, praebentesque concavam sui partem et aurae opponentes per summa aequorum velificant"; and further (9, 30 [49], 94): "in Propontide concham esse acatii modo carinatam inflexa puppe, prora rostrata, in hac condi nauplium animal saepiae simile ludendi societate sola. duobus hoc fieri generibus: tranquillum enim vectorem demissis palmulis ferire ut remis; si vero flatus invitet, easdem in usu gubernaculi porrigi pandique buccarum sinus aurae".

Tümpel claims (pp. 387 and 388) that this quotation settles the question. Aphrodite's "shell," according to him, is the *Nauplius* (depicted as a shell-fish, with its sail-like palmulæ spread out to the wind, but with the same sails flattened into plate-like arms for steering), clearly "a species of *Sepia*," wholly like Aphrodite herself, a ship-like shell-fish sailing over the surface of the water, the concha veneria. [The analogy to a ship bearing the Great Mother is extremely ancient and originally referred to the crescent moon carrying the moon-goddess across the heavenly ocean.]

[1] From ὠδινο—"to have the pains of childbirth".

Elsewhere (p. 399) he discusses the reasons for the connexion of Aphrodite with the "nautilus," by which is meant the argonaut of zoologists.

But if Jahn and Tümpel have thus clearly established the proof of the intimate association of Aphrodite with certain cephalopods, they are wholly unjustified in the assumption that their quotations from relatively modern authors disprove the reality of the equally close (though more ancient) relationship of the goddess to the cowry, the pearl-shell, the trumpet-shell, and the purple-shell.

It must not be forgotten that, as we have already seen, the primitive shell-cults of the Erythræan Sea had been diffused throughout the Mediterranean area long before Aphrodite was born upon the shores of the Levant, and possibly before Hathor came into existence in the south. The use of the cowry and gold models of the cowry goes back to an early time in Ægean history.[1] And the influence of Aphrodite's early associations had become blurred and confused by the development of new links with other shells and their surrogates.

But the connexion of Aphrodite with the octopus and its kindred played a very obtrusive part in Minoan and Mycenæan art; and its influence was spread abroad as far as Western Europe[2] and towards the East as far as America. In many ways it was a factor in the development of such artistic designs as the spiral and the volute, and not improbably also of the swastika.

Starting from the researches of Tümpel, a distinguished French zoologist, Dr. Frédéric Houssay,[3] sought to demonstrate that the cult of Aphrodite was "based upon a pre-existing zoological philosophy". The argument in support of his claim that Aphrodite was a personification of the octopus must be sharply differentiated into two parts: first, the reality of the association of the octopus with the goddess, of which there can be no doubt; and secondly, his explanation of it, which (however popular it may be with classical writers and modern scholars)[4] is not only a gratuitous assumption, but also, even if it were

---

[1] See Schliemann, "Ilios," p. 455; and Siret, *op. cit.*

[2] Siret, *op. cit. supra*, p. 59.

[3] "Les Théories de la Genèse à Mycènes et le sens zoologique de certains symboles du culte d'Aphrodite," *Revue Archéologique*, 3ie série, T. XXVI, 1895, p. 13.

[4] It was adduced also by Tümpel and others before him.

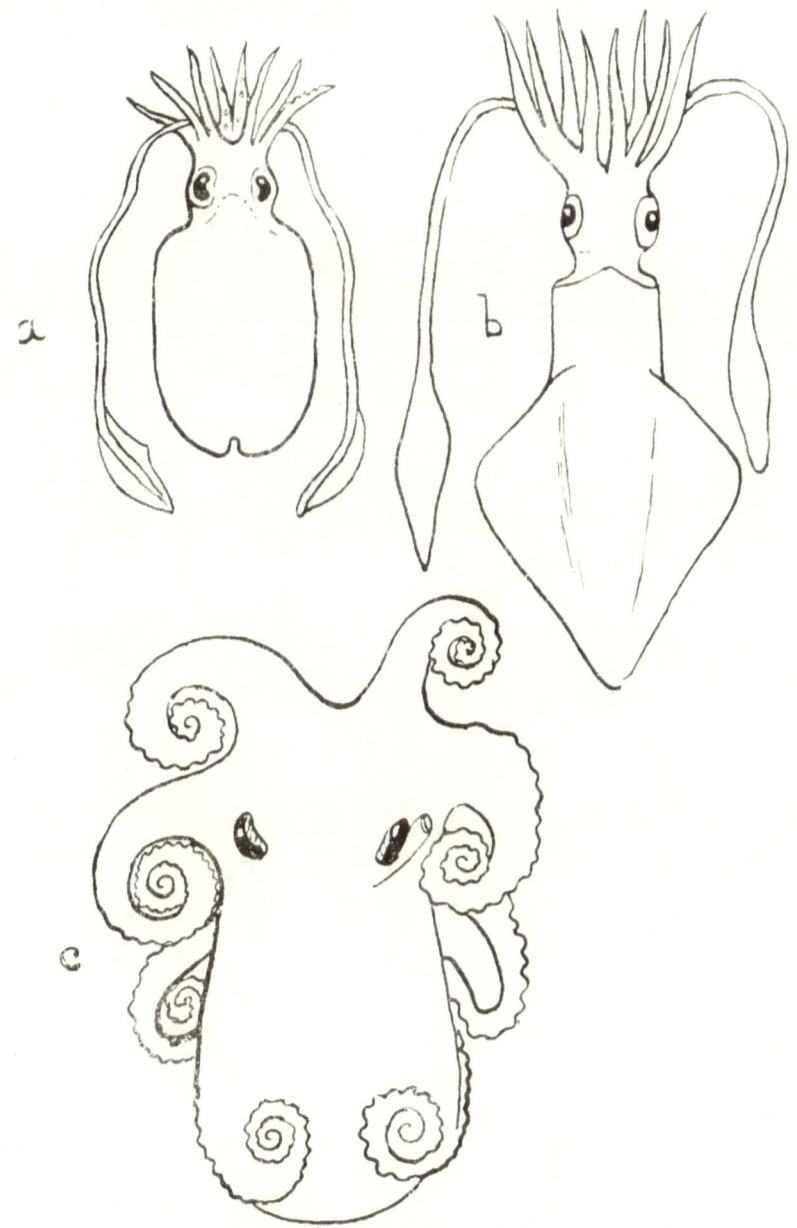

FIG. 22.—(a) SEPIA OFFICINALIS, AFTER TRYON, "CEPHALOPODA".
(b) LOLIGO VULGARIS, AFTER TRYON.
(c) THE POSITION USUALLY ADOPTED BY THE RESTING OCTOPUS, AFTER TRYON.

THE BIRTH OF APHRODITE

based upon more valid evidence than the speculations of such recent writers as Pliny, would not really carry the explanation very far.

I refer to his claim that " les premiers conquérants de la mer furent induits en vénération du poulpe nageur (octopus) parce qu'ils crurent que quelque-uns de ces céphalopodes, les poulpes sacrés (argonauta) avaient, comme eux et avant eux, inventé la navigation " (*op. cit.*, p. 15). Idle fancies of this sort do not help us to understand the arbitrary beliefs concerning the magical powers of the octopus.

The real problem we have to solve is to discover why, among all the multitude of bizarre creatures to be found in the Mediterranean Sea, the octopus and its allies should thus have been singled out for distinctive appreciation, and also acquired the same remarkable attributes as the cowry.

I believe that the Red Sea " Spider shell," *Pterocera*,[1] was the link between the cowry and the octopus. This shell was used, like the cowry, for funerary purposes in Egypt and as a trumpet in India.[2] But it was also depicted upon a series of remarkable primitive statues of the god Min, which were found at Coptos during the winter 1893-4 by Professor Flinders Petrie.[3] Some of these objects are now in the Cairo Museum and the others in the Ashmolean Museum in Oxford. They are supposed to be late predynastic representations of the god Min. If this supposition is correct they are the earliest idols (apart from mere amulets) that have been preserved from antiquity.

Upon these statues, representations of the Red Sea shell *Pterocera bryonia* are sculptured in low relief. Mr. F. Ll. Griffith is disinclined to accept my suggestion that the object of these pictures of the shell was to animate the statues. But whether this was their purpose or not, it is probably not without some significance that these life-giving shells were associated with so obtrusively phallic a deity as Min. In any case they afford concrete evidence of cultural contact between Coptos and the Red Sea, and indicate that these particular shells were chosen as symbols of that sea or its coast.

The distinctive feature of the *Pterocera* is that the mantle in the adult expands into a series of long finger-like processes each of which

---

[1] or *Pteroceras*. [2] Jackson, *op. cit.*, p. 38.
[3] " Koptos," pp. 7-9, Pls. III. and IV. : for a discussion of the significance of these statues see Jean Capart, " Les Débuts de l'Art en Égypte," Brussels, 1904, p. 216 *et seq*.

secretes a calcareous process or "claw". There are seven [1] of these claws as well as the long columella (Fig. 5). Hence, when the shell-cults were diffused from the Red Sea to the Mediterranean (where the *Pterocera* is not found), it is quite likely that the people of the Levant may have confused with the octopus some sailor's account of the eight-rayed shell (or perhaps representations of it on some amulet or statue). Whether this is the explanation of the confusion or not, it is certain that the beliefs associated with the cowry and the octopus in the Ægean area are identical with those linked up with the cowry and the *Pterocera* in the Red Sea.

FIG. 5.—*PTEROCERA BRYONIA*, THE RED SEA SPIDER-SHELL
Col.—the columella.
1-7—the "claws".

I have already mentioned that the mandrake is believed to possess the same magical powers. Sir James Frazer has called attention to the fact that in Armenia the bryony (*Bryonia alba*) is a surrogate of the mandrake and is credited with the same attributes.[2] Lovell Reeve ("Conchologia Iconica," VI, 1851) refers to the Red Sea *Pterocera* as the "Wild Vine Root" species, previously known as *Strombus radix bryoniae*; and Chemnitz ("Conch. Cab.," 1788, Vol. X, p. 227) says the French call it "Racine de brione femelle imparfaite," and refer to it as "the maiden". Here then is further evidence that this shell (*a*) was associated in some way with a surrogate of the mandrake (Aphrodite), and (*b*) was regarded as a maiden. Thus clearly it has a place in the chequered history of Aphrodite. I have suggested the possibility of its confusion with the octopus, which may have led to the inclusion of the latter within the scope of the marine creatures in Aphrodite's cultural equipment. According to Matthioli (Lib. 2, p. 135),

[1] This may help to explain the peculiar sanctity of the shell.
[2] Frazer, *op. cit.*, 4.

THE BIRTH OF APHRODITE 171

another of Aphrodite's creatures, the purple shell-fish, was also known as "the maiden". By Pliny it is called Pelogia, in Greek πορφυρα ; and πορφυρώματα was the term applied to the flesh of swine that had been sacrificed to Ceres and Proserpine (Hesych.). In fact, the purple-shell was "the maiden" and also "the sow": in other words it was Aphrodite. The use of the term "maiden" for the *Pterocera* suggests a similar identification. To complete this web of proof it may be noted that an old writer has called the mandrake the plant of Circe, the sorceress who turned men into swine by a magic draught.[1] Thus we have a series of shells, plants, and marine creatures accredited with identical magical properties, and each of them known in popular tradition as "the maiden". They are all culturally associated with Aphrodite.

I shall have occasion (*infra*, p. 177) to refer to M. Siret's account of the discovery of the Ægean octopus-motif upon Æneolithic objects in Spain, and of the widespread use in Western Europe of certain conventional designs derived from the octopus. M. Siret also (see the table, Fig. 6, on p. 34 of his book) makes the remarkable claim that the conventional form of the Egyptian Bes, which, according to Quibell,[2] is the god whose function it is to preside over sexual intercourse in its purely physical aspect, is derived from the octopus. If this is true—and I am bound to admit that it is far from being proved —it suggests that the Red Sea littoral may have been the place of origin of the cultural use of the octopus and an association with Hathor, for Bes and Hathor are said to have been introduced into Egypt from there.[3]

That the octopus was actually identified with the Great Mother and also with the dragon is revealed by the fact of the latter assuming an octopus-form in Eastern Asia and Oceania, and by the occurrence of octopus-motifs in the representation of the goddess in America. One of the most remarkable series of pictures depicting the Great Mother is found sculptured in low relief upon a number of stone slabs from Manabi in Central America,[4] one of which I reproduce here

---

[1] Just as Hathor (or her surrogate Horus) turned men into the creatures of Set, *i.e.* pigs, crocodiles, *et cetera*.
[2] " Excavations at Saqqara," 1905-1906, p. 14.
[3] Maspero, " The Dawn of Civilization," p. 34.
[4] Saville, " Antiquities of Manabi, Ecuador," 1907.

(Fig. 21*b*). The head of the goddess is a conventionalized octopus; to that was added a body consisting of a *Loligo ;* and, to give greater definiteness to this remarkable process of building up the form of the goddess, conventional representations of her arms and legs (and in some of the sculptures also the *pudendum muliebre*) were added. Thus there can be no doubt of the identification of this American Aphrodite and the octopus.

In the Polynesian Rata-myth there is a very instructive series of manifestations of the dragon.[1] The first form assumed by the monster in this story was a gaping shell-fish of enormous size; then it appeared as a mighty octopus; and lastly, as a whale, into whose jaws the hero Nganaoa sprang, as his representatives are said to have done elsewhere throughout the world (Frobenius, *op. cit.*, pp. 59-219).

Houssay (*op. cit. infra*) calls attention to the fact that at times Astarte was shown carrying an octopus as her emblem,[2] and has suggested that it was mistaken for a hand, just as in America the thunderbolt of Chac was given a hand-like form in the Dresden Codex (*vide supra*, Fig. 13), and elsewhere (*e.g.* Fig. 12).

If this suggestion should prove to be well founded it would provide a more convincing explanation of the girdle of hands worn by the Indian goddess Kali[3] than that usually given. If the "hands" really represent surrogates of the cowry, the wearing of such a girdle brings the Indian goddess into line, not only with Astarte and Aphrodite, but also with the East African maidens who still wear the girdle of cowries. Kali's exploits were in many respects identical with those of the bloodthirsty Sekhet-manifestation of the Egyptian goddess Hathor. Just as Sekhet had to be restrained by Re for her excess of zeal in murdering his foes, so Siva had to intervene with Kali upon the battle-

---

[1] A detailed summary of the literature relating to the world-wide distribution of certain phases of the dragon-myth is given by Frobenius, "Das Zeitalter des Sonnesgottes," Berlin, 1904: on pp. 63-5 he gives the Rata-myth.

[2] Which can also be compared with the conventional form of the thunderbolt.

[3] Of course the hands had the additional significance as trophies of her murderous zeal. But I think this is a secondary rationalization of their meaning. An excellent photograph of a bronze statue (in the Calcutta Art Gallery), representing Kali with her girdle of hands, is given by Mr. Donald A. Mackenzie, "Indian Myth and Legend," p. xl.

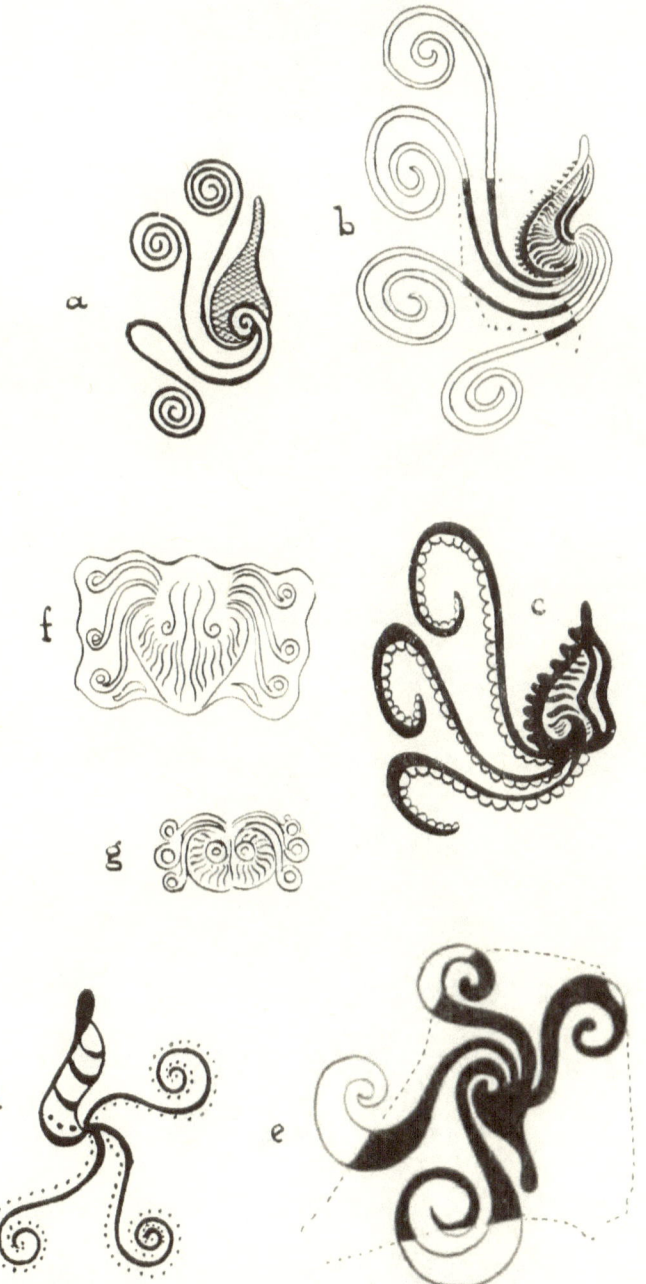

Fig. 23.—A series of Mycenæan conventionalizations of the Argonaut and the Octopus (after Tümpel), which provided the basis for Houssay's theory of the origin of the triskele (*a, c,* and *d*) and swastika (*b* and *e*), and Siret's theory to explain the design of Bes's face (*f* and *g*).

field flooded with gore (as also in the Egyptian story) to spare the remnant of his enemies.[1]

THE SWASTIKA.

Houssay (*op. cit. supra*) has made the interesting suggestion that the swastika may have been derived from such conventionalized representations of the octopus as are shown in Fig. 23. This series of sketches is taken from Tümpel's memoir, which provided the foundation for Houssay's hypothesis.

A vast amount of attention has been devoted to this lucky symbol,[2] which still enjoys a widespread vogue at the present day, after a history of several thousand years. Although so much has been written in attempted explanation of the swastika since Houssay made his suggestion, so far as I am aware no one has paid the slightest attention to his hypothesis or made even a passing reference to his memoir.[3] Fantastic and far-fetched though it may seem at first sight (though surely not more so than the strictly orthodox solar theory advocated by Mr. Cook or Mrs. Nuttall's astral speculations) Houssay's suggestion offers an explanation of some of the salient attributes of the swastika on which the alternative hypotheses shed little or no light.

Among the earliest known examples of the symbol are those

---

[1] F. T. Elworthy has summarized the extensive literature relating to hand-amulets ("The Evil Eye," 1895; and "Horns of Honour," 1900). Many of these hands have the definite reputation as fertility charms which one would expect if Houssay's hypothesis of their derivation from the octopus is well founded.

[2] Thomas Wilson ("The Swastika, the Earliest Known Symbol, and its Migrations; with Observations on the Migration of Certain Industries in Prehistoric Times," *Report of the U.S. National Museum for* 1894, Washington, 1896) has given a full and well-illustrated summary of most of the literature: further information is provided by Count d'Alviella (*op. cit. supra*), "The Migration of Symbols"; by Zelia Nuttall ("The Fundamental Principles of Old and New World Civilizations," *Archæological and Ethnological Papers of the Peabody Museum*, Cambridge, Mass., 1901); and Arthur Bernard Cook ("Zeus, A Study in Ancient Religion," Vol. I, Cambridge, 1914, pp. 472 *et seq.*).

[3] Since this has been printed Mr. W. J. Perry has called my attention to a short article by René Croste ("Le Svastika," *Bull. Trimestriel de la Société Bayonnaise d'Études Regionales*," 1918), in which Houssay's hypothesis is mentioned as having been adopted by Guilleminot ("Les Nouveaux Horizons de la Science").

engraved upon the so-called "owl-shaped" (but, as Houssay has conclusively demonstrated, really octopus-shaped) vases and a metal figurine found by Schliemann in his excavations of the hill at Hissarlik.[1] The swastika is represented upon the *mons Veneris* of these figures, which represent the Great Mother in her form as a woman or as a pot, which is an anthropomorphized octopus, one of the avatars of the Great Mother. The symbol seems to have been intended as a fertility amulet like the cowry, either suspended from a girdle or depicted upon a pubic shield or conventionalized fig-leaf.

Wherever it is found the swastika is supposed to be an amulet to confer "good luck" and long life. Both this reputation and the association with the female organs of reproduction link up the symbol with the cowry, the *Pterocera*, and the octopus. It is clear then that the swastika has the same reputation for magic and the same attributes and associations as the octopus; and it may be a conventionalized representation of it, as Houssay has suggested.

It must not be assumed that the identification of the swastika with the Great Mother and her powers of giving life and resurrection *necessarily* invalidates the solar and astral theories recently championed by Mr. Cook and Mrs. Nuttall respectively. I have already called attention to the fact that the Sun-god derived his existence and all his attributes from his mother. The whole symbolism of the Winged Disk and the Wheel of the Sun and their reputation for life-giving and destruction were adopted from the Great Mother. These well-established facts should prepare us to recognize that the admission of the truth of Houssay's suggestion would not necessarily invalidate the more widely accepted solar significance of the swastika.

Tümpel called attention to the fact that, when they set about conventionalizing the octopus, the Mycenæan artists often resorted to the practice of representing pairs of "arms" as units and so making four-limbed and three-limbed forms (Fig. 23), which Houssay regards as the prototypes of the swastika and the triskele respectively. That such a process may have played a part in the development of the symbol is further suggested by the form of a Transcaucasian swastika found by Rössler,[2] who assigns it to the Late Bronze or Early Iron Age. Each

---

[1] Wilson (*op. cit.*, pp. 829-33 and Figs. 125, 128, and 129) has collected the relevant passages and illustrations from Schliemann's writings.

[2] *Zeitschrift für Ethnologie*, Bd. 37, p. 148.

of the four limbs is bifurcated at its extremity. Moreover they exhibit
the series of spots, so often found upon or alongside the limbs of the
symbol, which suggest the conventional way of representing the suckers
of the octopus in the Mycenæan designs (Fig. 23).

Another remarkable picture of a swastika-like emblem has been
found in America.[1] The elephant-headed god sits in the centre and
four pairs of arms radiate from him, each of them equipped with definite suckers.

Another possible way in which the design of a four-limbed swastika may have been derived from an octopus is suggested by the
gypsum weight found in 1901 by Sir Arthur Evans[2] in the West
Magazine of the palace at Knossos (*circa* 1500 B.C.). Upon the
surface of this weight the form of an octopus has been depicted, four
of the arms of which stand out in much stronger relief than the others.

The number four has a peculiar mystical significance (*vide infra*,
p. 206) and is especially associated with the Sun-god Horus. This
fact may have played some part in the process of reduction of the
number of limbs of the octopus to four ; or alternatively it may have
helped to emphasize the solar associations of the symbol, which other
considerations were responsible for suggesting. The designs upon the
pots from Hissarlik show that at a relatively early epoch the swastika
was confused with the sun's disc represented as a wheel with four
spokes.[3] But the solar attributes of the swastika are secondary to
those of life-giving and luck-bringing, with which it was originally
endowed as a form of the Great Mother.

The only serious fact which arouses some doubt as to the validity
of Houssay's theory is the discovery of an early painted vase at Susa
decorated with an unmistakable swastika. Edmond Pottier, who has
described the ceramic ware from Susa,[4] regards this pot as Proto-
Elamite of the earliest period. If Pottier's claim is justified we have
in this isolated specimen from Susa the earliest example of the swastika.
Moreover, it comes from a region in which the symbol was supposed
to be wholly absent.

[1] Seler, *Zeitschrift für Ethnologie*, Bd., 41, p. 409.
[2] *Corolla Numismatica*, 1906, p. 342.
[3] A. B. Cook, " Zeus," pp. 198 *et seq.*
[4] " Etude Historique et Chronologique sur les Vases Peints de l'Acro-
pole de Suse," *Mémoires de la Délégation en Perse*, T. XIII, *Rech.
Archéol.*, 5e série, 1912, Plate XLI, Fig. 3.

This raises a difficult problem for solution. Is the Proto-Elamite swastika the prototype of the symbol whose world-wide migrations have been studied by Wilson (*op. cit. supra*)? Or is it an instance of independent evolution? If it falls within the first category and is really the parent of the early Anatolian swastikas, how is it to be explained? Was the conventionalization of the octopus design much more ancient than the earliest Trojan examples of the symbol? Or was the Susian design adopted in the West and given a symbolic meaning which it did not have before then?

These are questions which we are unable to answer at present because the necessary information is lacking. I have enumerated them merely to suggest that any hasty inferences regarding the bearing of the Susian design upon the general problem are apt to be misleading. Vincent[1] claims that the fact of the swastika having been in use by ceramic artists in Crete and Susiana many centuries before the appearance of Mycenæan art is fatal to Houssay's hypothesis. But I think it is too soon to make such an assumption. The swastika was already a rigidly conventionalized symbol when we first know it both in the Mediterranean and in Susiana. It may therefore have a long history behind it. The octopus may possibly have begun to play a part in the development of this symbolism before the Egyptian Bes (*vide supra*, p. 171) was evolved, perhaps even before the time of the Coptos statues of Min (*supra*, p. 169), or in the early days of Sumerian history when the conventional form of the water-pot was being determined (*infra*, p. 179). These are mere conjectures, which I mention merely for the purpose of suggesting that the time is not yet ripe for using such arguments as Vincent's finally to dispose of Houssay's octopus-theory.

There can be no doubt that the symbolism of the Mycenæan spiral and the volute is closely related to the octopus. In fact, the evidence provided by Minoan paintings and Mycenæan decorative art demonstrates that the spiral as a symbol of life-giving was definitely derived from the octopus. The use of the volute on Egyptian scarabs[2] and also in the decoration of an early Thracian statuette of a nude god-

---

[1] "Canaan," p. 340, footnote.
[2] Alice Grenfell, *Journal of Egyptian Archæology*, Vol. II, 1915, p. 217: and *Ancient Egypt*, 1916, Part I, p. 23.

THE BIRTH OF APHRODITE

dess[1] indicate that it was employed like the spiral and octopus as a life-symbol.

In Spanish graves of the Early and Middle Neolithic types M. Siret found cowry-shells in association with a series of flint implements, crude idols, and pottery almost precisely reproducing the forms of similar objects found with cowries and pecten shells at Hissarlik.[2] But when the Æneolithic phase of culture dawned in Spain, and the Ægean octopus-motif made its appearance there, the culture as a whole reveals unmistakable evidence of a predominantly Egyptian inspiration.

M. Siret claims, however, that, even in the Neolithic phase in Spain, the crude idols represent forms derived from the octopus in the Eastern Mediterranean (p. 59 *et seq.*). He regards the octopus as "a conventional symbol of the ocean, or, more precisely, of the fertilizing watery principle" (p. 19). He elucidates a very interesting feature of the Æneolithic representation of the octopus in Spain. The spiral-motif of the Ægean gives place to an angular design, which he claims to be due to the influence of the conventional Egyptian way of representing water (p. 40). If this interpretation is correct—and, in spite of the slenderness of the evidence, I am inclined to accept it—it affords a remarkable illustration of the effects of culture-contact in the conventionalization of designs, to which Dr. Rivers has called attention.[3] Whatever explanation may be provided of this method of representing the arms of the octopus with its angularly bent extremities, it seems to have an important bearing on Houssay's hypothesis of the swastika's origin. For it would reveal the means by which the spiral or volute shape of the limbs of the swastika became transformed into the angular form, which is so characteristic of the conventional symbol.[4]

The significance of the spiral as a form of the Great Mother inevitably led to its identification with the thunder weapon, like all her

[1] S. Reinach, *Revue Archéol.*, T. XXVI, 1895, p. 369.
[2] L. Siret, "Questions de Chronologie et d'Ethnographie Ibériques," 1913, p. 18, Fig. 3.
[3] Rivers, "History of Melanesian Society," Vol. II, p. 374; also *Report Brit. Association*, 1912, p. 599.
[4] M. Siret assigns the date of the appearance in Spain of the highly conventionalized angular form of octopus to the time between the fifteenth and the twelfth centuries B.C.; and he attributes it to Phœnician influence (p. 63).

178   THE EVOLUTION OF THE DRAGON

other surrogates. I have already referred (Chapter II, p. 98) to the association of the spiral with thunder and lightning in Eastern Asia. But other factors played a significant part in determining this specialization. In Egypt the god Amen was identified with the ram ; and this creature's spirally curved horn became the symbol of the thunder-god throughout the Mediterranean area,[1] and then further afield in Europe, Africa, and Asia, where, for instance, we see Agni's ram with the characteristic horn. This blending of the influence of the octopus- and the ram's-horn-motifs made the spiral a conventional representation of thunder. This is displayed in its most definite form in China, Japan, Indonesia, and America, where we find the separate spiral used as a thunder-symbol, and the spiral appendage on the side of the head as a token of the god of thunder.[2]

THE MOTHER POT.

In the lecture on "Incense and Libations" (Chapter I) I referred to the enrichment of the conception of water's life-giving properties which the inclusion of the idea of human fertilization by water involved. When this event happened a new view developed in explanation of the part played by woman in reproduction. She was no longer regarded as the real parent of mankind, but as the matrix in which the seed was planted and nurtured during the course of its growth and development. Hence in the earliest Egyptian hieroglyphic writing the picture of a pot of water was taken as the symbol of womanhood, the "vessel" which received the seed. A globular water-pot, the common phonetic value of which is Nw or Nu, was the symbol of the cosmic waters, the god Nw (Nu), whose female counterpart was the goddess Nut.

In his report, "A Collection of Hieroglyphs,"[3] Mr. F. Ll. Griffith discusses the bowl of water (a) and says that it stands for the female principle in the words for *vulva* and woman. When it is recalled that the cowry (and other shells) had the same double significance, the possibility suggests itself whether at times confusion may

---

[1] Cook, "Zeus," p. 346 *et seq.*
[2] This is well shown upon the Copan representations (Fig. 19) of the elephant-headed god—see *Nature*, November, 25, 1915, p. 340.
[3] *Archæol. Survey of Egypt*, 1898, p. 3.

THE BIRTH OF APHRODITE 179

not have arisen between the not very dissimilar hieroglyphic signs for "a shell" (*h*) and "the bowl of water" (woman) (*f*).[1]

Referring to the sign (*g* and *h*) for "a shell," Mr. Griffith says (p. 25): "It is regularly found at all periods in the word *hawt* = altar,[2] and perhaps only in this word: but it is a peculiarity of the Pyramid Texts that the sign shown in the text-figures *c*, *h*, and *i* is in them used very commonly, not as a word-sign, but also as a

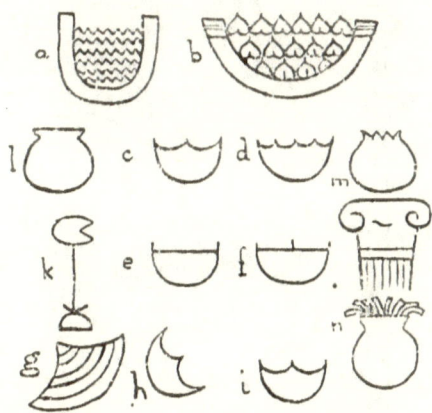

FIG. 6.

(*a*) Picture of a bowl of water—the hieroglyphic sign equivalent to *hm* (the word *hmt* means "woman")—Griffith, "Beni Hasan," Part III, Plate VI, Fig. 88 and p. 29.

(*b*) "A basket of sycamore figs"—Wilkinson's "Ancient Egyptians," Vol. I, p. 323.

(*c*) and (*d*) are said by Wilkinson to be hieroglyphic signs meaning "wife" and are apparently taken from (*b*). But (*c*) is identical with (*i*), which, according to Griffith (p. 14), represents a bivalve shell (*g*, from Plate III, Fig. 3), more usually placed obliquely (*h*). The varying conventionalizations of (*a*) or (*b*) are shown in (*d*), (*e*), and (*f*) (Griffith, "Hieroglyphics," p. 34).

(*k*) The sign for a lotus leaf, which is a phonetic equivalent of the sign (*h*), and, according to Griffith ("Hieroglyphics," p. 26), "is probably derived from the same root, on account of its shell-like outline".

(*l*) The hieroglyphic sign for a pot of water in such words as *Nu* and *Nut*.

(*m*) A "pomegranate" (replacing a bust of Tanit) upon a sacred column at Carthage (Arthur J. Evans, "Mycenæan Tree and Pillar Cult," p. 46).

(*n*) The form of the body of an octopus as conventionalized on the coins of Central Greece (compare Fig. 24 (*d*)). Its similarity to the Egyptian pot-sign (*l*) (which also has the significance of mother-goddess) is worthy of note.

phonetic equivalent to the sign labelled *k* (in the text-figure) for *ḫ* (*kha*), or apparently for *ḫ* alone in many words.

"The name of the lotus leaf is probably derived from the same root, on account of its shell-like outline or *vice versa*."

[1] Compare the two-fold meaning of the Latin *testa* as "shell" and "bowl".

[2] Compare the association of shells with altars in Minoan Crete and the widespread use of large shells as bowls for "holy water" in Christian churches.

The familiar representation of Horus (and his homologues in India and elsewhere) being born from the lotus suggests that the flower represents his mother Hathor. But as the argument in these pages has

FIG. 7.
(a) An Egyptian design representing the sun-god Horus emerging from a lotus, representing his mother Hathor (Isis).
(b) Papyrus sceptre often carried by goddesses and animistically identified with them either as an instrument of life-giving or destruction.
(c) Conventionalized lily—the prototype of the trident and the thunder-weapon.
(d) A water-plant associated with the Nile-gods.

led us towards the inference that the original form of Hathor was a shell-amulet,[1] it seems not unlikely that her identification with the lotus

[1] Miss Winifred M. Crompton, Assistant Keeper of the Egyptian Department of the Manchester Museum, has called my attention to a remarkable piece of evidence which affords additional corroboration of the view that Hathor was a development of the cowry-amulet. Upon the famous archaic palette of Narmer (Fig. 18), a sporran, composed of four representations of Hathor's head, takes the place of the original cowries that were suspended from more primitive girdles.
The cowries of the head ornament of primitive peoples of Africa and Asia (and of the Mediterranean area in early times—Schliemann's "Ilios," Fig. 685) are often replaced in Egypt by lotus flowers (W. D. Spanton, "Water Lilies of Egypt," *Ancient Egypt*, 1917, Part I, Figs. 19, 20, and 21). Upon the head-band of the statue of Nefert, which I have reproduced in Chapter I (Fig. 4), a conventional lotus design is found (see Spanton's Fig. 19), which is almost identical with the classical thunder-weapon.

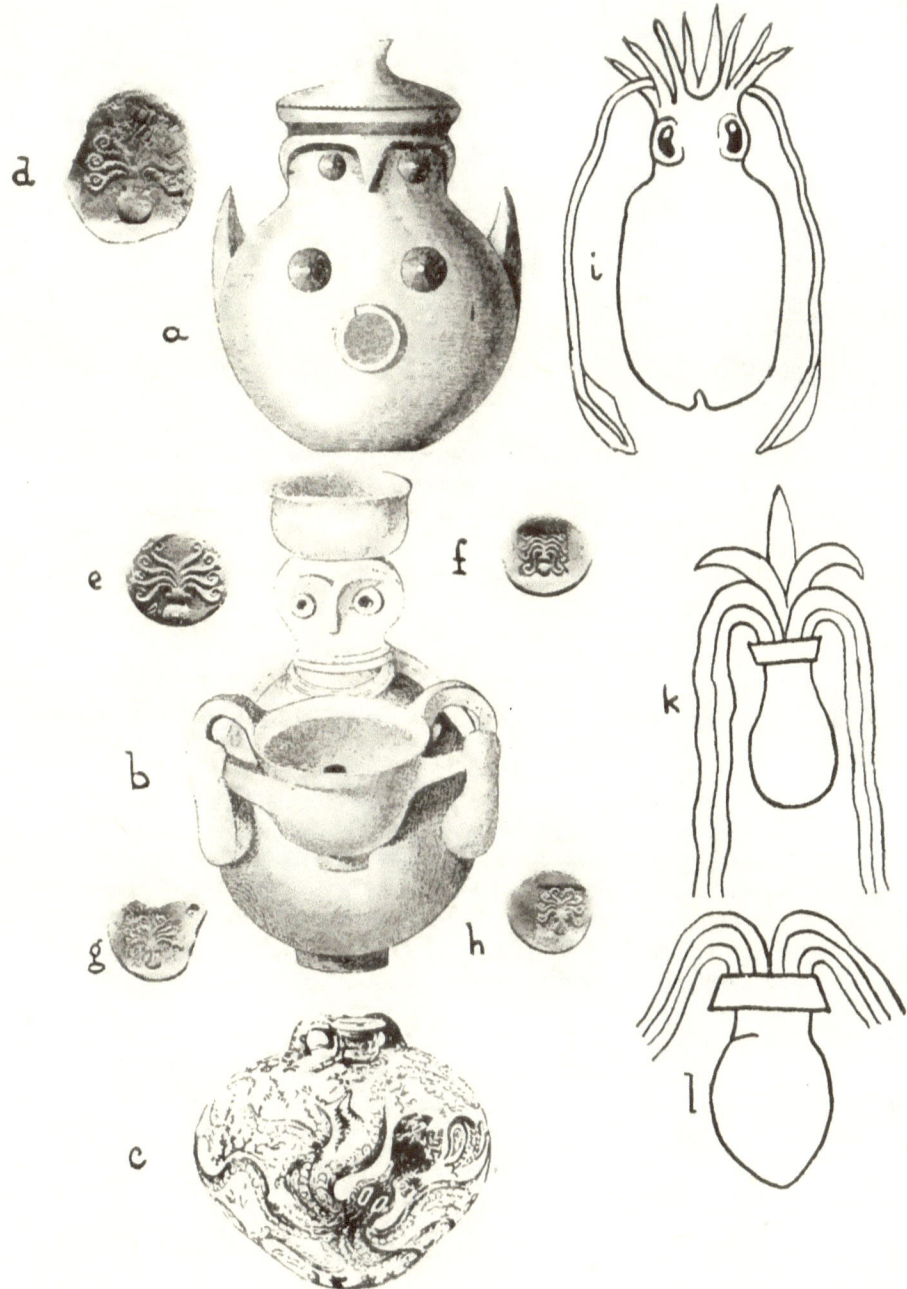

FIG. 24.

Fig. 24.

(*a*) and (*b*) Two Mycenæan pots (after Schliemann).

(*a*) The so-called "owl-shaped" vase is really a representation of the Mother-Pot in the form of a conventionalized Octopus (Houssay).

(*b*) The other vase represents the Octopus Mother-Pot, with a jar upon her head and another in her hands—a three-fold representation of the Great Mother as a pot.

(*c*) A Cretan vase from Gournia in which the Octopus-motive is represented as a decoration upon the pot instead of in its form.

(*d*), (*e*), (*f*), (*g*), and (*h*) A series of coins from Central Greece (after Head) showing a series of conventionalizations of the Octopus, with its pot-like body and palm-tree-like arms (*f*).

(*i*) *Sepia officinalis* (after Tryon).

(*h*) and (*l*) The so-called "spouting vases" in the hands of the Babylonian god Ea, from a cylinder seal of the time of Gudea, Patesi of Tello, after Ward ("Seal Cylinders, etc.," p. 215).

The "spouting vases" have been placed in conjunction with the Sepia to suggest the possibility of confusion with a conventionalized drawing of the latter in the blending of the symbolism of the water-jar and cephalopods in Western Asia and the Mediterranean.

THE BIRTH OF APHRODITE

may have arisen from the confusion between the latter and the cowry, which no doubt was also in part due to the belief that both the shell and the plant were expressions of the vital powers of the water in which they developed.

The identification of the Great Mother with a pot was one of the factors that played a part in the assimilation of her attributes with those of the Water God, who in early Sumerian pictures was usually represented pouring the life-giving waters from his pot (Fig. 24, *h* and *l*).

This idea of the Mother Pot is found not only in Babylonia, Egypt, India,[1] and the Eastern Mediterranean, but wherever the influence of these ancient civilizations made itself felt. It is widespread among the Celtic-speaking peoples. In Wales the pot's life-giving powers are enhanced by making its rim of pearls. But as the idea spread, its meaning also became extended. At first it was merely a jug of water or a basket of figs, but elsewhere it became also a witch's cauldron, the magic cup, the Holy Grail, the font in which a child is reborn into the faith, the vessel of water here being interpreted in the earliest sense as the uterus or the organ of birth. The Celtic pot, so Mr. Donald Mackenzie tells me, is closely associated with cows, serpents, frogs, dragons, birds, pearls, and " nine maidens that blow the fire under the cauldron " ; and, if the nature of these relationships be examined, each of them will be found to be a link between the pot and the Great Mother.

The witch's cauldron and the maidens who assist in the preparation of the witch's medicine seem to be the descendants respectively of Hathor's pots (in the story of the Destruction of Mankind) and the Sekti who churn up the *didi* and the barley with which to make the elixir of immortality and the sedative draught for the destructive goddess herself.

Mr. Donald Mackenzie has given me a number of additional references from Celtic and Indian literature in corroboration of these widespread associations of the pot with the Great Mother ; and he reminds me that in Oceania the coco-nut has the same reputation as the pot in the Indian *Mahābhārata*. It is the source of food and anything else that is wanted, and its supply can never be exhausted. [On some future occasion I hope to make use of the wonderful legends of the

---

[1] Among the Dravidian people at the present day the seven goddesses (corresponding to the seven Hathors) are often represented by seven pots.

pot's life-giving powers, to which Mr. Mackenzie has directed my attention. At present, however, I must content myself with the statement that the pot's identity with the Great Mother is deeply rooted in ancient belief throughout the greater part of the world.[1]]

The diverse conceptions of the Great Mother as a pot and as an octopus seem to have been blended in Mycenæan lands, where the so-called "owl-shaped" pots were clearly intended to represent the goddess in both these aspects united in one symbol. When the diffusion of these ideas into more remote parts of the world took place syntheses with other motives produced a great variety of most complex forms. In Honduras pottery vessels have been found[2] which give tangible expression to the blending of the ideas of the Mother Pot, the crocodile-like *Makara*, star-spangled like Hathor's cow, Aphrodite's

---

[1] The luxuriant crop of stories of the Holy Grail was not inspired originally by mere literary invention. A tradition sprung from the fountain-head of all mythology, the parent-story of the Destruction of Mankind, provided the materials which a series of writers elaborated into the varied assortment of legends of the Mother Pot. The true meaning of the Quest of the Holy Grail can be understood only by reading the fabled accounts of it in the light of the ancient search for the elixir of life and the historical development of the narrative describing that search.

A concise summary of the Grail literature will be found in Jessie L. Weston's "The Quest of the Holy Grail" (1913). Her theory will be found, after some slight modifications, to fall into line with the general argument of this book.

Mr. F. Ll. Griffith tells me that the Egyptian hieroglyphic for the verb "coire cum" gives frank expression to the real meaning of the symbolism of the pot as the matrix which receives the seed. The same idea provides the material for the incident of the birth of Drona (the pot-born) in the Adi Parva (Sections CXXXI, CXXXIX, and CLXVIII, in Roy's translation) of the Mahabharata, to which Mr. Donald A. Mackenzie has kindly called my attention. Drona was conceived in a pot from the seed of a Rishi. A widespread variant of the same story is the conception of a child from a drop of blood in a pot (see, for example, Hartland, "Legend of Perseus," Vol. I, pp. 98 and 144). If the pot can thus create a human being, it is easy to understand how it acquired its reputation of being also able to multiply food and provide an inexhaustible supply. Similarly, all substances, such as barley, rice, gold, pearls, and jade, to which the possession of a special vital essence or "soul substance" was attributed, were believed to be able to reproduce themselves and so increase in quantity of their own activities. As "givers of life" they were also able to add to their own life-substance, in other words to grow like any other living being.

[2] "An American Dragon," *Man*, November, 1918.

pig, and Soma's deer, and provided with the deer's antlers of the Eastern Asiatic dragon (see Chapter II, p. 103).

The New Testament sets forth the ancient conception of birth and rebirth. When Nicodemus asks: "How can a man be born again when he is old? Can he enter a second time into his mother's womb, and be born?" he is told: "Except a man be born of water and of the spirit, he cannot enter into the kingdom of God. That which is born of the flesh is flesh: and that which is born of the spirit is spirit" (John iii. 4, 5, and 6).

The phrase "born of water" refers to the birth "of the flesh"; and the mother's womb is the vessel containing "the water" from which the new life emerges. Plutarch states, with reference to the birth of Isis: "τετάρτη δε την Ἴσιν ἐν πανυγροις γενέσθαι". The great waters which produced all living things, the Egyptian god Nun and the goddess Nut, were expressed in hieroglyphic as pots of water. The goddess was identified with Hathor's celestial star-spangled cow, the original mother of the sun-god; and the word "Nun" was a symbol of all that was new, young, and fresh, and the fertilizing and life-giving waters of the annual inundation of the Nile. Hathor was the daughter of these waters, as Aphrodite was sprung from the sea-foam.

Artemis and the Guardian of the Portal.

Sir Gardner Wilkinson states (see text-figure, p. 179, *b*) that "a basket of sycamore figs" was originally the hieroglyphic sign for a woman, a goddess, or a mother. Later on (p. 199) I shall refer to the possible bearing of this Egyptian idea upon the origin of the Hebrew word for mandrakes and the allusion to "a basket of figs" in the Book of Jeremiah.

The life-giving powers attributed to "love-apples" and the association of these ideas with the fig-tree may have facilitated the transference of these attributes of "apples" to those actually growing upon a tree.

We know that Aphrodite was intimately associated, not only with "love-apples," but also with real apples. The sun-god Apollo's connexion with the apple-tree, which Dr. Rendel Harris, with great daring, wants to convert into an identity of name, was probably only one of the results of that long series of confusions between the Great

Mother (Hathor) and the Sun-god (Horus), to which I have referred in my discussion of the dragon-story.

But when Apollo's form emerges more clearly he is associated not with Aphrodite but with Artemis, whom Dr. Rendel Harris has shown to be identified with the mugwort, *Artemisia*. The association of the goddess with this plant is probably related to the identification of Sekhet with the marsh-plants of the Egyptian Delta and of Hathor and Isis with the lotus and other water plants. Any doubt as to the reality of these associations and Egyptian connexions is banished by the evidence of Artemis's male counterpart Apollo Hyakinthos and his relations to the sacred lily and other water plants.[1] Artemis was a gynæcological specialist : for she assisted women not only in childbirth and the expulsion of the placenta, but also in cases of amenorrhœa and affections of the uterus. She was regarded as the goddess of the portal, not merely of birth,[2] but also of gold and treasure, of which she possessed the key, and of the year (January).

This brings us back to the guardianship of gold and treasures which plays so vital a part in the evolution of the Mediterranean goddesses. For, like the story of the dog and the mandrake, it emphasizes the conchological ancestry of these deities and their connexion with the guardians of the subterranean palaces where pearls are found. But Artemis was not only the opener of the treasure-houses, but she also possessed the secret of the philosopher's stone : she could transmute base substances into gold,[3] for was she not the offspring of the Golden Hathor ? To open the portal either of birth or wealth she used her magic wand or key. As *Nūb*, the lady of gold, the Great Mother could not only change other substances into gold, but she was also the guardian of the treasure house of gold, pearls, and precious stones. Hence she could grant riches. Elsewhere in this chapter (p. 221) I shall explain how the goddess came to be identified with gold.

Just as Hathor, the Eye of Re, descended to provide the elixir of youth for the king who was the sun-god, so Artemis is described as

[1] Evans, *op. cit.*, p. 50.

[2] Her Latin representative, Diana, had a male counterpart and conjugate, Dianus, *i.e.* Janus, of whom it was said : " Ipse primum Janus cum puerperium concipitur . . . aditum aperit recipiendo semini ". For other quotations see Rendel Harris, *op. cit.*, p. 88 and the article " Janus " in Roscher's " Lexikon ".

[3] Rendel Harris, p. 73.

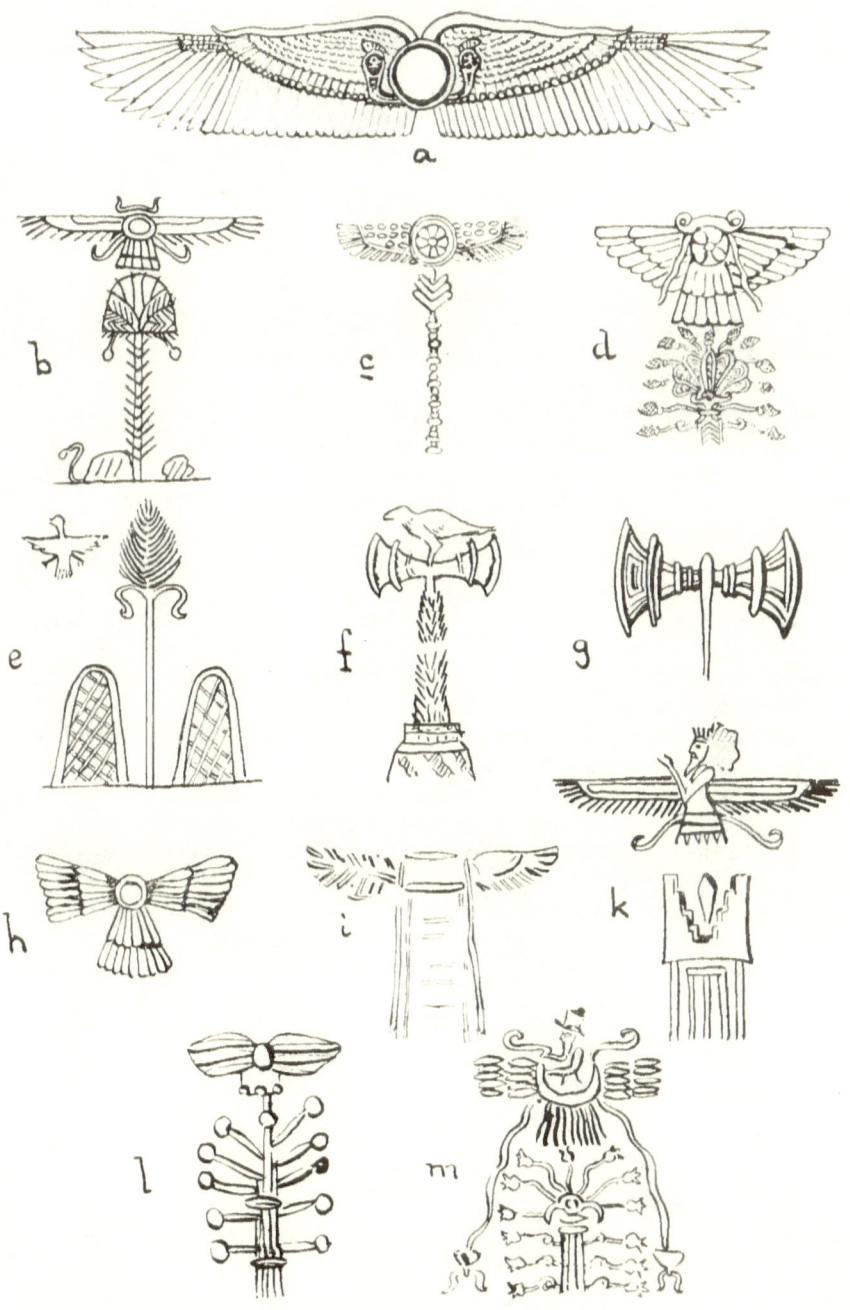

Fig. 25.

Fig. 25.

(*a*) Winged Disk from the Temple of Thothmes I.

(*b*) Persian design of Winged Disk above the Tree of Life (Ward, " Seal Cylinders of Western Asia," Fig. 1109).

(*c*) Assyrian or Syro-Hittite design of the Winged Disk and Tree of Life in an extremely conventionalized form (Ward, Fig. 1310).

(*d*) Assyrian conventionalized Winged Disk and Tree of Life, from the design upon the dress of Assurnazipal (Ward, Fig. 670).

(*e*) Part of the design from a tablet of the time of Dungi (Ward, Fig. 663). The Tree of Life (or the Great Mother) between the two mountains: alongside the tree is the heraldic eagle.

(*f*) Design on a Cretan sarcophagus from Hagia Triada (Blinckenberg, Fig. 9). The Tree of Life has now become the handle of the Double Axe, into which the Winged Disk has been transformed. But the bird which was the prototype of the Winged Disk has been added.

(*g*) Double axe from a gold signet from Acropolis Treasure, Mycenæ (after Sir Arthur Evans, " Mycenæan Tree and Pillar Cult," p. 10).

(*h*) Assyrian Winged Disk (Ward, Fig. 608) showing reduplication of the wing-pattern, possibly suggesting the doubling of each axe-blade in *g*.

(*i*) " Primitive Chaldean Winged Gate " (Ward, Fig. 349). The Gate as the Goddess of the Portal.

(*k*) Persian Winged Disk (Ward, Fig. 1144) above a fire-altar in the form suggestive of the mountains of dawn (compare Fig. 26, *c*).

(*l*) An Assyrian Tree of Life and Winged Disk crudely conventionalized (Ward, Fig. 691).

(*m*) Assyrian Tree of Life and " Winged Disk " in which the god is riding in a crescent replacing the Disk (Ward, Fig. 695).

THE BIRTH OF APHRODITE 185

travelling through the air in a car drawn by two serpents[1] seeking the most pious of kings in order that she might establish her cult with him and bless him with renewed youth.[2]

Artemis was a moon-goddess closely related to Britomartis and Diktynna, the Cretan prototype of Aphrodite. These goddesses afforded help to women in childbirth and were regarded as guardians of the portal. The goddess of streams and marshes was identified with the mugwort (*Artemisia*), which was hung above the door in the place occupied at other times by the winged disk, the thunder-stone, or a crocodile (dragon). As the guardian of portals Artemis's magic plant could open locks and doors. As the giver of life she could also withhold the vital essence and so cause disease or death; but she possessed the means of curing the ills she inflicted. Artemis, in fact, like all the other goddesses, was a witch.

In former lectures[3] I have often discussed the remarkable feature of Egyptian architecture, which is displayed in the tendency to exaggerate the door-posts and lintels, until in the New Empire the great temples become transformed into little more than monstrously overgrown doorways or pylons. I need not emphasize again the profound influence exerted by this line of development upon the Dravidian temples of India and the symbolic gateways of China and Japan.

This significance of gates was no doubt suggested by the idea that they represented the means of communication between the living and the dead, and, symbolically, the portal by which the dead acquired a rebirth into a new form of existence. It was presumably for this reason that the winged disk as a symbol of life-giving, was placed above the lintels of these doors, not merely in Egypt, Phœnicia, the Mediterranean Area, and Western Asia, but also in America,[4] and in modified forms in India, Indonesia, Melanesia, Cambodia, China, and Japan.

The discussion (Chapter II) of the means by which the winged disk came to acquire the power of life-giving, " the healing in its wings," will have made it clear that the sun became accredited with these virtues only when it assumed the place of the other " Eye of Re," the Great Mother. In fact, it was a not uncommon practice in Egypt

[1] No doubt the two uræi of the Saga of the Winged Disk.
[2] A. B. Cook, " Zeus," Vol. I, p. 244.
[3] *Journal of the Manchester Egyptian and Oriental Society*, 1916.
[4] " The Influence of Egyptian Civilization in the East and in America," *Bulletin of the John Rylands Library*, 1916.

to represent the eyes of Re or of Horus himself in place of the more usual winged disk. In the Ægean area the original practice of representing the Great Mother was retained long after it was superseded in Egypt by the use of the winged disk (the sun-god).

Over the lintel of the famous " Lion Gate" at Mycenæ, instead of the winged disk, we find a vertical pillar to represent the Mother Goddess, flanked by two lions which are nothing more than other representatives of herself (Fig. 26).

In his " Mycenæan Tree and Pillar Cult," Sir Arthur Evans has shown that all possible transitional forms can be found (in Crete and the Ægean area) between the representation of the actual goddess and her pillar- and tree-manifestations, until the stage is reached where the sun itself appears above the pillar between the lions.[1] In the large series of seals from Mesopotamia and Western Asia which have been described in Mr. William Hayes Ward's monograph,[2] we find manifold links between both the Egyptian and the Minoan cults.

The tree-form of the Great Mother there becomes transformed into the " tree of life " and the winged disk is perched upon its summit. Thus we have a duplication of the life-giving deities. The " tree of life " of the Great Mother surmounted by the winged disk which is really her surrogate or that of the sun-god, who took over from her the power of life-giving (Figs. 25 and 26).

In an interesting Cretan sarcophagus from Hagia Triada [3] the life-giving power is *tripled*. There is not only the tree representing the Great Mother herself ; but also the double axe (the winged-disk homologue of the sun-god) ; and the more direct representation of him as a bird perched upon the axe (Fig. 25, *f*).

The identification of the Great Mother with the tree or pillar seems also to have led to her confusion with the pestle with which the materials for her draught of immortality was pounded. She was also the bowl or mortar in which the pestle worked.[4]

---

[1] Evans's, Fig. 41, p. 63.
[2] " The Seal Cylinders of Western Asia," 1910.
[3] Paribeni, " Monumenti antichi dell' accademia dei Lincei." XIX, punt. 1, pll. 1-3 ; and V. Duhn, " Arch. f. Religionswissensch.," XII, p. 161, pll. 2-4 ; quoted by Blinkenberg, " The Thunder Weapon," pp. 20 and 21, Fig. 9.
[4] Without just reason, many writers have assumed that the pestle, which was identified with the handle used in the churning of the ocean (see de

THE BIRTH OF APHRODITE

As the Great Mother became confused with the pestle, so, "the Soma-plant, whose stalks are crushed by the priests to make the Soma-libation, becomes in the *Vedas* itself the Crusher or Smiter, by a very characteristic and frequent Oriental conceit in accordance with which the agent and the person or thing acted on are identified ".[1]

"The pressing-stones by means of which Soma is crushed typify thunderbolts." "In the *Rig-Veda*, we read of him [Soma] as *jyotih-rathah*, *i.e.* 'mounted on a car of light' (IX, 5, 86, verse 43); or again: 'Like a hero he holds weapons in his hand . . . mounted on a chariot' (IX, 4, 76, verse 2)"—(p. 171).

"Soma was the giver of power, of riches and treasures, flocks and herds, but above all, the giver of immortality" (p. 140).

Sir Arthur Evans is of opinion "that in the case of the Cypriote cylinders the attendant monsters and, to a certain extent, the symbolic column itself, are taken from an Egyptian solar cycle, and the inference has been drawn that the aniconic pillars among the Mycenæans of Cyprus were identified with divinities having some points in common with the sun-gods Ra, or Horus, and Hathor, the Great Mother" (*op. cit.*, pp. 63 and 64).

In attempting to find some explanation of how the tree or pillar of the goddess came to be replaced in the Indian legend by Mount Meru, the possibility suggests itself whether the aniconic form of the Great Mother placed between two relatively diminutive hills may not have helped, by confusion, to convert the cone itself into a yet bigger hill, which was identified with Mount Meru, the summit of which in other legends produced the *amrita* of the gods, either in the form of the soma plant that grew upon its heights, or the rain clouds which collected there. But, as the subsequent argument will make clear, the real reason for the identification of the Great Mother with a mountain was the belief that the sun was born from the splitting of the eastern mountain, which thus assumed the function of the sun-god's mother. Possibly the association of the tops of mountains with cloud-and rain-phenomena and the gods that controlled them played some part in the

Gubernatis, "Zoological Mythology." Vol II, p. 361), was a phallic emblem. This meaning may have been given to the handle of the churn at a later period, when the churn itself was regarded as the Mother Pot or uterus; but we are not justified in assuming that this was its primary significance.

[1] Gladys M. N. Davis, "The Asiatic Dionysos," p. 172.

development of the symbolism of mountains. [When I referred (in Chapter II, p. 98) to the fact that what Sir Arthur Evans calls "the horns of consecration" was primarily the split mountain of the dawn, I was not aware that Professor Newberry ("Two Cults of the Old Kingdom," *Annals of Archæology and Anthropology*, Liverpool, Vol. I, 1908, p. 28) had already suggested this identification.]

In the Egyptian story the god Re instructed the Sekti of Heliopolis to pound the materials for the food of immortality. In the Indian version, the gods, aware of their mortality, desired to discover some elixir which would make them immortal. To this end, Mount Meru [the Great Mother] was cast into the sea [of milk]. Vishnu, in his second avatar as a tortoise[1] supported the mountain on his back; and the Naga serpent Vasuki was then twisted around the mountain, the gods seizing its head and the demons his tail twirled the mountain until they had churned the amrita or water of life. Wilfrid Jackson has called attention to the fact that this scene has been depicted, not only in India and Japan, but also in the Precolumbian *Codex Cortes* drawn by some Maya artist in Central America.[2]

The horizon is the birthplace of the gods; and the birth of the deity is depicted with literal crudity as an emergence from the portal between its two mountains. The mountain splits to give birth to the sun-god, just as in the later fable the parturient mountain produced the "ridiculous mouse" (Apollo Smintheus). The Great Mother is described as giving birth—" the gates of the firmament are undone for Teti himself at break of day" [that is when the sun-god is born on the horizon]. "He comes forth from the Field of Earu" (Egyptian Pyramid Texts—Breasted's translation).

In the domain of Olympian obstetrics the analogy between birth and the emergence from the door of a house or the gateway of a temple is a common theme of veiled reference. Artemis, for instance, is a goddess of the portal, and is not only a helper in childbirth, but also grows in her garden a magical herb which is capable of opening locks. This reputation, however, was acquired not merely by reason of her skill in midwifery, but also as an outcome of the legend[3] of the treasure-house of pearls which was under the guardianship of the great " giver

---

[1] The tortoise was the vehicle of Aphrodite also and her representatives in Central America.

[2] Jackson, "Shells, etc.," pp. 57 *et seq*.   [3] *Vide supra*, p. 158.

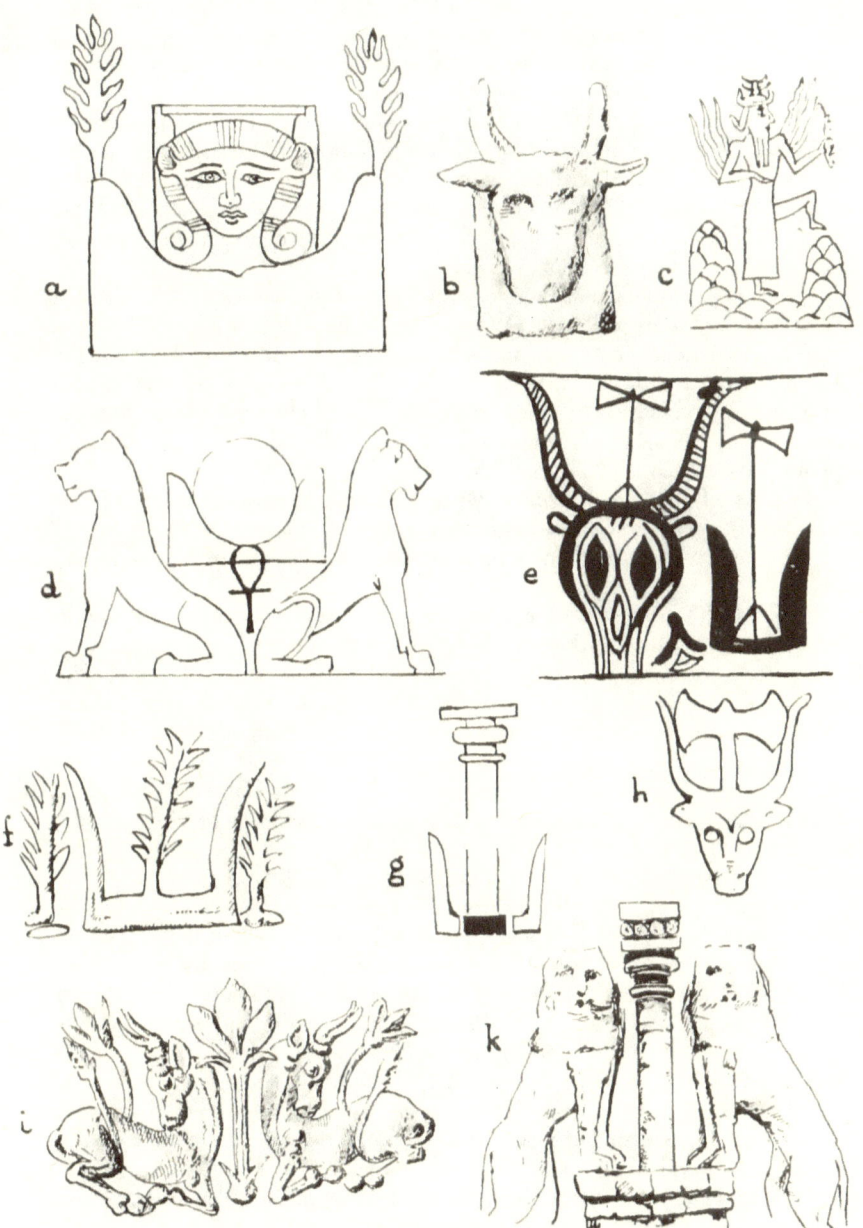

Fig. 26.

Fig. 26.

(*a*) An Egyptian picture of Hathor between the mountains of the horizon (on which trees are growing) (after Budge, "Gods of the Egyptians," Vol. II. p. 101). [This is a part only of a scene in which the goddess Nut is giving birth to the sun, whose rays illuminate Hathor on the horizon, as Sothis, the "Opener of the Way" for the sun.]

(*b*) The mountains of the horizon supporting a cow's head as a surrogate of Hathor, from a stele found at Teima in Northern Arabia, now in the Louvre (after Sir Arthur Evans, *op. cit.*, p. 39). This indicates the identity of what Evans calls "the horns of consecration" and the "mountains of the horizon," and also suggests how confusion may have arisen between the mountains and the cow's horns.

(*c*) The Mesopotamian sun-god Shamash rising between the Eastern Mountains, the Gates of Dawn (Ward, *op. cit.*, p. 373).

(*d*) The familiar Egyptian representation of the sun rising between the Eastern Mountains (the splitting of the mountain giving birth to "the ridiculous mouse"—Smintheus). The *ankh* (life-sign) below the sun is the determinative of the act of giving birth or life. The design is heraldically supported by the Great Mother's lionesses.

(*e*) Part of the design from a Mycenæan vase from Old Salamis (after Evans, p. 9). The cow's head and the Eastern Mountains are shown alongside one another, each of them supporting the Double Axe representing the god.

(*f*) Part of the design from a lentoid gem from the Idæan Cave, now in the Candia Museum (after Evans, Fig. 25). If this design be compared with the Egyptian picture (*a*), it will be seen that Hathor's place is taken by the tree-form of the Great Mother, and the trees which in the former (*a*) are growing upon the Eastern Mountains are now placed alongside the "horns". In the complete design (*vide* Evans, *op. cit.*, p. 44) a votary is represented blowing a conch-shell trumpet to animate the deity in the sacred tree.

(*g*) The Eastern Mountains supporting the pillar-form of the goddess (after Evans, Fig. 66).

(*h*) Another Mycenæan design comparable with (*e*).

(*i*) Design from a signet-ring from Mycenæ (after Evans, Fig. 34). If this be compared with the Egyptian picture (*a*) it will be noted that the Great Mother is now replaced by a tree: the Eastern Mountains by bulls, from whose backs the trees of the Eastern Mountains are sprouting. This design affords interesting corroboration of the suggestion that the Eastern Mountains may be confused with the cow's head (see *b* and *c*) or with the cow itself. Newberry (*Annals of Archæology and Anthropology*, Liverpool, Vol. I, p. 28) has called attention to the intimate association (in Protodynastic Egypt) of the Eastern Mountains, the Bull and the Double Axe—a certain token of cultural contact with Crete.

(*k*) The famous sculpture above the Lion Gate at Mycenæ. The pillar form of the Great Mother heraldically supported by her lioness-avatars, which correspond to the cattle of the design (*i*) and the Eastern Mountains of (*a*). The use of this design above the lintel of the gate brings it into homology with the Winged Disk. The Pillar represents the Goddess, as the Disk represents her Egyptian *locum tenens*, Horus; her destructive representatives (the lionesses) correspond to the two uræi of the Winged Disk design.

of life" and of which she kept the magic key. She was in fact the feminine form of Janus, the doorkeeper who presided over all beginnings, whether of birth, or of any kind of enterprise or new venture, or the commencement of the year (like Hathor). Janus was the guardian of the door of Olympus itself, the gate of rebirth into the immortality of the gods.

The ideas underlying these conceptions found expression in an endless variety of forms, material, intellectual, and moral, wherever the influence of civilization made itself felt. I shall refer only to one group of these expressions that is directly relevant to the subject-matter of this book. I mean the custom of suspending or representing the life-giving symbol above the portal of temples and houses. Thus the plant peculiar to Artemis herself, the mugwort or Artemisia, was hung above the door,[1] just as the winged disk was sculptured upon the lintel, or the thunder-stone was placed above the door of the cowhouse[2] to afford the protection of the Great Mother's powers of life-giving to her own cattle.

In the Pyramid Texts the rebirth of a dead pharaoh is described with vivid realism and directness. "The waters of life which are in the sky come. The waters of life which are in the earth come. The sky burns for thee, the earth trembles for thee, before the birth of the god. The two hills are divided, the god comes into being, the god takes possession of his body. The two hills are divided, this Neferkere comes into being, this Neferkere takes possession of his body. Behold this Neferkere—his feet are kissed by the pure waters which are from Atum, which the phallus of Shu made, which the vulva of Tefnut brought into being. They have come, they have brought for thee the pure waters from their father."[3]

[1] Rendel Harris, "The Ascent of Olympus," p. 80. In the building up of the idea of rebirth the ancients kept constantly before their minds a very concrete picture of the actual process of parturition and of the anatomy of the organs concerned in this physiological process. This is not the place to enter into a discussion of the anatomical facts represented in the symbolism of the "giver of life" presiding over the portal and the "two hills" which are divided at the birth of the deity: but the real significance of the primitive imagery cannot be wholly ignored if we want to understand the meaning of the phraseology used by the ancient writers.

[2] Blinckenberg, "The Thunder-weapon," p. 72.

[3] Aylward M. Blackman, "Sacramental Ideas and Usages in Ancient Egypt," *Proceedings of the Society of Biblical Archæology*, March, 1918, p. 64.

The Egyptians entertained the belief[1] that the sun-god was born of the celestial cow Mehetwēret, a name which means "Great Flood," and is the equivalent of the primeval ocean Nun. In other words the celestial cow Hathor, the embodiment of the life-giving waters of heaven and earth, is the mother of Horus. So also Aphrodite was born of the "Great Flood" which is the ocean.

In his report upon the hieroglyphs of Beni Hasan,[2] Mr. Griffith refers to the picture of "a woman of the marshes," which is read *sekht*, and is "used to denote the goddess Sekhet, the goddess of the marshes, who presided over the occupations of the dwellers there. Chief among these occupations must have been the capture of fish and fowl and the culture and gathering of water-plants, especially the papyrus and the lotus". Sekhet was in fact a rude prototype of Artemis in the character depicted by Dr. Rendel Harris.[3]

It is perhaps not without significance that the root of a marsh plant, the *Iris pseudacorus*[4] is regarded in Germany as a luck-bringer which can take the place of the mandrake.[5]

The Great Mother wields a magic wand which the ancient Egyptian scribes called the "Great Magician". It was endowed with the two-fold powers of life-giving and opening, which from the beginning were intimately associated the one with the other from the analogy of the act of birth, which was both an opening and a giving of life. Hence the "magic wand" was a key or "opener of the ways," wherewith, at the ceremonies of resurrection, the mouth was opened for speech and the taking of food, as well as for the passage of the breath of life, the eyes were opened for sight, and the ears for hearing. Both the physical act of opening (the "key" aspect) as well as the vital aspect of life-giving (which we may call the "uterine" aspect) were implied in this symbolism. Mr. Griffith suggests that the form of the magic wand may have been derived from that of a con-

---

[1] *Op. cit.*, p. 60.

[2] "Archæol. Survey of Egypt," 5th Memoir, 1896, p. 31.

[3] See especially *op. cit.*, p. 35, the goddess of streams and marshes, who was also herself "the mother plant," like the mother of Horus.

[4] Whose cultural associations with the Great Mother in the Eastern Mediterranean littoral has been discussed by Sir Arthur Evans, "Mycenæan Tree and Pillar Cult," pp. 49 *et seq.* Compare also *Apollo hyakinthos* as further evidence of the link with Artemis.

[5] P. J. Veth, "Internat. Arch. f. Ethnol.," Bd. 7, pp. 203 and 204.

THE BIRTH OF APHRODITE

ventionalized picture of the uterus,[1] in its aspect as a giver of life. But it is possible also that its other significance as an "opener of the ways" may have helped in the confusion of the hieroglyphic uterus-symbol with the key-symbol, and possibly also with double-axe symbol which the vaguely defined early Cretan Mother-Goddess wielded. For, as we have already seen (*supra*, p. 122), the axe also was a life-giving divinity and a magic wand (fig. 8).

In his chapter on "the Origin of the Cult of Artemis," Dr. Rendel Harris refers to the reputation of Artemis as the patron of travellers, and to Parkinson's statement: "It is said of Pliny that if a traveller binde some of the hearbe [Artemisia] with him, he shall feele no weariness at all in his journey" (p. 72). Hence the high Dutch name *Beifuss* is applied to it.

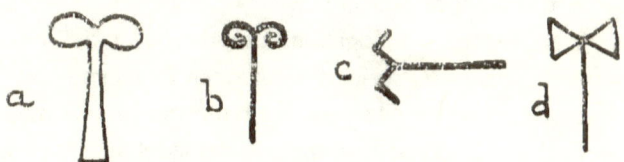

FIG. 8.

(a) "Ceremonial forked object," or "magic wand," used in the ceremony of "opening the mouth," possibly connected with (b) (a bicornuate uterus), according to Griffith ("Hieroglyphics," p. 60).
(c) The Egyptian sign for a key.
(d) The double axe of Crete and Egypt.

The left foot of the dead was called "the staff of Hathor" by the Egyptians; and the goddess was said "to make the deceased's legs to walk".[2]

It was a common practice to tie flowers to a mummy's feet, as I discovered in unwrapping the royal mummies. According to Moret (*op. cit.*) the flowers of Upper and Lower Egypt were tied under the king's feet at the celebration of the Sed festival.

Mr. Battiscombe Gunn (quoted by Dr. Alan Gardiner) states that the familiar symbol of life known as the *ankh* represents the string of a sandal.[3]

It seems to be worth considering whether the symbolism of the sandal-string may not have been derived from the life-girdle, which in

---

[1] "Hieroglyphics," p. 60.
[2] Budge, "The Gods of the Egyptians," Vol. I, pp. 436 and 437.
[3] Alan Gardiner, "Life and Death (Egyptian)," Hastings' *Encyclopædia of Religion and Ethics*.

ancient Indian medical treatises was linked in name with the female organs of reproduction and the pubic bones. According to Moret (*op. cit.*, p. 91) a girdle furnished with a tail was used as a sign of consecration or attainment of the divine life after death. Jung (*op. cit.*, p. 270), who, however, tries to find a phallic meaning in all symbolism, claims that reference to the foot has such a significance.

THE MANDRAKE.

We have now given reasons for believing that the personification of the mandrake was in some way brought about by the transference to the plant of the magical virtues that originally belonged to the cowry shell.

The problem that still awaits solution is the nature of the process by which the transference was effected.

When I began this investigation the story of the Destruction of Mankind (see Chapter II) seemed to offer an explanation of the confusion. Brugsch, Naville, Maspero, Erman, and in fact most Egyptologists, seemed to be agreed that the magical substance from which the Egyptian elixir of life was made was the mandrake. As there was no hint [1] in the Egyptian story of the derivation of its reputation from the fancied likeness to the human form, its identification with Hathor seemed to be merely another instance of those confusions with which the pathway of mythology is so thickly strewn. In other words, the plant seemed to have been used merely to soothe the excited goddess: then the other properties of "the food of the gods," of which it was an ingredient, became transferred to the mandrake, so that it acquired the reputation of being a "giver of life" as well as a sedative. If this had been true it would have been a simple process to identify this "giver of life" with the goddess herself in her rôle as the "giver of life," and her cowry-ancestor which was credited with the same reputation.

But this hypothesis is no longer tenable, because the word *d'd'* (variously transliterated *doudou* or *didi*), which Brugsch [2] and his followers interpreted as "mandragora," is now believed to have another meaning.

---

[1] As Maspero has specifically mentioned ("Dawn of Civilization," p. 166).

[2] "Die Alraune als altägyptische Zauberpflanze," *Zeitsch. f. Ægypt. Sprache*, Bd. XXIX, 1891, pp. 31-3.

THE BIRTH OF APHRODITE

In a closely reasoned memoir, Henri Gauthier[1] has completely demolished Brugsch's interpretation of this word. He says there are numerous instances of the use of *d'd'* (which he transliterates *doudouiou*) in the medical papyri. In the Ebers papyrus "*doudou* d'Eléphantine broyé" is prescribed as a remedy for external application in diseases of the heart, and as an astringent and emollient dressing for ulcers. He says the substance was brought to Elephantine from the interior of Africa and the coasts of Arabia.

Mr. F. Ll. Griffith informs me that Gauthier's criticism of the translation "mandrakes" is undoubtedly just: but that the substance referred to was most probably "red ochre" or "hæmatite".[2]

The relevant passage in the Story of the Destruction of Mankind (in Seti I's tomb) will then read as follows: "When they had brought the red ochre, the Sekti of Heliopolis pounded it, and the priestesses mixed the pulverized substance with the beer, so that the mixture resembled human blood".

I would call special attention to Gauthier's comment that the blood-coloured beer "had *some magical and marvellous property which is unknown to us*".[3]

In his dictionary Brugsch considered the determinative to refer to the fruits of a tree which he called "apple tree," on the supposed analogy with the Coptic ⲬⲒⲬⲒ, *fructus autumnalis, pomus*, the Greek ὀπώρα; and he proposed to identify the supposed fruit, then transliterated *doudou*, with the Hebrew *doudaïm*, and translate it *poma amatoria*, mandragora, or in German, *Alraune*. This interpretation was adopted by most scholars until Gauthier raised objections to it.

As Loret and Schweinfurth have pointed out, the mandrake is not found in Egypt, nor in fact in any part of the Nile Valley.[4]

But what is more significant, the Greeks translated the Hebrew

---

[1] "Le nom hiéroglyphique de l'argile rouge d'Eléphantine," *Revue Egyptologique*, XIᵉ Vol., Nos. i.-ii., 1904, p. 1.

[2] It is quite possible that the use of the name "hæmatite" for this ancient substitute for blood may itself be the result of the survival of the old tradition.

[3] It is very important to keep in mind the two distinct properties of *didi*: (*a*) its magical life-giving powers, and (*b*) its sedative influence.

[4] In Chapter II, p. 118, I have given other reasons of a psychological nature for minimizing the significance of the geographical question.

dūdā'im by μανδράγορας and the Copts did not use the word ⲝⲓⲝⲓ in their translations, but either the Greek word or a term referring to its sedative and soporific properties. Steindorff has shown (*Zeitsch. f. Ægypt. Sprache*, Bd. XXVII, 1890, p. 60) that the word in dispute would be more correctly transliterated "*didi*" instead of "*doudou*".

Finally, in a letter Mr. Griffith tells me the identification of *didi* with the Coptic ⲝⲓⲝⲓ, "apple (?)" is philologically impossible.

Although this red colouring matter is thus definitely proved not to be the fruit of a plant, there are reasons to suggest that when the story of the Destruction of Mankind spread abroad—and the whole argument of this book establishes the fact that it did spread abroad—the substance *didi* was actually confused in the Levant with the mandrake. We have already seen that in the Delta a prototype of Artemis was already identified with certain plants.

In all probability *didi* was originally brought into the Egyptian legend merely as a surrogate of the life-blood, and the mixture of which it was an ingredient was simply a restorer of youth to the king. But the determinative (in the tomb of Seti I)—a little yellow disc with a red border, which misled Naville into believing the substance to be yellow berries—may also have created confusion in the minds of ancient Levantine visitors to Egypt, and led them to believe that reference was being made to their own yellow-berried drug, the mandrake. Such an incident might have had a two-fold effect. It would explain the introduction into the Egyptian story of the sedative effects of *didi*, which would easily be rationalized as a means of soothing the maniacal goddess; and in the Levant it would have added to the real properties of mandrake[1] the magical virtues which originally belonged to *didi* (and blood, the cowry, and water).

In my lecture on "Dragons and Rain Gods" (Chapter II) I explained that the Egyptian story of the Destruction of Mankind is merely one version of a saga of almost world-wide currency. In many of the non-Egyptian versions[2] the rôle of *didi* in the Egyptian story is taken

---

[1] For the therapeutic effects of mandrake see the *British Medical Journal*, 15 March, 1890, p. 620.

[2] Even in Egypt itself *didi* may be replaced by fruit in the more specialized variants of the Destruction of Mankind. Thus, in the Saga of the Winged Disk, Re is reported to have said to Horus: "Thou didst put grapes in the water which cometh forth from Edfu". Wiedemann ("Religion of the Ancient Egyptians," p. 70) interprets this as meaning: "thou didst cause

THE BIRTH OF APHRODITE

by some *vegetable* product of a *red* colour; and many of these versions reveal a definite confusion between the red fruit and the red clay, thus proving that the confusion of *didi* with the mandrake is no mere hypothetical device to evade a difficulty on my part, but did actually occur.

In the course of the development of the Egyptian story the red clay from Elephantine became the colouring matter of the Nile flood, and this in turn was rationalized as the blood or red clay into which the bodies of the slaughtered enemies of Re were transformed,[1] and the material out of which the new race of mankind was created.[2] In other words, the new race was formed of *didi*. There is a widespread legend that the mandrake also is formed from the substance of dead bodies[3]

---

the red blood of the enemy to flow into it". But by analogy with the original version, as modified by Gauthier's translation of *didi*, it should read: "thou didst make the water blood-red with grape-juice"; or perhaps be merely a confused jumble of the two meanings.

[1] In the Babylonian story of the Deluge "Ishtar cried aloud like a woman in travail, the Lady of the gods lamented with a loud voice (saying): The old race of man hath been turned back into clay, because I assented to an evil thing in the council of the gods, and agreed to a storm which hath destroyed my people that which I brought forth" (King, "Babylonian Religion," p. 134).

The Nile god, Knum, Lord of Elephantine, was reputed to have formed the world of alluvial soil. The coming of the waters from Elephantine brought life to the earth.

[2] In the Babylonian story, Bêl "bade one of the gods cut off his head and mix the earth with the blood that flowed from him, and from the mixture he directed him to fashion men and animals" (King, "Babylonian Religion," p. 56). Bêl (Marduk) represents the Egyptian Horus who assumes his mother's rôle as the Creator. The red earth as a surrogate of blood in the Egyptian story is here replaced by earth *and* blood.

But Marduk created not only men and animals but heaven and earth also. To do this he split asunder the carcase of the dragon which he had slain, the Great Mother Tiamat, the evil *avatar* of the Mother-Goddess whose mantle had fallen upon his own shoulders. In other words, he created the world out of the substance of the "giver of life" who was identified with the red earth, which was the elixir of life in the Egyptian story. This is only one more instance of the way in which the same fundamental idea was twisted and distorted in every conceivable manner in the process of rationalization. In one version of the Osirian myth Horus cut off the head of his mother Isis and the moon-god Thoth replaced it with a cow's head, just as in the Indian myth Ganesa's head was replaced by an elephant's.

[3] See Frazer, *op. cit.*, p. 9.

often represented as innocent or chaste men wrongly killed, just as the red clay was the substance of mankind killed to appease Re's wrath, "the blood of the slaughtered saints".[1]

But the original belief is found in a more definite form in the ancient story that "the mandrake was fashioned out of the same earth whereof God formed Adam".[2] In other words the mandrake was part of the same substance as the earth *didi*.[3]

Further corroboration of this confusion is afforded by a story from Little Russia, quoted by de Gubernatis.[4] If bryony (a widely recognized surrogate of mandrake) be suspended from the girdle all the dead Cossacks (who, like the enemies of Re in the Egyptian story, had been killed and broken to pieces in the earth) will come to life again. *Thus we have positive evidence of the homology of the mandrake with red clay or hæmatite.*

The transference to the mandrake of the properties of the cowry (and the goddesses who were personifications of the shell) and blood (and its surrogates) was facilitated by the manifold homologies of the Great Mother with plants. We have already seen that the goddess was identified with : (*a*) incense-trees and other trees, such as the sycamore, which played some definite part in the burial ceremonies, either by providing the divine incense, the materials for preserving the body, or for making coffins to ensure the protection of the dead, and so make it possible for them to continue their existence ; and (*b*) the

---

[1] Compare with this the story of Picus the giant who fled to Kirke's isle and there was slain by Helios, the plant μῶλυ springing from his blood (A. B. Cook, "Zeus," p. 241, footnote 15). For a discussion of *moly* see Andrew Lang's "Custom and Myth".

[2] Frazer, p. 6.

[3] In Socotra a tree (dracæna) has been identified with the dragon, and its exudation, "dragon's blood," was called cinnabar, and confused with the mineral (red sulphide of mercury), or simply with red ochre. In the Socotran dragon-myth the elephant takes the hero's rôle, as in the American stories of Chac and Tlaloc (see Chapter II). The word *kinnabari* was applied to the thick matter that issues from the dragon when crushed beneath the weight of the dying elephant during these combats (Pliny, XXXIII, 28 and VIII, 12). The dragon had a passion for elephant's blood. Any thick red earth attributed to such combats was called *kinnabari* (Schoff, *op. cit.*, p. 137). This is another illustration of the ancient belief in the identification of blood and red ochre.

[4] "Mythologie des Plantes," Vol. II, p. 101.

THE BIRTH OF APHRODITE

lotus, the lily, the iris, and other marsh plants,[1] for reasons that I have already mentioned (p. 184).

The Babylonian poem of Gilgamesh represents one of the innumerable versions of the great theme which has engaged the attention of writers in every age and country attempting to express the deepest longings of the human spirit. It is the search for the elixir of life. The object of Gilgamesh's search is a magic *plant* to prolong life and restore youth. The hero of the story went a voyage by water in order to obtain what appears to have been a marsh plant called *dittu*.[2] The question naturally arises whether this Babylonian story and the name of the plant played any part in Palestine in blending the Egyptian and Babylonian stories and confusing the Egyptian elixir of life, the red earth *didi*, with the Babylonian elixir, the plant *dittu*?

In the Babylonian story a serpent-demon steals the magic plant, just as in India *soma*, the food of immortality, is stolen. In Egypt Isis steals Re's name,[3] and in Babylonia the Zu bird steals the tablets of

---

[1] In an interesting article on "The Water Lilies of Ancient Egypt" (*Ancient Egypt*, 1917, Part I, p. 1) Mr. W. D. Spanton has collected a series of illustrations of the symbolic use of these plants. In view of the fact that the papyrus- and lotus-sceptres and the lotus-designs played so prominent a part in the evolution of the Greek thunder-weapon, it is peculiarly interesting to find (in the remote times of the Pyramid Age) lotus designs built up into the form of the double-axe (Spanton's Figs. 28 and 29) and the classical *keraunos* (his Fig. 19).

[2] The Babylonian magic plant to prolong life and renew youth, like the red mineral *didi* of the Egyptian story. It was also "the plant of birth" and "the plant of life".

[3] Müller, Quibell, Maspero, and Sethe regard the "round cartouche," which the divine falcon often carries in place of the *ankh*-symbol of life, as a representation of the royal name (R. Weill, "Les Origines de l'Egypte pharaonique," *Annales du Musée Guimet*, 1908, p. 111). The analogous Babylonian sign known as "the rod and ring" is described by Ward (*op. cit.*, p. 413) as "the emblem of the sun-god's supremacy," a "symbol of majesty and power, like the tablets of destiny".

As it was believed in Egypt and Babylonia that the possession of a name "was equivalent to being in existence," we can regard the object carried by the hawk or vulture as a token of the giving of life and the controlling of destiny. It can probably be equated with the "tablets of destiny" so often mentioned in the Babylonian stories, which the bird god *Zu* stole from Bēl and was compelled by the sun-god to restore again. Marduk was given the power to destroy or to create, *to speak the word of command* and to control fate, to wield the invincible weapon and to be able to render objects invisible. This form of the weapon, "the word" or *logos*,

destiny, the *logos*. In Greek legend apples are stolen from the garden of Hesperides. Apples are surrogates of the mandrake and *didi*.

We have now seen that the mandrake is definitely a surrogate (*a*) of the cowry and a series of its shell-homologues, and (*b*) of the red substance in the Story of the Destruction of Mankind.

There still remain to be determined (i) the means by which the mandrake became identified with the goddess, (ii) the significance of the Hebrew word *dūdā-īm*, and (iii) the origin of the Greek word *mandragora*.

The answer to the first of these three queries should now be obvious enough. As the result of the confusion of the life-giving magical substance *didi* with the sedative drug, mandrake, the latter acquired the reputation of being a " giver of life " and became identified with *the* " giver of life," the Great Mother, the story of whose exploits was responsible for the confusion.

The erroneous identification of *didi* with the mandrake was originally suggested by Brugsch from the likeness of the word (then transliterated *doudou*) with the Hebrew word *dūdā-īm* in Genesis, usually translated " mandrakes". I have already quoted the opinion of Gauthier and Griffith as to the error of such identification. But the evidence now at our disposal seems to me to leave no doubt as to the reality of the confusion of the Egyptian red substance with the mandrake. This naturally suggests the possibility that the similarity of the sounds of the words *may* have played some part in creating the confusion : but it is impossible to admit this as a factor in the development of the story, because the Hebrew word probably arose out of the identification of the mandrake with the Great Mother and not by any confusion of names. In other words the similarity of the names of these homologous substances is a mere coincidence.

Dr. Rendel Harris claims (and Sir James Frazer seems to approve of the suggestion) that the Hebrew word *dūdā-īm* was derived from *dōdīm*, " love " ; and, on the strength of this derivation, he soars into a lofty flight of philological conjecture to transmute *dōdīm* into *Aphro-*

like all the other varieties of the thunder-weapon, could " become flesh," in other words, be an animate form of the god.

In Egyptian art it is usually the hawk of Horus (the homologue of Marduk) which carries the " round cartouche," which is the *logos*, the tablets of destiny.

THE BIRTH OF APHRODITE

dite, "love" into the "goddess of love". It would be an impertinence on my part to attempt to follow these excursions into unknown heights of cloudland.

But my colleagues Professor Canney and Principal Bennett tell me that the derivation of *dūdā-īm* from *dōdīm* is improbable; and the former authority suggests that *dūdā-īm* may be merely the plural of *dūd*, a "pot".[1] Now I have already explained how a pot came to symbolize a woman or a goddess, not merely in Egypt, but also in Southern India, and in Mycenæan Greece, and, in fact, the Mediterranean generally.[2] Hence the use of the term *dūd* for the mandrake implies either (*a*) an identification of the plant with the goddess who is the giver of life, or (*b*) an analogy between the form of the mandrake-fruit and a pot, which in turn led to it being called a pot, and from that being identified with the goddess.[3]

I should explain that when Professor Canney gave me this state-

[1] I quote Professor Canney's notes on the word *dūdā'īm* (Genesis xxx. 14) verbatim: "The *Encyclopædia Biblica* says (s.v. 'Mandrakes'): 'The Hebrew name, *dūdā'īm*, was no doubt popularly associated with *dōdīm*, הוֹדִים, "love"; but its real etymology (like that of μανδραγόρας) is obscure'.

"The same word is translated 'mandrakes' in Song of Songs vii. 13.

"*Dūdā'īm* occurs also in Jeremiah xxiv, 1, where it is usually translated 'baskets' ('baskets of figs'). Here it is the plural of a word *dūd*, which means sometimes a 'pot' or 'kettle,' sometimes a 'basket'. The etymology is again doubtful.

"I should imagine that the words in Jeremiah and Genesis have somehow or other the same etymology, and that *dūdā-īm* in Genesis has no real connexion with *dōdīm* 'love'.

"The meaning 'pot' (*dūd*, plur. *dūdā-īm*) is probably more original than 'basket'. Does *dūdā-īm* in Genesis and Song of Songs denote some kind of pot or caldron-shaped flower or fruit?"

[2] The Mother Pot is really a fundamental conception of all religious beliefs and is almost worldwide in its distribution.

[3] The fruit of the lotus (which is a form of Hathor) assumes a form (Spanton, *op. cit.*, Fig. 51) that is identical with a common Mediterranean symbol of the Great Mother, called "pomegranate" by Sir Arthur Evans (see my text-fig. 6, p. 179, *m*), which is a surrogate of the apple and mandrake. The likeness to the Egyptian hieroglyph for a jar of water (text-fig. 6, *l*) and the goddess *Nu* of the fruit of the poppy (which was closely associated with the mandrake by reason of its soporific properties) may have assisted in the transference of their attributes. The design of the water-plant (text-fig. 7, *d*) associated with the Nile god may have helped such a confusion and exchange.

ment he was not aware of the fact that I had already arrived at the conclusion that the Great Mother was identified with a pot and also with the mandrake ; but in ignorance of the meaning of the Hebrew words I had hesitated to equate the pot with the mandrake. As soon as I received his note, and especially when I read his reference to the second meaning, "basket of figs," in Jeremiah, I recalled Mr. Griffith's discussion of the Egyptian hieroglyphic (" a pot of water ") for woman, wife, or goddess, and the claim made by Sir Gardner Wilkinson that this manner of representing the word for " wife " was apparently taken from a conventionalized picture of " a basket of sycamore figs ".[1] The interpretation has now clearly emerged that the mandrake was called $dūdā'īm$ by the Hebrews because it was identified with the Mother Pot. The symbolism involved in the use of the Hebrew word also suggests that the inspiration may have come from Egypt, where a woman was called " a pot of water " or " a basket of figs ".

When the mandrake acquired the definite significance as a symbol of the Great Mother and the power of life-giving, its fruit, " the love apple," became the quintessence of vitality and fertility. The apple and the pomegranate became surrogates of the " love apple," and were graphically represented in forms hardly distinguishable from pots, occupying places which mark them out clearly as homologues of the Great Mother herself.[2]

But once the mandrake was identified with the Great Mother in the Levant the attributes of the plant were naturally acquired from her local reputation there. This explains the pre-eminently conchological aspect of the magical properties of the mandrake and the bryony.

I shall not attempt to refer in detail to the innumerable stories of red and brown apples, of rowan berries, and a variety of other red fruits that play a part in the folk-lore of so many peoples, such as *didi* played in the Egyptian myth. These fruits can be either elixirs of life and food of the gods, or weapons for overcoming the dragon as Hathor (Sekhet) was conquered by her sedative draught.[3]

[1] " A Popular Account of the Ancient Egyptians," revised and abridged, 1890, Vol. I, p. 323.
[2] See, for example, Sir Arthur Evans, " Mycenæan Tree and Pillar Worship," Fig. 27, p. 46.
[3] In a Japanese dragon-story the dragon drinks " sake " from pots set out on the shore (as Hathor drank the *didi* mixture from pots associated

THE BIRTH OF APHRODITE

In his account of the peony, Pliny ("Nat. Hist.," Book XXVIII, Chap. LX) says it has " a stem two cubits in length, accompanied by two or three others, and of a reddish colour, with a bark like that of the laurel. . . . the seed is enclosed in capsules, *some being red* and *some black* . . . it has an *astringent taste*. The leaves of the female plant *smell like myrrh*". Bostock and Riley, from whose translation I have made this quotation, add that in reality the plant is destitute of smell. In the Ebers papyrus *didi* was mixed with incense in one of the prescriptions;[1] and in the Berlin medical papyrus it was one of the ingredients of a fumigation used for treating heart disease. If my contention is justified, it may provide the explanation of how the confusion arose by which the peony came to have attributed to it a " smell like myrrh ".

Pliny proceeds: " Both plants [*i.e.* male and female] grow in the woods, and they should always be taken up at night, it is said; as it would be dangerous to do so in the day-time, the woodpecker of Mars being sure to attack the person so engaged.[2] It is stated also that the person, while taking up the root, runs great risk of being attacked with [prolapsus ani]. . . . Both plants are used[3] for various purposes: the red seed, taken in red wine, about fifteen in number, arrest menstruation; while the black seed, taken in the same proportion, in either raisin or other wine, are curative of diseases of the uterus." I refer to these red-coloured beverages and their therapeutic use in women's complaints to suggest the analogy with that other red drink administered to the Great Mother, Hathor.

In his essay, " Jacob and the Mandrakes,"[4] Sir James Frazer has called attention to the homologies between the attributes of the peony and the mandrake and to the reasons for regarding the former as Aelian's *aglaophotis*.

Pliny states (" Nat. Hist.," Book XXIV, Chap. CII) that the *aglao-*

with the river); and the intoxicated monster was then slain. From its tail the hero extracted a sword (as in the case of the Western dragons), which is now said to be the Mikado's state sword.

[1] See Gauthier, *op. cit.*, pp. 2 and 3.
[2] Compare the dog-incident in the mandrake story.
[3] Bostock and Riley add the comment that " the peony has no medicinal virtues whatever ".
[4] *Proceedings of the British Academy*, Vol. VIII, 1917, p. 16 (in the reprint).

photis " is found growing among the marble quarries of Arabia, on the side of Persia," just as the Egyptian *didi* was obtained near the granite quarries at Aswan. " By means of this plant [aglaophotis], according to Democritus, the Magi can summon the deities into their presence when they please," just as the users of the conch-shell trumpet believed they could do with this instrument. I have already (p. 196) emphasized the fact that all of these plants, mandrake, bryony, peony, and the rest, were really surrogates of the cowry, the pearl, and the conch-shell. The first is the ultimate source of their influence on womankind, the second the origin of their attribute of *aglaophotis*, and the third of their supposed power of summoning the deity. The attributes of some of the plants which Pliny discusses along with the peony are suggestive. Pieces of the root of the *achaemenis* (? perhaps *Euphorbia antiquorum* or else a night-shade) taken in wine, torment the guilty to such an extent in their dreams as to extort from them a confession of their crimes. He gives it the name also of "hippophobas," it being an especial object of terror to mares. The complementary story is told of the mandrake in mediæval Europe. The decomposing tissues of the body of an innocent victim on the gallows when they fall upon the earth can become reincarnated in a mandrake —the *main de gloire* of old French writers.

Then there is the plant *adamantis*, grown in Armenia and Cappadocia, which when *presented to a lion makes the beast fall upon its back*, and drop its jaws. Is this a distorted reminiscence of the lion-manifestation of Hathor who was calmed by the substance *didi*? A more direct link with the story of the destruction of mankind is suggested by the account of the *ophiusa*, " which is found in Elephantine, an island of Ethiopia". This plant is of a livid colour, and hideous to the sight. Taken by a person in drink, it inspires such a horror of serpents, which his imagination continually represents as menacing him that he commits suicide at last : hence it is that persons guilty of sacrilege are compelled to drink an infusion of it (Pliny, "Nat. Hist.," XXIV, 102). I am inclined to regard this as a variant of the myth of the Destruction of Mankind in which the "snake-plant" from Elephantine takes the place of the uraei of the Winged Disk Saga, and punishes the act of sacrilege by driving the delinquent into a state of delirium tremens.

The next problem to be considered is the derivation of the word *mandragora*. Dr. Mingana tells me it is a great puzzle to discover any adequate meaning. The attempt to explain it through the Sanskrit *mand*, "joy," "intoxication," or *mantasana*, "sleep," "life," or *mandra*, "pleasure," or *mantara*, "paradise tree," and *agru*, "unmarried, violently passionate," is hazardous and possibly far-fetched.

The Persian is *mardumgiah*, "man-like plant".

The Syro-Arabic word for it is *Yabrouh*, Aramaic *Yahb-kouh*, "giver of life". This is possibly the source of the Chinese *Yah-puh-lu* (Syriac *ya-bru-ha*) and *Yah-puh-lu-Yak*. The termination *Yak* is merely the Turanian termination meaning "diminutive".

The interest of the Levantine terms for the mandrake lies in the fact that they have the same significance as the word for pearl, *i.e.* "giver of life". This adds another argument (to those which I have already given) for regarding the mandrake as a surrogate of the pearl. But they also reveal the essential fact that led to the identification of the plant with the Mother-Goddess, which I have already discussed.

In Arabic the mandrake is called *abou ruhr*, "father of life," *i.e.* "giver of life".[1]

In Arabic *margan* means "coral" as well as "pearl". In the Mediterranean area coral is explained as a new and marvellous plant sprung from the petrified blood-stained branches on which Perseus hung the bleeding head of Medusa. Eustathius ("Comment. ad Dionys. Perieget." 1097) derives κοράλιον from κόρη, personifying the monstrous virgin: but Chæroboscos claims that it comes from κόρη and ἅλιον, because it is a maritime product used to make ornaments for maidens. In any case coral is a "giver of life" and as such identified with a maiden,[2] as the most potential embodiment of life-giving force. But this specific application of the word for "giver of life" was due to the fact that in all the Semitic languages, as well as in literary references in the Egyptian Pyramid Texts, this phrase was understood as a reference to the female organs of reproduction. The

---

[1] I am indebted to Dr. Alphonse Mingana for this information. But the philological question is discussed in a learned memoir by the late Professor P. J. Veth, "De Leer der Signatuur," *Internationales Archiv für Ethnographie*, Leiden, Bd. VII, 1894, pp. 75 and 105, and especially the appendix, p. 199 *et seq.*, "De Mandragora, Naschrift op het tweede Hoofdstuk der Verhandeling over de Leer der Signatur".

[2] Like the *Purpura* and the *Pterocera*, the bryony and other shells and plants.

same *double entendre* is implied in the use of the Greek word for "pig" and "cowry," these two surrogates of the Great Mother, each of which can be taken to mean the "giver of life" or the "pudendum muliebre".

Perhaps the most plausible suggestion that has been made as to the derivation of the word "mandragora" is Delâtre's claim [1] that it is compounded of the words *mandros*, "sleep," and *agora*, "object or substance," and that mandragora means "the sleep-producing substance".

This derivation is in harmony with my suggestion as to the means by which the plant acquired its magical properties. The sedative substance that, in the Egyptian hieroglyphs (of the Story of the Destruction of Mankind), was represented by yellow spheres with a red covering was confused in Western Asia with the yellow-berried plant which was known to have sedative properties. Hence the plant was confused with the mineral and so acquired all the magical properties of the Great Mother's elixir. But the Indian name is descriptive of the actual properties of the plant and is possibly the origin of the Greek word.

Another suggestion that has been made deserves some notice. It has been claimed that the first syllable of the name is derived from the Sanskrit *mandara*, one of the trees in the Indian paradise, and the instrument with which the churning of the ocean was accomplished.[2] The mandrake has been claimed to be the tree of the Hebrew paradise; and a connexion has thus been instituted between it and the *mandara*. This hypothesis, however, does not offer any explanation of how either the mandrake or the *mandara* acquired its magical attributes. The Indian tree of life was supposed to "sweat" *amrita* just as the incense trees of Arabia produce the divine life-giving incense.

But there are reasons [3] for the belief that the Indian story of the churning of the sea of milk is a much modified version of the old Egyptian story of the pounding of the materials for the elixir of life. The *mandara* churn-stick, which is often supposed to represent the

---

[1] Larousse, Article "Mandragore".

[2] I have already referred to another version of the churning of the ocean in which Mount Meru was used as a churn-stick and identified with the Great Mother, of whom the *mandara* was also an avatar.

[3] Which I shall discuss in my forthcoming book on "The Story of the Flood".

THE BIRTH OF APHRODITE

phallus,[1] was originally the tree of life, the tree or pillar which was animated by the Great Mother herself.[2] So that the *mandara* is homologous with the *mandragora*. But so far as I am aware, there is no adequate reason for deriving the latter word from the former.

The derivation from the Sanskrit words *mandros* and *agora* seems to fit naturally into the scheme of explanation which I have been formulating.

In the Egyptian story the Sekti of Heliopolis pounded the *didi* in a mortar to make "the giver of life," which by a simple confusion might be identified with the goddess herself in her capacity as "the giver of life". This seems to have occurred in the Indian legend. Lakshmi, or Sri, was born at the churning of the ocean. Like Aphrodite, who was born from the sea-foam churned from the ocean, Lakshmi was the goddess of beauty, love, and prosperity.

Before leaving the problems of mandrake and the homologous plants and substances, it is important that I should emphasize the rôle of blood and blood-substitutes, red-stained beer, red wine, red earth, and red berries in the various legends. These life-giving and death-dealing substances were all associated with the colour red, and the destructive demons Sekhet and Set were given red forms, which in turn were transmitted to the dragon, and to that specialized form of the dragon which has become the conventional way of representing Satan.

[The whole of the mandrake legend spread to China and became attached to the plants *ginseng* and *shang-luh*—see de Groot, Vol. II, p. 316 *et seq.*; also Kumagusu Minakata, *Nature*, Vol. LI, April 25, 1895, p. 608, and Vol. LIV, Aug. 13, 1896, p. 343. The

---

[1] The phallic interpretation is certainly a secondary rationalization of an incident which had no such implication originally.

[2] The "tree of the knowledge of good and evil" (Genesis ii. 17) produced fruit the eating of which opened the eyes of Adam and Eve, so that they realized their nakedness: they became conscious of sex and made girdles of fig-leaves (*vide supra*, p. 155). In other words, the tree of life had the power of love-provoking like the mandrake. In Henderson's "Celtic Dragon Myth" (p. xl) we read: "The berries for which she [Medb] craved were from the Tree of Life, the food of the gods, the eating of which by mortals brings death," and further: "The berries of the rowan tree are the berries of the gods" (p. xliii). I have already suggested the homology between these red berries, the mandrake, and the red ochre of Hathor's elixir. Thus we have another suggestion of the identity of the tree of paradise and the mandrake.

fact that the Chinese make use of the Syriac word *yabruha* (*vide supra*) suggests the source of these Chinese legends.]

The Measurement of Time.

It was the similarity of the periodic phases of the moon and of womankind that originally suggested the identification of the Great Mother with the moon, and originated the belief that the moon was the regulator of human beings.[1] This was the starting-point of the system of astrology and the belief in Fates. The goddess of birth and death controlled and measured the lives of mankind.

But incidentally the moon determined the earliest subdivision of time into months; and the moon-goddess lent the sanctity of her divine attributes to the number twenty-eight.

The sun was obviously the determiner of day and night, and its rising and setting directed men's attention to the east and the west as cardinal points intimately associated with the daily birth and death of the sun. We have no certain clue as to the factors which first brought the north and the south into prominence. But it seems probable that the direction of the river Nile,[2] which was the guide to the orientation of the corpse in its grave, may have been responsible for giving special sanctity to these other cardinal points. The association of the direction of the deceased's head with the position of the original homeland and the eventual home of the dead would have made the south a "divine" region in Predynastic times. For similar reasons the north may have acquired special significance in the Early Dynastic period.[3]

When the north and the south were added to the other two cardinal points the intimate association of the east and the west with the measurement of time would be extended to include all the four cardinal points.[4] Four became a sacred number associated with time-measurement, and especially with the sun.[5]

Many other factors played a part in the establishment of the

[1] The Greek Chronus was the son of Selene.
[2] Or possibly the situations of Upper and Lower Egypt.
[3] See G. Elliot Smith, "The Ancient Egyptians".
[4] The association of north and south with the primary subdivision of the state probably led to the inclusion of the other two cardinal points to make the subdivision four-fold.
[5] The number four was associated with the sun-god. There were four "children of Horus" and four spokes to the wheel of the sun.

THE BIRTH OF APHRODITE

sanctity of the number four. Professor Lethaby has suggested[1] that the four-sided building was determined by certain practical factors, such as the desirability of fashioning a room to accommodate a woven mat, which was necessarily of a square or oblong form. But the study of the evolution of the early Egyptian grave and tomb-superstructures suggests that the early use of slabs of stone, wooden boards, and mud-bricks helped in the process of determining the four-sided form of house and room.

When, out of these rude beginnings, the vast four-sided pyramid was developed, the direction of its sides was brought into relationship with the four cardinal points; and there was a corresponding development and enrichment of the symbolism of the number four. The form of the divine house of the dead king, who was the god, was thus assimilated to the form of the universe, which was conceived as an oblong area at the four corners of which pillars supported the sky, as the four legs supported the Celestial Cow.

Having invested the numbers four and twenty-eight with special sanctity and brought them into association with the measurement of time, it was a not unnatural proceeding to subdivide the month into four parts and so bring the number seven into the sacred scheme. Once this was done the moon's phases were used to justify and rationalize this procedure, and the length of the week was incidentally brought into association with the moon-goddess, who had seven *avatars*, perhaps originally one for each day of the week. At a later period the number seven was arbitrarily brought into relationship with the Pleiades.

The seven Hathors were not only mothers but fates also. Aphrodite was chief of the fates.

The number seven is associated with the pots used by Hathor's priestesses at the celebration inaugurating the new year; and it plays a prominent part in the Story of the Flood. In Babylonia the sanctity of the number received special recognition. When the goddess became the destroyer of mankind, the device seems to have been adopted of intensifying her powers of destruction by representing her at times as seven demons.[2]

[1] "Architecture," p. 24.
[2] See the chapter on "Magic" in Jevons, "Comparative Religion". In his article "Magic (Egyptian)," in Hastings' *Encyclopædia of Religion and Ethics* (p. 266), Dr. Alan Gardiner makes the following statement:

But the Great Mother was associated not only with the week and month but also with the year. The evidence at our disposal seems to suggest that the earliest year-count was determined by the annual inundation of the river. The annual recurrence of the alternation of winter and summer would naturally suggest in a vague way such a subdivision of time as the year; but the exact measurement of that period and the fixing of an arbitrary commencement, a New Year's day, were due to other reasons. In the Story of the Destruction of Mankind it is recorded that the incident of the soothing of Hathor by means of the blood-coloured beer (which, as I have explained elsewhere,[1] is a reference to the annual Nile flood) was celebrated annually on New Year's day.

Hathor was regarded in tradition as the cause of the inundation. She slaughtered mankind and so caused the original "flood": in the next phase she was associated with the 7000 jars of red beer; and in the ultimate version with the red-coloured river flood, which in another story was reputed to be "the tears of Isis".

Hathor's day was in fact the date of the commencement of the inundation and of the year; and the former event marked the beginning of the year and enabled men for the first time to measure its duration. Thus Hathor[2] was the measurer of the year, the month, and the week; while her son Horus (Chronus) was the day-measurer.

"The mystical potency attaching to certain *numbers* doubtless originated in associations of thought that to us are obscure. The number seven, in Egyptian magic, was regarded as particularly efficacious. Thus we find references to the seven Hathors: *cf.* αἱ ἑπτὰ Τύχαι τοῦ οὐρανοῦ (A. Dieterich, *Eine Mithrasliturgie*, Leipzig, 1910, p. 71): 'the seven daughters of Re,' who 'stand and weep and make seven knots in their seven tunics'; and similarly 'the seven hawks who are in front of the barque of Re'."

Are the seven daughters of Re the seven days of the week, or the representatives of Hathor corresponding to the seven days?

[1] Chapter II, p. 118.

[2] We have already seen that the primitive aspect of life-giving that played an essential part in the development of the story we are considering was the search for the means by which youth could be restored. It is significant that Hathor's reputed ability to restore youth is mentioned in the Pyramid Texts in association with her functions as the measurer of years: for she is said "to turn back the years from King Teti," so that they pass over him without increasing his age (Breasted, "Thought and Religion in Ancient Egypt," p. 124).

THE BIRTH OF APHRODITE

In Tylor's "Early History of Mankind" (pp. 352 *et seq.*) there is a concise summary of some of the widespread stories of the Fountain of Youth which restores youthfulness to the aged who drank of it or bathed in it. He cites instances from India, Ethiopia, Europe, Indonesia, Polynesia, and America. "The Moslem geographer, Ibn-el-Wardi, places the Fountain of Life in the dark south-western regions of the earth" (p. 353).

The star Sothis rose heliacally on the first day of the Egyptian New Year.[1] Hence it became "the second sun in heaven," and was identified with the goddess of the New Year's Day. The identification of Hathor with this "second sun"[2] may explain why the goddess is said to have entered Re's boat. She took her place as a crown upon his forehead, which afterwards was assumed by her surrogate, the fire-spitting uræus-serpent. When Horus took his mother's place in the myth, he also entered the sun-god's boat, and became the prototype of Noah seeking refuge from the Flood in the ship the Almighty instructed him to make.

In memory of the beer-drinking episode in the Destruction of Mankind, New Year's Day was celebrated by Hathor's priestesses in wild orgies of beer drinking.

This event was necessarily the earliest celebration of an anniversary, and the prototype of all the incidents associated with some special day in the year which have been so many milestones in the historical progress of civilization.

The first measurement of the year also naturally forms the starting-point in the framing of a calendar.

Similar celebrations took place to inaugurate the commencement of the year in all countries which came, either directly or indirectly, under Egyptian influence.

The month Ἀφροδίσια (so-called from the festival of the goddess) began the calendar of Bithynia, Cyprus, and Iasos, just as Hathor's feast was a New Year's celebration in Egypt.

---

[1] Breasted ("Religion and Thought in Ancient Egypt," p. 22) states that as the inundation began at the rising of Sothis, the star of Isis, sister of Osiris, they said to him [*i.e.* Osiris] : "The beloved daughter, Sothis, makes thy fruits (rnpwt) in her name of ' Year ' (rnpt) ".

[2] The Great Mother was identified with the moon, but when she became specialized, her representative adopted Sothis or Venus as her star.

In the celebration of these anniversaries the priestesses of Aphrodite worked themselves up in a wild state of frenzy ; and the term ὑστήρια[1] became identified with the state of emotional derangement associated with such orgies. The common belief that the term " hysteria " is derived directly from the Greek word for uterus is certainly erroneous. The word ὑστήρια was used in the same sense as Ἀφροδίσια, that is, as a synonym for the festivals of the goddess. The " hysteria " was the name for the orgy in celebration of the goddess on New Year's day : then it was applied to the condition produced by these excesses ; and ultimately it was adopted in medicine to apply to similar emotional disturbances. Thus both the terms " hysteria " and " lunacy "[2] are intimately associated with the earliest phases in the moon-goddess's history ; and their survival in modern medicine is a striking tribute to the strong hold of effete superstition in this branch of the diagnosis and treatment of disease.[3]

I have already referred to the association of Artemis with the portal of birth and rebirth. As the guardian of the door her Roman representative Diana and her masculine *avatar* Dianus or Janus gave the name to the commencement of the year. The Great Mother not only initiated the measurement of the year, but she (or her representative) lent her name to the opening of the year in various countries.

But the story of the Destruction of Mankind has preserved the record not only of the circumstances which were responsible for originating the measurement of the year and the making of a calendar, but also of the materials out of which were formed the mythical epochs pre-

---

[1] " At Argos the principal fête of Aphrodite was called ὑστήρια because they offered sacrifices of pigs (" Athen." III, 49, 96 ; " Clem. Alex. Protr." 33) "—Article " Aphrodisia," *Dict. des Antiquités*, p. 308. The Greek word for pig had the double significance of " pig " and " female organs of reproduction ".

[2] Aphrodite sends Aphrodisiac " mania " (see Tümpel, *op. cit.*, pp. 394 and 395).

[3] There is still widely prevalent the belief in the possibility of being " moonstruck," and many people, even medical men who ought to know better, solemnly expound to their students the influence of the moon in producing " lunacy ". If it were not invidious one could cite instances of this from the writings of certain teachers of psychological medicine in this country within the last few months. The persistence of these kinds of traditions is one of the factors that make it so difficult to effect any real reform in the treatment of mental disease in this country.

THE BIRTH OF APHRODITE

served in the legends of Greece and India and many other countries further removed from the original centre of civilization When the elaboration of the early story involved the destruction of mankind, it became necessary to provide some explanation of the continued existence of man upon the earth. This difficulty was got rid of by creating a new race of men from the fragments of the old or from the clay into which they had been transformed (*supra*, p. 196). In course of time this *secondary* creation became the basis of the familiar story of the *original* creation of mankind. But the story also became transformed in other ways. Different versions of the process of destruction were blended into one narrative, and made into a series of catastrophes and a succession of acts of creation. I shall quote (from Mr. T. A. Joyce's "Mexican Archæology," p. 50) one example of these series of mythical epochs or world ages to illustrate the method of synthesis :—

When all was dark Tezcatlipoca transformed himself into the sun to give light to men.

1. This sun terminated in the destruction of mankind, including a race of giants, by *jaguars*.

2. The second sun was Quetzalcoatl, and his age terminated in a terrible *hurricane*, during which mankind was transformed into monkeys.

3. The third sun was Tlaloc, and the destruction came by a *rain of fire*.

4. The fourth was Chalchintlicue, and mankind was finally destroyed by a *deluge*, during which they became fishes.

The first episode is clearly based upon the story of the lioness-form of Hathor destroying mankind : the second is the Babylonian story of Tiamat, modified by such Indian influences as are revealed in the *Ramayana :* the third is inspired by the Saga of the Winged Disk ; and the fourth by the story of the Deluge.

Similar stories of world ages have been preserved in the mythologies of Eastern Asia, India, Western Asia, and Greece, and no doubt were derived from the same original source.

THE SEVEN-HEADED DRAGON.

I have already referred to the magical significance attached to the number seven and the widespread references to the seven Hathors, the seven winds to destroy Tiamat, the seven demons, and the seven fates.

In the story of the Flood there is a similar insistence on the seven-fold nature of many incidents of good and ill meaning in the narrative. But the dragon with this seven-fold power of wrecking vengeance came to be symbolized by a creature with seven heads.

A Japanese story told in Henderson's notes to Campbell's "Celtic Dragon Myth"[1] will serve as an introduction to the seven-headed monster :—

"A man came to a house where all were weeping, and learned that the last daughter of the house was to be given to a dragon with *seven or eight*[2] heads who came to the sea-shore yearly to claim a victim. He went with her, enticed the dragon to drink *sake* from pots set out on the shore, and then he slew the monster. From the end of his tail he took out a sword, which is supposed to be the Mikado's state sword. He married the maiden, and with her got a jewel or talisman which is preserved with the regalia. A third thing of price so preserved is a mirror."

The seven-headed dragon is found also in the Scottish dragon-myth, and the legends of Cambodia, India, Persia, Western Asia, East Africa, and the Mediterranean area.

The seven-headed dragon probably originated from the seven Hathors. In Southern India the Dravidian people seem to have borrowed the Egyptian idea of the seven Hathors. "There are seven Mari deities, all sisters, who are worshipped in Mysore. All the seven sisters are regarded vaguely as wives or sisters of Siva."[3] At one village in the Trichinopoly district Bishop Whitehead found that the goddess Kāliamma was represented by seven brass pots, and adds: "It is possible that the seven brass pots represent seven sisters or the seven virgins sometimes found in Tamil shrines" (p. 36). But the goddess who animates seven pots, who is also the seven Hathors, is probably well on the way to becoming a dragon with seven heads.

There is a close analogy between the Swahili and the Gaelic stories that reveals their ultimate derivation from Babylonia. In the Scottish

---

[1] "The Celtic Dragon Myth," by J. F. Campbell, with the "Geste of Fraoch and the Dragon," translated with introduction by George Henderson, Edinburgh, 1911, p. 134.

[2] My italics.

[3] Henry Whitehead (Bishop of Madras), "The Village Gods of South India," Oxford, 1916, p. 24.

THE BIRTH OF APHRODITE 213

story the seven-headed dragon comes in a storm of wind and spray. The East African serpent comes in a storm of wind and dust.[1] In the Babylonian story seven winds destroy Tiamat.

"The famous legend of the seven devils current in antiquity was of Babylonian origin, and belief in these evil spirits, who fought against the gods for the possession of the souls and bodies of men, was widespread throughout the lands of the Mediterranean basin. Here is one of the descriptions of the seven demons :—

"Of the seven the first is the south wind. . . .

"The second is a dragon whose open mouth. . . .

"The third is a panther whose mouth spares not.

"The fourth is a frightful python. . . .

"The fifth is a wrathful . . . who knows no turning back.

"The sixth is an on-rushing . . . who against god and king [attacks].

"The seventh is a hurricane, an evil wind which [has no mercy].

"The Babylonians were inconsistent in their description of the seven devils, describing them in various passages in different ways. In fact they actually conceived of a very large number of these demons, and their visions of the other evil spirits are innumerable. According to the incantation of Shamash-shum-ukin fifteen evil spirits had come into his body and

"'My God who walks at my side they drove away.'

"The king calls himself 'the son of his God'. We have here the most fundamental doctrines of Babylonian theology, borrowed originally from the religious beliefs of the Sumerians. For them man in his natural condition, at peace with the gods and in a state of atonement, is protected by a divine spirit whom they conceived of as dwelling in their bodies along with their souls or 'the breath of life'. In many ways the Egyptians held the same doctrine, in their belief concerning the *ka*[2] or the soul's double. According to the beliefs of the Sumerians and Babylonians these devils, evil spirits, and all evil powers stand for ever waiting to attach (*sic*) (? attack) the divine genius with each man. By means of insinuating snares they entrap mankind in the meshes of their magic. They secure possession of his soul and body by leading him into sin, or bringing him into contact with tabooed things, or by overcoming his divine protector with sympathetic magic.

---

[1] "The Celtic Dragon Myth," p. 136.　　[2] See Chapter I, p. 47.

... These adversaries of humanity thus expel a man's god, or genius, or occupy his body. These rituals of atonement have as their primary object the ejection of the demons and the restoration of the divine protector. Many of the prayers end with the petition, 'Into the kind hands of his god and goddess restore him'.

"Representations of the seven devils are somewhat rare.... The Brit. Mus. figurine represents the demon of the winds with body of a dog, scorpion tail, bird legs and feet" (S. Langdon, "A Ritual of Atonement for a Babylonian King," *The Museum Journal* [University of Pennsylvania], Vol. VIII, No. 1, March, 1917, pp. 39-44).

But the Babylonians not only adopted the Egyptian conception of the power of evil as being seven demons, but they also seem to have fused these seven into one, or rather given the real dragon seven-fold attributes.[1]

In "The Cuneiform Inscriptions of Western Asia"[2] (British Museum), Marduk's weapon is compared to "the fish with seven wings".

The god himself is represented as addressing it in these words: "The tempest of battle, my weapon of fifty heads, which like the great serpent of seven heads is yoked with seven heads, which like the strong serpent of the sea (sweeps away) the foe".

In the Japanese story which I have quoted, the number of the dragon's heads is given as *seven* or *eight*; and de Visser is at a loss to know why "the number eight should be stereotyped in these stories of [Japanese] dragons".[3]

I have already emphasized the worldwide association of the seven-

---

[1] I do not propose to discuss here the interesting problems raised by this identification of the dragon with a man's good or evil spirit. But it is worthy of note that while the Babylonian might be possessed by seven evil spirits, the Egyptian could have as many as fourteen good spirits or *kas*. In a form somewhat modified by the Indian and Indonesian channels, through which they must have passed, these beliefs still persist in Melanesia; and the illuminating account of them given by C. E. Fox and F. W. Drew ("Beliefs and Tales of San Cristoval," *Journ. Roy. Anthropol. Inst.*, Vol. XLV, 1915, p. 161), makes it easier to us to form some conception of their original meaning in ancient Babylonia and Egypt. The *ataro* which possesses a man (and there may be as many as a hundred of these "ghosts") leaves his body at death and usually enters a shark (or in other cases an octopus, skate, turtle, crocodile, hawk, kingfisher, tree, or stone).

[2] Vol. II, 19, 11-18, and 65, quoted by Sayce, *Hibbert Lectures*, p. 282.

[3] *Op. cit.*, p. 150.

headed dragon with storms. The Argonaut (usually called "Nautilus" by classical scholars) was the prophet of ill-luck and the storm-bringer: but, true to the paradox that runs through the whole tissue of mythology, this form of the Great Mother is also a benevolent warner against storms. This seems to be another link between the seven-headed dragon and these cephalopoda.

I would suggest, merely as a tentative working hypothesis, that the process of blending the seven *avatars* of the dragon into a seven-headed dragon may have been facilitated by its identification with the *Pterocera* and the octopus. We know that the octopus and the shell-fish were forms assumed by the dragon (see p. 172): the confusion between the numbers seven and eight is such as might have been created during the transference of the *Pterocera's* attributes to the octopus (*vide supra*, p. 170); and the Babylonian reference to "the fish with seven wings," which was afterwards rationalized into "a great serpent with seven heads," seems to provide the clue which explains the origin of the seven-headed dragon. If Hathor was a seven-fold goddess and at the same time was identified with the seven-spiked spider-shell (*Pterocera*), the process of converting the shell-fish's seven "wings" into seven heads would be a very simple one for an ancient story-teller. If this hypothesis has any basis in fact, the circumstance that the beliefs concerning the *Pterocera* must (from the habitat of the shell-fish) have come into existence upon the shores of Southern Arabia would explain the appearance of the derived myth of the seven-headed dragon in Babylonia.

My attention was first called to the possibility of the octopus being the parent of the seven-headed dragon, and one of the forms assumed by the thunderbolt, by the design upon a krater from Apulia.[1] The weapon seemed to be a conventionalization of the octopus. Though further research has led me to distrust this interpretation, it has convinced me of the intimate association of the octopus and the derived spiral ornament with thunder and the dragon, and has suggested that the process of blending the seven demons into a seven-headed demon has been assisted by the symbolism of the octopus and the *Pterocera*.

---

[1] A. B. Cook, "Zeus," Vol. I, p. 337, in which (Fig. 269) the rider in the car is *welcoming* the thunderbolt as a divine gift from heaven, *i.e.* as a life-amulet, a giver of fertility and good luck. For a design representing the octopus as a weapon of the god Eros see the title-page of Usener's "Die Sintfluthsagen," 1899.

The Pig.

I have already referred to the circumstances that were responsible for the identification of the cow with the Great Mother, the sky, and the moon. Once this had happened, the process seems to have been extended to include other animals which were used as food, such as the sheep, goat, pig, and antelope (or gazelle and deer). In Egypt the cow continued to occupy the pre-eminent place as a divine animal; and the cow-cult extended from the Mediterreanean to equatorial Africa, to Western Europe, and as far East as India. But in the Mediterranean area the pig played a more prominent part than it did in Egypt.[1] In the latter country Osiris, Isis, and especially Set, were identified with the pig; and in Syria the place of Set as the enemy of Osiris (Adonis) was taken by an actual pig. But throughout the Eastern Mediterranean the pig was also identified with the Great Mother and associated with lunar and sky phenomena. In fact at Troy the pig was represented[2] with the star-shaped decorations with which Hathor's divine cow (in her rôle as a sky-goddess) was embellished in Egypt. To complete the identification with the cow-mother Cretan fable represents a sow suckling the infant Minos or the youthful Zeus-Dionysus as his Egyptian prototype was suckled by the divine cow.

Now the cowry-shell was called χοῖρος by the Greeks. The pig, in fact, was identified both with the Great Mother and the shell; and it is clear from what has been said already in these pages that the reason for this strange homology was the fact that originally the Great Mother was nothing more than the cowry-shell.

But it was not only with the shell itself that the pig was identified but also with what the shell symbolized. Thus the term χοῖρος had an obscene significance in addition to its usual meaning "pig" and its acquired meaning "cowry". This fact seems to have played some part in fixing upon the pig the notoriety of being "an unclean animal".[3] But it was mainly for other reasons of a very different kind that the eating of swine-flesh was forbidden. The tabu seems to have arisen

---

[1] And also, in a misunderstood form, even as far as America.

[2] Schliemann, "Ilios," Fig. 1450, p. 616.

[3] This is seen in the case of the Persian word *khor*, which means both "pig" and "harlot" or "filthy woman". The possibility of the derivation of the old English word "[w]hore" from the same source is worth considering.

THE BIRTH OF APHRODITE

originally because the pig was a sacred animal identified with the Great Mother and the Water God, and especially associated with both these deities in their lunar aspects.

According to a Cretan legend the youthful god Zeus-Dionysus was suckled by a sow. For this reason "the Cretans consider this animal sacred, and will not taste of its flesh ; and the men of Præsos perform sacred rites with the sow, making her the first offering at the sacrifice".[1]

But when the pig also assumed the rôle of Set, as the enemy of Osiris, and became the prototype of the devil, an active aversion took the place of the sacred tabu, and inspired the belief in the unwholesomeness of pig flesh. To this was added the unpleasant reputation as a dirty animal which the pig itself acquired, for the reasons which I have already stated.

I have already referred to the irrelevance of Miss Jane Harrison's denial of the birth of Aphrodite from the sea (p. 141). Miss Harrison does not seem to have realized that in her book[2] she has collected evidence which is much more relevant to the point at issue. For, in the interesting account of the Eleusinian Mysteries (pp. 150 *et seq.*), she has called attention to the important rite upon the day " called in popular parlance ' ἅλαδε μύσται,' ' to the sea ye mystics ' " (p. 152), which, I think, has a direct bearing upon the myth of Aphrodite's birth from the sea.

The Mysteries were celebrated at full moon ; and each of the candidates for admission " took with him his own pharmakos,[3] a young pig ".

" Arrived at the sea, each man bathed with his pig " (p. 152). On one occasion, so it is said, " when a mystic was bathing his pig, a sea-monster ate off the lower part of his body " (p. 153). So important was the pig in this ritual " that when Eleusis was permitted (B.C. 350-327) to issue her autonomous coinage it is the pig she chooses as the sign and symbol of her mysteries " (p. 153).

" On the final day of the Mysteries, according to Athenæus, two vessels called *plemochoæ* are emptied, one towards the East and the other towards the West, and at the moment of outpouring a mystic

---

[1] L. R. Farnell, "Cults of the Greek States." Vol. I, p. 37.
[2] "Prolegomena to the Study of Greek Religion."
[3] Which, in fact, was intended as the equivalent of φάρμακον ἀθανασίας, " the redeeming blood ".

formulary was pronounced. . . . What the mystic formulary was we cannot certainly say, but it is tempting to connect the libation of the *plemochoæ* with a formulary recorded by Proclos. He says ' In the Eleusinian mysteries, looking up to the sky they cried aloud " Rain," and looking down to earth they cried " Be fruitful " ' " (p. 161).

In these latter incidents we see, perhaps, a distant echo of Hathor's pots of blood-coloured beer that were poured out upon the soil, which in a later version of the story became the symbol of the inundation of the river and the token of the earth's fruitfulness. The personification in the Great Mother of these life-giving powers of the river occurred at about the same time ; and this was rationalized by the myth that she was born of the sea. She was also identified with the moon and a sow. Hence these Mysteries were celebrated, both in Egypt and in the Mediterranean, at full moon, and the pig played a prominent part in them. The candidates washed the sacrificial pig in the sea, not primarily as a rite of purification,[1] as is commonly claimed, but because the sacrificial animal was merely a surrogate of the cowry, which lived in the sea, and of the Great Mother,[2] who was sprung from the cowry and hence born of the sea. In the story of the man carrying the pig being attacked by a sea-monster, perhaps we have an incident of that widespread story of the shark guarding the pearls. We have already seen how it was distorted into the fantastic legend of the dog's rôle in the digging up of mandrakes. In the version we are now considering the pearl's place is taken by the pig, both of them surrogates of the cowry.

The object of the ceremony of carrying the pig into the sea was not the cleansing of " the unclean animal," nor was it *primarily* a rite of purification in any sense of the term : it was simply a ritual procedure for identifying the sacrifice with the goddess by putting it in her own medium, and so transforming the surrogate of the sea-shell, the prototype of the sea-born goddess, into the actual Great Mother.

The question naturally arises : what was the real purpose of the sacrifice of the pig ?

---

[1] Blackman (" Sacramental Ideas and Usages in Ancient Egypt," *Proceedings of the Society of Biblical Archæology*, March, 1918, p. 57 ; and May, 1918, p. 85) has shown that the idea of purification was certainly entertained.

[2] In some places an image of the goddess was washed in the sea.

THE BIRTH OF APHRODITE

In the story of the Destruction of Mankind we have seen that originally a human victim was slain for the purpose of obtaining the life-giving human blood to rejuvenate the ageing king. Two circumstances were responsible for the modification of this procedure. In the first place, there was the abandonment of human sacrifice and the substitution of either beer coloured red with ochre to resemble blood (or in other cases red wine) or the actual blood of an animal sacrifice in place of the human blood. Secondly, the blood of the Great Mother herself (personified in the special *avatar* that was recognized in a particular locality, the cow in one place, the pig in another, and so on) was regarded as more potent as a life-giving force than that of a mere mortal human being. It is possible, perhaps even probable, that this was the real reason for the abandoning of human sacrifice and the substitution of an animal for a human being. For it is unlikely that, in the rude state of society which had become familiarized with and brutalized by the practice of these bloody rites of homicide, ethical motives alone would have prompted the abolition of the custom of human sacrifice, to which such deep significance was attached. The substitution of the animal was prompted rather by the idea of obtaining a more potent elixir from the life-blood of the Great Mother herself in her cow- or sow-forms.

In the transitional stage of the process of substitution of an animal for a human being some confusion seems to have arisen as to the ritual meaning of the new procedure. If Moret's account of the Egyptian Mysteries [1] is correct—and without a knowledge of Egyptian philology I am not competent to express an opinion upon this matter—the attempt was made to identify the animal victim of sacrifice with the human being whose place it had taken. In the procession a human being wore the skin of an animal; and, according to Moret, there was a ceremony of passing a human being through the skin as a ritual procedure for transforming the mock victim into the animal which was to be sacrificed in his place. If there is any truth in this interpretation, such a ceremony must have been prompted by a misunderstanding of the meaning of the sacrifice, unless the identification of the sacrificial animal with the goddess was merely a secondary rationalization of the substitution which had been made for ethical or some other reasons.

We know that the dead were often buried in the skins of sacrificial

[1] "Mystères Égyptiens."

animals, and so identified with the life-giving deities and given rebirth. We know also that in certain ceremonies the appropriate skins were worn by those who were impersonating particular gods or goddesses. The wearing of these skins of divine animals seems to have been prompted not so much by the idea of a reincarnation in animal form as by the desire for identification and communion with the particular deity which the animal represented. The whole question, however, is one of great complexity, which can only be settled by a critical study of the texts by some scholar who keeps clearly before his mind the real issues, and refuses to take refuge in the stereotyped evasions of conventional methods of interpretation.

The sacrifice of the sow to Demeter is merely a late variant of Hathor's sacrifice of a human being to rejuvenate the king Re. How the real meaning of the story became distorted I have already explained in Chapter II ("Dragons and Rain Gods"). The killing of the sow to obtain a good harvest is homologous with the sacrifice of a maiden to obtain a good inundation of the river. The sow is the surrogate of the beautiful princess of the fairy tale. Instead of the maiden being slain, in one case, as Andromeda, she is rescued by the hero, in the other her place is taken by a sow. These late rationalizations are merely glosses of the deep motives which more than fifty centuries ago seem to have prompted early pharmacologists to obtain a more potent elixir than human blood by stealing from the heights of Olympus the divine blood of the life-giving deities themselves.

The pig was identified not only with the Great Mother, but with Osiris and Set also. With the pig's lunar and astral associations I do not propose to deal in these pages, as the astronomical aspects of the problems are so vast as to need much more space than the limits imposed in this statement. But it is important to note that the identification of Set with a pig was perhaps the main factor in riveting upon this creature the fetters of a reputation for evil. The evil dragon was the representative of both Set and the Great Mother (Sekhet or Tiamat); and both of them were identified with the pig. Just as Set killed Osiris, so the pig gave Adonis his mortal injury.[1] When these earthly incidents were embellished with a celestial significance, the con-

---

[1] Mr. Donald Mackenzie has collected a good deal of folklore concerning the pig ("Myths of Egypt," pp. 66 *et seq.*; also his books on Babylonian, Indian, and Cretan myths, *op. cit. supra*).

THE BIRTH OF APHRODITE

flict of Horus with Set was interpreted as the struggle between the forces of light and order and the powers of darkness and chaos. When worshipped as a tempest-god the Mesopotamian Rimmon was known as "the pig"[1] and, as "the wild boar of the desert," was a form of Set.

I have discussed the pig at this length because the use of the words χοῖρος by the Greeks, and *porcus* and *porculus* by the Romans, reveals the fact that the terms had the double significance of "pig" and "cowry-shell". As it is manifestly impossible to derive the word "cowry" from the Greek word for "pig," the only explanation that will stand examination is that the two meanings must have been acquired from the identification of both the cowry and the pig with the Great Mother and the female reproductive organs. In other words, the pig-associations of Aphrodite afford clear evidence that the goddess was originally a personification of the cowry.[2]

The fundamental nature of the identification of the cowry, the pig, and the Great Mother, the one with the other, is revealed not merely in the archæology of the Ægean, but also in the modern customs and ancient pictures of the most distant peoples. For example, in New Guinea the place of the sacrificial pig may be taken by the cowry-shell;[3] and upon the chief façade of the east wing of the ancient American monument, known as the Casa de las Monjas at Chichen Itza, the hieroglyph of the planet Venus is placed in conjunction with a picture of a wild pig.[4]

Gold and the Golden Aphrodite.

The evidence which has been collected by Mr. Wilfrid Jackson seems to suggest that the shell-cults originated in the neighbourhood of the Red Sea.

With the introduction of the practice of wearing shells on girdles

---

[1] According to Sayce, "Hibbert Lectures," p. 153, note 6.
[2] In Egypt not only was the sow identified with Isis, but "lucky pigs" were worn on necklaces just like the earlier cowry-amulets (Budge, "Guide to the Egyptian Collections" (British Museum), p. 96).
[3] Malinowski, *Trans. and Proc. Royal Society, South Australia*, XXXIX, 1915, p. 587 *et. seq.*
[4] Seler, "Die Tierbilder der mexikanischen und der Maya-Handschriften," *Zeitsch. f. Ethnologie*, Bd. 41, 1909, p. 405, and Fig. 242 in Maudslay, "Biologia Centrali-Americana, Vol. III, Pl. 13.

and necklaces and as hair ornaments the time arrived when people living some distance from the sea experienced difficulty in obtaining these amulets in quantities sufficient to meet their demands. Hence they resorted to the manufacture of imitations of these shells in clay and stone. But at an early period in their history the inhabitants of the deserts between the Nile and the Red Sea (Hathor's special province) discovered that they could make more durable and attractive models of cowries and other shells by using the plastic yellow metal which was lying about in these deserts unused and unappreciated. This practice first gave to the metal gold an arbitrary value which it did not possess before. For the peculiar life-giving attributes of the shells modelled in the yellow metal came to be transferred to the gold itself. No doubt the lightness and especially the beauty of such gold models appealed to the early Egyptians, and were in large measure responsible for the hold gold acquired over mankind. But this was an outcome of the empirical knowledge gained from a practice that originally was inspired purely by cultural and not æsthetic motives. The earliest Egyptian hieroglyphic sign for gold was a picture of a necklace of such amulets; and this emblem became the determinative of the Great Mother Hathor, not only because she was originally the personification of the life-giving shells, but also because she was the guardian deity both of the Eastern wadys where the gold was found and of the Red Sea coasts where the cowries were obtained. Hence she became the "Golden Hathor," the prototype of the "Golden Aphrodite".

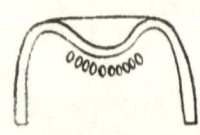

FIG. 9.—THE EGYPTIAN EMBLEM FOR GOLD, THE SIGN *nub*. IT REPRESENTS A COLLAR FROM WHICH GOLDEN AMULETS, PROBABLY REPRESENTING COWRIES, ARE SUSPENDED.

It is a significant token of the influence of these Egyptian incidents upon the history of the Ægean that among the earliest gold ornaments found by Schliemann at Troy were a series of crude representations of cowries worn as pendants to a hair ornament.[1]

It is hardly necessary to insist upon the vast influence upon the history of civilization which this arbitrary value of gold has been responsible for exerting. For more than fifty centuries men have been

---

[1] So far as I am aware the fact that these objects were intended to represent cowries does not appear to have been recognized hitherto. I am indebted to Mr. Wilfrid Jackson for calling my attention to the figures 685 and 832 in Schliemann's "Ilios" (1880), and for identifying the objects.

THE BIRTH OF APHRODITE

searching for the precious metal, and have been spreading abroad throughout the world the elements of our civilization. It has been not only the chief factor in bringing about the contact of peoples[1] and incidentally in building up our culture, but it has been the cause, directly or indirectly, of most of the warfare which has afflicted mankind. Yet these mighty forces were let loose upon the world as the result of the circumstance that early searchers for an elixir of life used the valueless metal to make imitations of their shell amulets!

The identification of gold with cowries may not have been the primary reason for the invention of gold currency. In fact, Professor Ridgeway has called attention to certain historical events which in his opinion forced men to convert their jewellery into coinage. But the fact that cowries were the earliest form of currency may have prepared the way for the recognition of the use of gold for a similar purpose. Moreover, we know that long before a real gold currency came into being rings of gold were in Egypt a form of tribute and a sign of wealth. Cowries acquired their significance as currency as the result of incidents in some respects analogous to those which impelled the early Egyptians to make gold models of the shells. In places in Africa far removed from the sea where the practice has grown up of offering vast numbers of cowries to brides on the occasion of their marriage (as fertility amulets) or of putting the shells in the grave (to secure for the dead fresh vital energy), the people offered their most treasured possessions, such as their cattle, in exchange for the amulets which were believed to confer such priceless social and religious boons. Cattle were therefore given in exchange for cowries, or the shells were used for the purchaes of wives. When the new significance as currency developed a remarkable confusion occurred. In many places cowries were placed in the mouth of the dead to confer the breath of life: but when the cowries acquired the new meaning as currency, the people who had lost all knowledge of the original significance of this practice explained the cowries as money with which to pay Charon's fare to the other world. Then, in many places, the cowry was replaced by an actual metallic coin. Most scholars fall into the same error as these ancient rationalists,

---

[1] See Perry, " Megalithic Monuments and Ancient Mines," *Proceedings and Memorials of the Manchester Literary and Philosophical Society,* 1916: also " War and Civilization," *Bulletin of the John Rylands Library,* 1918.

and accept their explanation of the *obolus* as though it were the real meaning of the act.

Another result of the use of gold models of shells as life-giving amulets was that the metal also acquired the reputation of being a giver of life,[1] which originally belonged merely to the shell or the imitation of its form, whatever the substance used for making the model.

Thus gold came to share the same magical reputation as the cowry and the pearl. It was also put to the same use: it was buried with the dead to confer a continuation of existence.

Not only was Hathor called *Nūb*, *i.e.* "gold" or the golden Hathor: but the place where the funerary statue was made ("born") in Egypt was called the "House of Gold" and personified as a goddess who gave rebirth to the dead (Alan Gardiner, "The Tomb of Amenemhēt," p. 95; and A. M. Blackman, *Journal of Egyptian Archæology*, Vol. IV, p. 127).

When ancient prospectors from the South exploited the rivers of Turkestan for alluvial gold and fresh water pearls, incidentally they also collected pebbles of jade for the purpose of making seals. The local inhabitants confused the properties of the stone with the magical reputation of the gold and the pearls. One outcome of this jade-fishing in Turkestan was the transference of the credit of life-giving to jade. Prospectors searching for these precious materials gradually made their way east past Lob Nor, and eventually discovered the deposits of gold and jade in the Shensi province. Thus jade became the nucleus around which the distinctive civilization of China became crystallized. It played an obtrusive part not only in attracting men from the West and in determining the locality where the germs of Western civilization were planted in China, but also in giving Chinese culture its distinctive shape.

"The ancient Chinese, wishing to facilitate the resurrection of the dead, surrounded them with jade, gold, pearls, timber, and other things imbued with influences emitted from the heavens, or, in other words, with such objects as are pervaded with vital energy derived from the *Yang* matter of which the heavens are the principal depository" (De Groot, *op. cit.*, p. 316).

By a similar process diamonds acquired the same reputation in India when searchers after gold discovered the precious metal in Hyderabad,

---

[1] "Danæ pregnant with immortal gold."

THE BIRTH OF APHRODITE

and the diamonds of Golconda came to be accredited with life-giving powers.[1]

According to the beliefs of the Indians " the Naga owns riches, the water of life, and a jewel that restores the dead to life ".

Thus gold, pearls, jade, and diamonds in course of time acquired the reputation of elixirs of life, but the hold they established upon mankind was due to the fact (*a*) that the amulets made of these materials made a strong appeal to the æsthetic sense, and (*b*) the arbitrary value assigned to them made them desirable objects to search for.

In his " Mycenæan Tree and Pillar Cult " (1901) Sir Arthur Evans gives cogent reasons for the view that at the time when Mycenæan influence was powerful in Cyprus " the ' golden Aphroditê ' of the Egyptians seems to play a much more important part than any form of Astarte or Mylitta " (p. 52). " The Cypriote parallels will be found to have a fundamental importance as demonstrating in detail that these [' a simple form of the palmette pillar, approaching a fleur-de-lys in outline,' in association with its guardian monsters] are in fact taken over from the cult of Mentu-Ra, the Warrior Sun-god of Egypt, of Hathor, and of Horus " (p. 52).

APHRODITE AS THE THUNDER-STONE.

As a surrogate of the Great Mother, the Eye of Re, the thunder-weapon was also identified with any of her varied manifestations.

The thunderbolt is one of the manifestations of the life-giving and death-dealing Divine Cow, and therefore is able specially to protect mundane cows.[2]

There are numerous hints in the ancient literature of other countries in confirmation of the association of the Great Mother with " falling stars ". " In a fragment of Sanchoniathon, Astarte, travelling about the habitable world, is said to have found a star falling through the air, which she took up and consecrated."[3]

Aphrodite also was looked upon as a meteoric stone that fell from

---

[1] See Laufer, " The Diamond," also Munn, " The Ancient Gold Mines of Hyderabad," paper now being published in the *Proceedings of the Manchester Literary and Philosophical Society*.

[2] Blinckenberg, *op. cit.*, p. 70 *et seq.*

[3] Quoted by Layard, " Nineveh and its Remains," Vol. II, p. 457.

the moon. In the "Iliad," Zeus is said to have sent Athena as a meteorite from heaven to earth.[1]

The association of Aphrodite with meteoric stones and the ancient belief that they fell from the moon serve to confirm the identification of these life-giving and death-dealing objects with the pearl and the thunderbolt. In Southern India the goddesses may be represented either by small stones or by pots of water, usually seven in number. During the ceremony around the stone-form of the goddess the *kappukaran* runs thrice around the stone, as the mandrake-digger does around the plant. The *pujari* who represents the goddess is painted like a leopard (Hathor's lioness) and kills the sacrificial sheep. The goddess (like Hathor) is supposed to drink the blood of the sacrificial victims (Whitehead, *op. cit.*, pp. 164-8).

Many factors played a part in the development of the beliefs about the origin of mankind from stones, with which the identification of the thunderbolt with the winged disk plays a part.

The idea that the cowry was the giver of life and the parent of men was also transferred to crude stone imitations of the shell. Perhaps the belief in such stones as creators of human beings may have been reinforced by finding actual fossilized shells within pebbles.[2]

A further corroboration of this theory was provided when the pearl came to be regarded as the quintessence of the life-giving substance of shells and as a little particle of moon-substance which fell as a drop of dew into the gaping oyster. Perry (*op. cit.*, p. 78) refers to an Indonesian belief among the Tsalisen that their ancestors came out of the moon; and the chief of this people has a spherical stone which is said to represent the moon.

This association of the moon with round stones may be connected with the identification of the sun (as the winged disk) with a stone axe,

---

[1] Cook, "Zeus," I, p. 760.

[2] Striking examples of these stories about birth from split stones have been given by Perry, "Megalithic Culture of Indonesia," Chapter X, and de Groot's "Religious System of China". It is possible that the double meaning of the Egyptian word *set*, as "stone" and "mountain" played a part in originating these stories. I have already quoted from the Pyramid Texts the account of the daily birth of the sun-god by a splitting of the "mountain" of the dawn. By a pun on this word the god's origin might have been interpreted as having taken place from a split "stone". The fact that the Great Mother was identified with a "mountain" (*set*) may also have facilitated the homology with the other meaning of *set*, *i.e.* "a stone".

THE BIRTH OF APHRODITE

when they came to be regarded as alternative weapons for the destruction or the creation of men. Perry records a story of a rock being lowered down from the sun, from which it was born, and out of a cleft in it man and woman emerged, as they were believed to have been born from the cleft in the cowry.

Then there are the Egyptian beliefs concerning stone statues, obelisks, or even unshaped blocks of stone which could be animated by human beings or gods.[1]

The cycle of these stories was completed when the " Eye of Re " slaughtered the enemies of the god and they became identified with the followers of Set, " creatures of stone ". Thus the evil eye petrified rebellious men : and so was launched upon its course the peculiar group of legends which in time encircled the world.

It is particularly significant that in Indonesia, in association with these ideas about stone-origins and petrifaction, Perry (p. 133) found also the clear-cut belief that the thunder-weapon was a stone, or the tooth of a cloud-dragon in the sky.

In Indonesia also petrifaction, thunder-stones, rain, floods, lightning, and an arrow shot to the accompaniment of thunder and lightning were the punishments traditionally assigned for certain offences, such as incest and laughing at animals.

The same people who introduced into the Malay Archipelago these characteristic fragments of the dragon-myth also believed that certain animals were impersonations of their gods : they also brought stories of incestuous unions on the part of their deities and rulers. To laugh at their sacred animals, or to imitate privileged customs permitted to their deities, but not to ordinary mortals, merited the same sort of punishments as were meted out to those other rebels against the ruling class and the gods in the home of these beliefs.[2]

[1] " Incense and Libations ".

[2] As the character and attributes of the early goddesses became more complex, and contradictory traits were more sharply contrasted, the inevitable tendency developed to differentiate the goddesses themselves, and provide distinctive names for the new personalities thus split off from the common parent. We see this in Egypt in the case of Hathor and Sekhet, and in Babylonia in Ishtar and Tiamat. But the process of specialization and differentiation might even involve a change of sex. There can be no doubt that the *god* Horus was originally a differentiation of certain of the aspects of the sky-goddess Hathor, at first as a brother " Eye ". But as the *king* Horus was the son of Osiris (as the dead king), when the confusion of the attributes

To laugh at the divine animals, or to commit incest, which was a divine prerogative, was analogous to "the blasphemy against the Holy Ghost," which in the New Testament is proclaimed an unpardonable offence, and in pagan legend was punished by the divine wrath, thunder, lightning, rain, floods, or petrifaction being the avenging instruments. Œdipus put out his own eyes to forestall the traditional wrath of the gods.

The Serpent and the Lioness.

When the development of the story of the Destruction of Mankind necessitated the finding of a human sacrifice and drove the Great Mother to homicide, this side of her character was symbolized by identifying her with a man-slaying lion and the venomous uræus-serpent.

She had previously been represented by such beneficent food-providing and life-sustaining creatures as the cow, the sow, and the gazelle (antelope or deer) : but when she developed into a malevolent creature and became the destroyer of mankind it was appropriate that she should assume the form of such man-destroyers as the lion and the cobra.

Once the reason for such identifications grew dim, the uræus-form of the Great Mother became her symbol in either of her aspects, good or bad, although the legend of her poison-spitting, man-destroying powers persisted.[1] The identification of the destroying-goddess with the moon, "the Eye of the Sun-god," prepared the way for the rationalization of her character as a uræus-serpent spitting venom and the sun's Eye spitting fire at the Sun-god's enemies. Such was the

---

of Osiris and Hathor—the actual father and the divine mother of Horus—made their marriage inevitable, the maternal relationship of the goddess to her "brother" was emphasized. But as the Great Mother, Hathor was the parent of the universe, and the mother not only of Horus but also of his father Osiris. This complicated rationalization made Hathor the sister, mother, and grandmother of Horus, and was responsible for originating the belief in the incestuous practices of the divine family. When the royal family assumed the rôle of gods and goddesses they were bound by these traditions (which had their origin purely in theological sophistry) and were driven to indulge in actual incest, as we know from the records of the Egyptian royal family and their imitators in other countries. But incest became a royal and divine prerogative which was sternly forbidden to mere mortals and regarded as a peculiarly detestable sin.

[1] Sethe, " Zur altägyptische Sage von Sonnenaugen das im Fremde war," *Untersuchungen zur Geschichte und Altertumskunde Ægyptens*, V, p. 23.

THE BIRTH OF APHRODITE 229

goddess of Buto in Lower Egypt, whose uræus-symbol was worn on the king's forehead, and was misinterpreted by the Greeks as not merely a symbolic "eye," but an actual median eye upon the king's or the god's forehead.

It is not without special significance that in the ancient legend (see Sethe, *op. cit.*) the lioness-goddess Tefnut was reputed to have come from Elephantine (or at any rate the region of Sehêl and Biga, which has the same significance), which serves to demonstrate her connexion with the story of the Destruction of Mankind and to corroborate the inference as to its remote antiquity. She was identified with Hathor, Sekhet, Bast, and other goddesses.

But the uræus was not merely the goddess who destroyed the king's enemies and the emblem of his kingship : in course of time the cobra became identified with the ruler himself and the dead king, who was the god Osiris. When this happened the snake acquired the god's reputation of being the controller of water.

The fashionable speculation of modern scholars that the movements of the snake naturally suggest rippling water [1] and provide "the obvious reason" which led many people quite independently the one of the other to associate the snake with water, is thus shown to have no foundation in fact.

One would have imagined that, if any natural association between snakes and water was the reason for this association, a water-snake would have been chosen to express the symbolism ; or, if it was the mere rippling motion of the reptile, that all snakes or any snake would have been drawn into the analogy. But primarily only one kind of snake, a cobra, was selected [2] ; and it is not a water snake, and cannot live in or under water. It was selected *because it was venomous* and the appropriate symbol of man-slaying.

The circumstances which led to the identification of this particular serpent with water were the result of a process of legend-making of so arbitrary and eccentric a nature as to make it impossible seriously to pretend that so tortuous a ratiocination should have been exactly followed to the same unexpected destination also in Crete and Western

---

[1] See especially the claims put forward by Brinton, which have been accepted by Spinden, Joyce, and many other recent writers.

[2] Possibly also the Cerastes. At a relatively late period other snakes were adopted as surrogates of the cobra and Cerastes.

Europe, in Babylonia and India, in Eastern Asia, and in America, without prompting the one of the other. No serious investigator who is capable of estimating the value of evidence can honestly deny that the belief in the serpent's control over water was diffused abroad from one centre where a concatenation of peculiar circumstances and beliefs led to the identification of the ruler with the cobra and the control of water.

We are surely on safe ground in assuming the improbability of such a wholly fortuitous set of events happening a second time and producing the same result elsewhere. Thus when we find in India the Nâga rajas identified with the cobra, and credited with the ability to control the waters, we can confidently assume that in some way the influence of these early Egyptian events made itself felt in India. As we compare the details of the Nâga worship in India [1] with early Egyptian beliefs, all doubt as to their common origin disappears.

The Nâga rulers were closely associated with springs, streams, and lakes. " To this day the rulers of the Hindu Kush states, Hunza and Nagar, though now Mohammedans, are believed, by their subjects, to be able to command the elements."

Oldham adds : " This power is still ascribed to the serpent-gods of the sun-worshipping countries of China, Manchuria, and Korea, and was so, until the introduction of Christianity, in Mexico and Peru ". This is put forward in support of his argument that the Nâga kings' " supposed ability to control the elements, and especially the waters," arose " from their connexion with the sun ". But this is not so.[2] The belief in the Egyptian king's power over water was certainly older than sun-worship, which did not begin until Osirian beliefs and the personification of the moon as the Great Mother brought the sky-deities and the control of water into correlation the one with the other. The association of the sun and the serpent in the royal insignia was a later development.

The early Egyptian goddess was identified with the uræus-serpent in that vitally important nodal point of primitive civilization, Buto, in Lower Egypt. The earliest deity in Crete and the Eastern Mediter-

---

[1] See Oldham, " Sun and Serpent," p. 51 *inter alia*.
[2] Blackman, however, has recently advanced this claim in reference to Egypt (*op. cit., Proc. Soc. Bibl. Archæology*, 1918, p. 57), as Breasted and others have done before.

ranean seems to have been a goddess who was also closely associated with the serpent. According to Langdon " the ophidian nature of the earliest Sumerian mother-goddess *Innini* is unmistakable. . . . She carries the caduceus in her hand, two serpents twining about a staff." [1]

The earliest Indian deities also were goddesses, and the first rulers of whom any record has been preserved were regarded as divine cobras, to whom was attributed the power of controlling water. These Nāgas, whether kings or queens, gods or goddesses, were the prototypes of the Eastern Asiatic dragon, whose origin is discussed in Chapter II.

In Japan the earliest sun-deity was a goddess who was identified with a snake. Elsewhere in this volume (Chapter II) I have referred to the completeness of the transference to America of these Old World ideas of the serpent. Right on the route taken by the main stream of cultural diffusion across the Pacific we still find in their fully-developed form the old beliefs concerning the good Mother Serpent of the ancient civilizations (C. E. Fox and F. H. Drew, *op. cit. supra*, p. 139). She could be re-incarnated as a coconut : she controlled crops ; she was associated with the coming of death into the world, with the introduction of agriculture and the discovery of fire. Like her predecessors in the West she was also a Mother Pot or Basket that never emptied.

All the *hiona* or *figona* (*i.e.* spirits) of San Cristoval have a serpent incarnation from Agunua the creator, worshipped by every one, to Oharimae and others, only known to particular persons. Other spirits, called *ataro*, might be incarnate in almost any animal. Agunua, who took the form of a serpent, was good, not evil (p. 134). Very many pools, rocks, water-falls, or large trees were thought to be the abode of *figona*. These serpent spirits could take the form of a stone, or retire within a stone, and sacred stones seem to be connected with *figona* rather than with *ataro* (p. 135). Almost all the local *figona* are represented as female snakes, but Agunua is a male snake (p. 137).

As the real significance of the snake's symbolism originated from its identification with the Great Mother in her destructive aspect, it is not surprising that the snake is the most primitive form of the evil

[1] S. Langdon, " A Seal of Nidaba, the Goddess of Vegetation," *Proceedings of the Society of Biblical Archæology*, Vol. XXXVI, 1914, p. 281.

dragon. The Babylonian Tiamat was originally represented as a huge serpent,[1] and throughout the world the serpent is pre-eminently a symbol of the evil dragon and the powers of evil.

The serpent that tempted Eve was the homologue both of the mother of mankind herself and also of the tree of paradise. It was the representative of the dragon-protector of pearls and of other kinds of treasure: it was also the goddess who animated the sacred tree as well as the protector who attacked all who approached it. It was the evil dragon that tempted Eve to eat of the forbidden fruit which brought her mortality.

The identification of the Great Mother with the lioness (and the secondary association of her husband and son with the lion) was responsible for a widespread relationship of these creatures with the gods and goddesses in Egypt and the Mediterranean, in Western Asia, in Babylonia and India, in Eastern Asia [tiger] and America [ocelot, and forms borrowed from the conventionalized lions and tigers of the Old World].

The account of the Great Mother's attributes and associations throws into clear relief certain aspects of the evolution of the dragon which were left in a somewhat nebulous state in Chapter II. The earliest form assumed by the power of evil was the serpent or the lion, because these death-dealing creatures were adopted as symbols of the Great Mother in her rôle as the Destroyer of Mankind. When Horus was differentiated from the Great Mother and became her *locum tenens*, his falcon (or eagle) was blended with Hathor's lioness to make the composite monster which is represented on Elamite and Babylonian monuments (see p. 79). But when the rôle of water as the instrument of destruction became prominent, Ea's antelope and fish were blended to make a monster, usually known as the "goat-fish," which in India and elsewhere assumed a great variety of forms. Some of the varieties of *makara* were sufficiently like a crocodile to be confused or identified with this representative of the followers of Set.

The real dragon was created when all three larval types—serpent, eagle-lion, and antelope-fish—were blended to form a monster with bird's feet and wings, a lion's forelimbs and head, the fish's scales, the antelope's horns, and a more or less serpentine form of trunk and tail,

---

[1] L. W. King, "Babylonian Religion," p. 58.

and sometimes also of head. Repeated substitution of parts of other animals, such as the spiral horn of Amen's ram, a deer's antlers, and the elephant's head, led to endless variation in the dragon's traits.

The essential unity of the motives and incidents of the myths of all peoples and of every age is a token, not of independent origin or the result of "the similarity of the working of the human mind," but of their derivation from the same ultimate source.

The question naturally arises: what is a myth? The dragon-myth of the West is the religion of China. The literature of every religion is saturated with the influence of the myth. In what respect does religion differ from myth? In Chapter I, I attempted to explain how originally science and religion were not differentiated. Both were the outcome of man's attempt to peer into the meaning of natural phenomena, and to extract from such knowledge practical measures for circumventing fate. His ever-insistent aim was to combat danger to life.

Religion was differentiated from science when the measures for controlling fate became invested with the assurance of supernatural help, for which the growth of a knowledge of natural phenomena made it impossible for the mere scientist to be the sponsor. It became a question of faith rather than knowledge; and man's instinctive struggle against the risk of extinction impelled him to cling to this larger hope of salvation, and to embellish it with an ethical and moral significance which at first was lacking in the eternal search for the elixir of life.

If religion can be regarded as archaic science enriched with the belief in supernatural control, the myth can be regarded as effete religion which has been superseded by the growth of a loftier ethical purpose. The myth is to religion what alchemy is to chemistry or astrology is to astronomy. Like these sciences, religion retains much of the material of the cruder phase of thought that is displayed in myth, alchemy, and astrology, but it has been refined and elaborated. The dross has been to a large extent eliminated, and the pure metal has been moulded into a more beautiful and attractive form. In searching for the elixir of life, the makers of religion have discovered the philosopher's stone, and with its aid have transmuted the base materials of myth into the gold of religion.

If we seek for the deep motives which have prompted men in all ages so persistently to search for the elixir of life, for some means of averting the dangers to which their existence is exposed, it will be found in the instinct of self-preservation, which is the fundamental factor in the behaviour of all living beings, the means of preservation of the life which is their distinctive attribute and the very essence of their being.

The dragon was originally a concrete expression of the divine powers of life-giving ; but with the development of a higher conception of religious ideals it became relegated to a baser rôle, and eventually became the symbol of the powers of evil.

CORRIGENDA.

P. xix (also the description of Fig. 25 facing p. 184 and the footnotes on pp. 189 and 225). For Blinckenberg read Blinkenberg.
P. 77.   „ Yung   „ Jung.
P. 82.   „ Tristam   „ Tristram.
P. 137.   „ Pl. VI.   „ Fig. 17.
   „   „ Pl. VII.   „ Fig. 16.
P. 158.   „ Hadramant   „ Hadramaut.
P. 181.   „ Fig. 24, h and l   „ Fig. 24, k and l.
P. 223.   „ purchaes   „ purchase.
   „   „ Proceedings and Memoirs „ Memoirs and Proceedings.

NOTES.

a. The publication of the memoir to which reference is made in the footnote on p. 99 and of Major Munn's paper mentioned in footnote 1 on p. 225 has been unavoidably delayed.

b. Since the book has been printed I have obtained further corroboration of the explanation proposed (on pp. 199 and 200) for the special meaning acquired by the Hebrew word for "pots" (dūdā'im). The use of the plural form of this word for the mandrake-avatar of the Great Mother is due to the fact that in Western Asia and elsewhere the goddess was usually identified not with a single pot (dūd) but with several (most commonly seven) pots (dūdā'im).

About the Author

Sir Grafton Elliot Smith, FRS, FRCP (1871 –1937) was an Australian-British anatomist and a proponent of the hyperdiffusionist view of prehistory.

Smith was born in Grafton, New South Wales. He attended Sydney Boys High School, he was awarded a degree in medicine at the University of Sydney and developed an interest in the anatomy of the human brain. He held a travelling scholarship at Cambridge in 1896. From 1900 to 1909 he was the first chairholder of anatomy at the Cairo School of Medicine and investigated the brains of Egyptian mummies. He was the first scholar to x-ray a mummy.

In 1907 he became archaeological advisor to the archaeological survey of Nubia. From 1909 to 1919 he was Professor in anatomy in Manchester, 1919–1937 he held the chair of Anatomy at the University College London. He was elected President of the Anatomical Society of Great Britain and Ireland for 1924 to 1927. During World War I he attended military hospitals for shell shock and served on the British General Medical Council.

G. E. Smith's father had migrated to New South Wales from London. He had attended a workingman's college under John Ruskin and later became teacher and headmaster in Grafton, New South Wales. His older brother (S. H. Smith) was Director of Education in New South Wales; his younger brother (S. A. Smith) was Acting Professor of Anatomy at the University of Sydney.

G. E. Smith married Kathleen Macredie in 1902. During his time in London, he lived in Hampstead, Gower Street, and at Regent's Park. During his London years, he became a friend of Dr. W. H. R. Rivers.

Smith's youngest son, Stephen Smith, died in an accident in 1936 and G. E Smith spent his final year in a nursing home in London, where he died.

Smith was the leading specialist on the evolution of the brain of his day. Many of his ideas on the evolution of the primate brain still form the core of present scholarship.

He was decorated by the Khedive of Egypt, Abbas Hilmy in 1909. He became Fellow of the Royal Society in 1907, FRCP, cross of the French Legion of Honour, and was knighted in 1934. In 1912 he received the Royal Medal of the Royal Society, in 1930 the Honorary Gold Medal of the Royal College of Surgeons, in 1936 the Huxley Memorial Medal from the Royal Anthropological Institute of Great Britain and Ireland.

Bibliography
Among the most important of his publications are:

- The Natural Subdivision of the Cerebral Hemisphere (1901).
- The Primary Subdivisions of the Mammalian Cerebellum (1902).
- The Ancient Egyptians and the origin of Civilization (London/New York, Harper & Brother 1911).
- Catalogue of the Royal Mummies in the Museum of Cairo (Cairo 1912).
- On the Significance of the geographical distribution of Mummification – a study of the migrations of peoples and the spread of certain customs and beliefs (1916).
- The Evolution of the Dragon (1919). (Project Gutenberg copy of book) (Hathitrust copy)
- Evolution of the Dragon at sacred-texts.com
- Tutankhamen and the Discovery of his Tomb (1923).
- Evolution of Man: Essays (1924, 2nd edition 1927).
- Human History (1930).
- The Diffusion of Culture (London, Watts 1933).
- Elephants and Ethnologists.[9]
- Serle, Percival (1949). "Smith, Grafton Elliot". Dictionary of Australian Biography. Sydney: Angus and Robertson.
- P. Elkin/N. W. G. Macintosh, Grafton Elliot Smith, The Man and his Work (Sydney University Press 1974).
- W. R. Dawson, Sir Grafton Elliot Smith: a Biographical Record by his Colleagues (London, Cape 1938).